P9-CIW-433

ROMANTIC PERSPECTIVES

ROMANTIC PERSPECTIVES

The work of
Crabbe, Blake, Wordsworth, and Coleridge
as seen by their contemporaries
and by themselves

EDITED BY

PATRICIA HODGART M.A.
Formerly Scholar of Girton College, Cambridge

AND

THEODORE REDPATH M.A. Ph.D.
Fellow and Tutor of Trinity College, Cambridge, and Lecturer
in English in the University of Cambridge

BARNES & NOBLE, Inc. · New York
Booksellers · Publishers · Founded 1873

132372

First published in the United States 1964

© *Patricia Hodgart and Theodore Redpath* 1964

Made in Great Britain

Preface

THIS is the first of two companion volumes, consisting substantially of passages concerning the poetry of the chief poets of the Romantic Period. These passages were written by their contemporaries, and in a few cases by the poets themselves. The passages are briefly annotated, and there are also short introductions to those concerning the work of each poet, and a general introduction to each volume.

The passages in this volume are about Crabbe, Blake, Wordsworth, and Coleridge (to name them in order of birth). The passages chiefly concern the *work* of the poets—either their poetry in general or particular poems. On the other hand, some passages have been included which refer rather to the *characters* and *personalities* of the poets than directly to their work. This has been done in the belief that such passages may sometimes indirectly throw light on the spirit of the poets' work, or at least afford some explanation why it was received by contemporaries in the way it was. The general design of the present project, indeed, is twofold —first, to show how the work of these poets appeared to some of the leading minds of their time; and, secondly, to help to throw light on the poetry itself, by making conveniently available a record of the impressions it made when it had freshly appeared—impressions which in some instances have not since been excelled in justice or subtlety. The first of these two objects, then, falls within the scope of literary and critical *history*; the second belongs to literary *criticism*. Where a piece of criticism included here is unjust it has been selected for a historical purpose—to show what was said; where, on the other hand, it is valid, it has been included not only for the sake of historical truth but also for the sake of its contribution to criticism.

As far as we know, the present anthology differs in character from any which has so far appeared. The two anthologies which might be thought most similar to ours will be seen even on cursory comparison to be quite different. The two anthologies referred to are Mr E. H. Lacon Watson's *Contemporary Comments* (London, 1931) and Mr John Wain's *Contemporary Reviews of Romantic Poetry* (London, 1953), two valuable collections, themselves diverse in scope. Mr Lacon Watson's anthology concerns no fewer than eighteen writers of the early nineteenth century, and the passages chosen criticize both prose and verse. Moreover, the passages themselves are generally much shorter than many of those offered here. Again, Mr Lacon Watson does not include Crabbe among the writers dealt with. Mr Wain includes neither Crabbe nor, of course, Blake, and he deliberately draws his passages only from the two dominant reviews (the *Edinburgh* and the *Quarterly*) and from the most important magazine (*Blackwood's*), whereas the passages here reprinted come not only from these and other reviews and magazines but also from books, essays, letters, and reminiscences. The divergence of choice represents a divergence of purpose. We have been concerned to offer a fairly representative cross-section of critical opinion, and to illustrate the complexity of the impressions the poets' work made on their contemporaries.

As to the public we have had in mind, it is of two kinds. On the one hand, we have hoped to interest the general reader curious to know something more precise and extensive about the reception accorded to the work of these poets than is generally available in manuals or literary histories. On the other hand, we have had especially in mind the needs of boys and girls in schools studying the poets of the Romantic

Period. We have been anxious to help to prevent them from forming too simple a picture of the impact which the work of these poets had on the critics and public of their time. We have hoped that our anthology may offer them a welcomely direct contact with the rich array of critical attitudes and discriminations which marked that important period in the history of English poetry. We have also hoped that it may afford an insight into the working of the various factors which so often help to determine the character of literary critiques, such as political and religious views, traditional criteria of literary value, personal animosity and partisanship, each of which sometimes frustrates and sometimes furthers that work of critical exploration and judgment which must always depend primarily on critical intelligence and sensibility. If our anthology is found really helpful towards a better understanding of the poetry of the writers considered, and also of the critical standards and tendencies which pressed for its acceptance or rejection, we shall be satisfied.

P.H.
T.R.

PUBLISHER'S NOTE

The two editors are jointly responsible for the total conception of the book, but in the detailed work there has been a division of labour. Mrs Hodgart has selected and edited the great majority of the extracts, and has written the separate Introductions concerning each poet. Dr Redpath has selected and edited a few of the extracts and written the General Introduction.

The publishers and both the editors wish to record their gratitude to Miss Marie Overton for her valuable advice during the preparation of this book.

CAMBRIDGE,
May 1964

Contents

LIST OF ABBREVIATIONS

B: *Blackwood's Magazine*
BC: *The British Critic*
BC and Theol. Rev.: *The British Critic and Theological Review*
CR: *The Critical Review*
ER: *The Edinburgh Review*
Ecl.R.: *The Eclectic Review*
LM: *The London Magazine*
MR: *The Monthly Review*
N.S.: New Series
QR: *The Quarterly Review*

Introduction

I

Preliminary Considerations

When we have been reading poems by distinguished poets of the past it is natural that we should come to wonder sometimes how their poetry struck their contemporaries. The primary purpose of the present collection of extracts is to help towards answering this question in the case of four poets of the Early Romantic period: Crabbe, Blake, Wordsworth, and Coleridge. Another question, however, which may also readily occur to a reader of past poets, especially where the work of the poet effected a literary revolution, is: What did the poet himself think he was trying to do in his poetry? Some passages have therefore been included here in which the poets write of their poetic intentions. It is, in addition, also natural to wonder what kind of people the poets seemed to their contemporaries to be. No attempt has been made here to satisfy this particular kind of curiosity, except by including a comparatively small number of passages describing the personalities of the poets in such a way as to throw light on the spirit of their work. In the case of Blake, however, the comments of his contemporaries most often concern his personality and intentions. Though he was quite well known as an engraver, he was scarcely known at all as a poet. One of the chief reasons for this was that, though a number of his best poetical works appeared in his lifetime, only his *Poetical Sketches* (1783) was printed in the usual way. The rest, which included *Songs of*

Innocence (1789), *The Book of Thel* (1789), *America* (1793), *Songs of Experience* (1794), *The First Book of Urizen* (1794), *The Book of Los* (1795), *Milton* (1804), and *Jerusalem* (1804), he printed by a special process, and published them himself, together with his own illustrations; and few people saw the comparatively small number of copies of these. Moreover, even those who did see them seem to have generally paid more attention to the illustrations than to the text. Landor was a notable exception, on one occasion maintaining Blake to be the greatest of poets; and Hazlitt was also deeply struck by some of the poems Crabb Robinson read to him. Southey, Lamb, Coleridge, and Wordsworth all saw a few of the poems, and their interest was stirred more or less strongly, but in no case did enthusiasm lead them to recognize Blake's real stature as one of the great poets of that time and of all time. His name occurs but seldom in their correspondence or in records of their conversation. The poetry of Crabbe, Wordsworth, and Coleridge, on the other hand, was regularly reviewed and well known to the reading public. Wordsworth's work made the greatest stir, and the criticism of it in the reviews thrusts us at once into fundamental issues about the nature of poetry, and as to what gives individual poems their value. Some of the reviewers, faced with work sharply differing from any previously known in the history of English poetry, sometimes got so angry that their strictures lost discrimination, though in some cases the adverse critiques not only made well-judged exceptions for particular poems, but also offered general criticisms which are still worth consideration even where they may not seem to us to deserve the emphasis which was laid on them. Despite the fact that the attitudes expressed in reviews were sometimes based partly on personal rancour or goodwill or on the political standpoint of the reviewer or of the periodical for which he was writing, there was often plenty of genuine critical comment even where such bias was at work. Important clashes were occurring between sincerely held critical attitudes, and this gives the criticism of the period, and particularly the criticism of Wordsworth's work, a very special interest. It is essential to a proper understanding of the literary history of the period, however, not to simplify unduly the nature of the battles and of the standards involved. It would be a gross mistake, for instance, to think that the situation could be satisfactorily summed up by saying that the influential reviewers were maintaining the standards of the eighteenth century against what they considered to be the undesirable innovations of Romanticism. Such a diagnosis would fit certain elements in certain critiques, but it would be quite inadequate even as a succinct account of the situation, which was far more complex. Different periodicals had different critical standpoints, and even the same periodical did not always adopt the same critical attitudes, either because various reviewers were employed, or because the critical views of the editor changed. Indeed, on occasion even the same reviewer changed his standpoint from one critique to another. Finally, it is hard to find critical writing where the critical standards adopted are wholly what could be helpfully described as 'eighteenth-century standards.' Some of these complexities will appear in concrete instances when we come to consider more closely a few of the individual periodicals. Meanwhile, however, it will be worth taking a rapid survey of the field of literary periodicals and of their position in the life of the time.

II

The Position of Literary Periodicals in the Early Nineteenth Century

The periodicals can be fairly clearly divided into three kinds: reviews, magazines, and weeklies. The difference between reviews and magazines is now somewhat blurred, but at that time a review contained only articles and reviews, whereas a magazine contained both creative and critical work, and sometimes also even news items and stock-exchange quotations. During the early nineteenth century the reviews with by far the largest circulation were *The Edinburgh Review* (founded 1802) and *The Quarterly Review* (founded 1809). The *Edinburgh* was originally intended to be politically neutral, but soon acquired a Whig bias, which was rapidly accentuated. This led to the founding of the *Quarterly* in London as a Tory counterblast. The *Edinburgh* and the *Quarterly* were both, however, brilliant newcomers in a field by no means empty. Oldest among the already established reviews was *The Monthly Review*, founded in 1749, which had by 1790 developed from a collection of abstracts of books into a publication in which an attempt was made to review all British books published during the last month. The dozen works which seemed most important were reviewed at some length, and shorter notices were given of the rest. The political colour of the *Monthly* was Whig, and there was a tendency to freethinking among some of its contributors. The most important of the other older reviews was *The Critical Review*, founded in 1756. This had been started under Tory and Church patronage, and maintained conservative principles in religion and politics. But the *Critical* had seen its best days in the eighteenth century, and its place as a Tory organ was first gradually taken by *The British Critic*, founded in 1793. Finally, in 1817, less than a decade after the founding of the Tory *Quarterly*, the *Critical* was discontinued. Only three other reviews require mention: *The Annual Review*, *The Eclectic Review*, and *The Westminster Review*. *The Annual Review* only ran for a few years (1803–8), and is substantially of interest for our purposes solely for the sake of its review of Wordsworth's *Poems in Two Volumes* (1807). *The Eclectic Review*, founded in 1805, represented the views of the Dissenters. *The Eclectic Review* and *The British Critic*, both religious reviews, though of different persuasions, often contained literary criticism which did more justice to the merits of work of an unfamiliar kind (such as much of the work of Wordsworth) than was sometimes done in the smarter criticism of the two great reviews. The *Westminster* was started much later (in 1824). Its politics were Radical. Its founder was James Mill, a Utilitarian and disciple of Bentham, and father of the more famous John Stuart Mill. During this early phase of the *Westminster*'s career, however, its literary criticism was rather crudely derived from Utilitarian principles, and certainly not very perceptive.

As to magazines, that with the largest circulation was *Blackwood's Edinburgh Magazine*, commonly known as '*Maga*,' founded in 1817 by the Tory publisher Blackwood as an Edinburgh counter-attraction to the Whig *Edinburgh*. There were, however, other magazines whose critical reviews and articles were sometimes juster than those in *Blackwood's*, though generally not so vigorous. Chief among these were *The London Magazine* (1820–29), which was particularly distinguished during its first year or two; *The New Monthly Magazine*, founded in 1814, though not really important as a critical organ till Thomas Campbell became editor in 1820; and Leigh Hunt's and Byron's *The Liberal* (1822), which only appeared for four numbers.

Finally, there were the literary weeklies, which included John and Leigh Hunt's *The Examiner* (1808–81), which was only of literary interest until 1830; *The Literary Gazette* (1817–62), which performed most usefully the same kind of function fulfilled by *The Times Literary Supplement* to-day; *The Literary Journal* (1818–19), short-lived but of good quality; the lively *Literary Chronicle and Weekly Review* (1819–28, when it was incorporated in *The Athenaeum* (1828–1921)); and *The Edinburgh Literary Journal* (1828–31).

Thus the bulk of periodical criticism in the early nineteenth century was considerable. It was, indeed, far greater than in the eighteenth century. The growth seems to have been rapid. Perhaps the prime cause was the swift increase in sales of books during the last years of the eighteenth century. The bookseller Lackington, writing in 1803, estimated that four times as many books were being sold then as had been twenty years before. This expansion of the reading public was part and parcel of the rapidly expanding economy following on the industrial and agricultural revolutions. The vastly increased demand for books naturally encouraged authorship, and the spate of literary products had to be brought to the attention of the public. The problem of selecting the best works also began to make itself felt more acutely. It was, moreover, now essential to use the medium of print both to convey to the reading public expert opinion on new books and also to educate their literary taste. The public were no longer concentrated in the coffee-houses of the metropolis, even though these now numbered several thousand. And readers were far from being as homogeneous in background and culture as they had been a few decades before. Many of them were in need of guidance not only as to what to read but even as to what to think of it. Furthermore (a point sometimes neglected in literary discussions of the rise of periodical criticism), this large reading public was becoming more and more important as a political force, a body of voters amenable to direction by the persuasive powers of journalism. It is worth remembering that when some of the contributors to the *Edinburgh* complained to its editor, Jeffrey, at the increasingly Whig tendencies of the periodical, he replied that, though it might have two legs, literature and politics, the "right leg" was politics. Yet the leading periodicals are not simply to be thought of as political powerhouses with literary façades. They met, and, on the whole, met admirably, a genuine need for a regular flow of well-informed and well-written comment on current affairs and current literature by some of the acutest critical minds of the time.

To command the services of high-grade editors and contributors it was evidently advisable to pay well, though sometimes sounder literary criticism was written for periodicals which could not afford inflated remuneration. In the case of the few leading reviews and magazines scintillating rewards proved amply possible. Jeffrey's regular editorial salary once the *Edinburgh* was well under way was £300[1] per annum, and articles in the *Edinburgh* were paid at the average rate of 20–25 guineas a sheet (sixteen pages).[2] Gifford, the editor of the *Quarterly*, received £200 per annum at first, but after four years his salary was doubled, and in the meantime Murray, the *Quarterly*'s publisher, had given him a present of £500. When Lockhart took over in 1825 he was offered £1000 per annum. The *Quarterly* usually paid 10 guineas a sheet for contributions, but some long articles brought their writers as much as £100. As to *Blackwood's*, it

[1] The modern equivalents for this and the other figures given are probably between five and six times as great. Retail prices are now only three to four times as great as in 1815; but the price of services is seven to eight times as great.

[2] A rough average number of words per page was 500.

sometimes paid 16 guineas a sheet.[1] The result was that it was possible for writers of critical articles and reviews to earn livings which can only be described as more than handsome. John Wilson ("Christopher North"), one of the pioneers of *Blackwood's*, said that for some time he was able to make 600 guineas a year, of which we can reckon at least 400 guineas to be payment for contributions. Even at present rates of income-tax the modern equivalent of 600 guineas (probably over £3000) would be quite a tidy sum, but, being virtually tax-free, it was imposing.

These very high rates of payment were made possible by the remarkable circulations these periodicals achieved quite soon after their foundation. Of the first number of the *Edinburgh* in 1802, admittedly, only 750 copies were printed, but by 1808 the issues had reached 9000 per quarter; and the competition of the *Quarterly* did not result in a decline. By 1814 the *Edinburgh* was printing nearly 13,000, and in 1818 sales attained the peak of about 14,000. The *Quarterly*'s circulation had reached 9000 by 1816, and drew roughly level with that of the *Edinburgh* two years later. The combined circulation of the two leading reviews in 1815 has been estimated as 20,000, and the total of their readers as possibly 100,000.[2] Now, the population of the British Isles at that time was apparently about 19,000,000, and that of England and Wales about 10,000,000. The ratio between the number of readers of these two reviews and the total population was therefore astonishingly high. In estimating the number of people who had access to serious critical journals, moreover, one would need to take into account all the other periodicals already mentioned, apart from others not spoken

[1] The usual rate of payment of the old-established *Critical* was only two guineas a sheet, and of the *Monthly* four guineas a sheet.

[2] É. Halévy, *A History of the English People in 1815*, tr. E. I. Watkin (London, 1924), III, 134.

of. The circulation of *Blackwood's*, for instance, reached an even higher peak than those of the two great reviews. Three years after its foundation it was selling 17,000 copies in a quarter. It is an interesting reflection on the difference between the civilization of this country then and now that the circulation of these periodicals was then higher than that of any daily newspaper.[1] Still more striking perhaps is the probability that, even allowing for considerable overlap among the readers of the various periodicals, well over one-half of the reading public around the time of Waterloo (possibly about 220,000[2]) were readers of periodicals in which appeared intelligent discussion of current literature. It would be quite impossible to say the same to-day.[3] On the other hand, we have the consolation, which should not, however, be overvalued, that the proportion of illiterates to the total population is far smaller.

It will be obvious that these periodicals were well placed to have a powerful influence on what the reading public read, and on its literary judgments. Their influence was, moreover, strengthened by certain features of policy. Before the beginning of the century the *Monthly* and *Critical* had adopted the policy of printing longer articles on works deemed more important and shorter notices of the rest. *The British Critic* took a further step by introducing half-yearly prefaces, in which attention was drawn to recent work which seemed to stand out from the general run. A more radical move, however, was made by the *Edinburgh* in its very first number. It entirely abandoned the practice of reviewing every printed

[1] The circulation of *The Times* in 1816 was 8000 (L. E. Gates, *Three Studies in Literature*, 1899).

[2] So estimated by Jeffrey in *ER*, XX, November 1812, 280.

[3] Even comparatively widely circulated weeklies which review current literature now have circulations far less than those of the leading daily and weekly newspapers. The following are average figures for 1961: *The New Statesman:* 77,077; *The Spectator:* 43,538; *The Daily Express:* 4,269,704; *The Daily Mirror:* 4,648,768; *The Daily Mail:* 2,449,712; *The Daily Telegraph:* 1,205,855; *The Times:* 259,961; *The News of the World:* 6,664,035.

work that appeared. Indeed, although its first number contained twenty-nine articles in its 252 pages, the number of works reviewed each quarter, once the periodical had settled down, was seldom more than a dozen. The total number of works it reviewed in any one year was only about a tenth of the number reviewed by the periodicals which kept to the old policy of a complete survey of publications. The *Quarterly* followed the policy of the *Edinburgh*, and *Blackwood's* was even more selective in its reviewing. Now, these were, as has been said, the most widely circulated periodicals; and it can easily be seen that the tendency of this new policy would be to promote very strongly the sales of works favourably reviewed and to depreciate the sales of works not noticed. Moreover, such was the authority that the *Edinburgh* and *Quarterly* soon acquired that a condemnatory review in one of them, unless counterbalanced by a favourable review in the other, could have a crippling effect on sales. This authority was partly acquired owing to the already current practice of reviewing being anonymous.[1] But the special authority of these two periodicals was obtained largely through the clearly talented character of their contributors, who could spread themselves in the long articles permitted by the reviews' selective policy. It is quite certain that the *Edinburgh* and *Quarterly* soon came to enjoy from many of their readers an awestruck respect.

The consequent sense of power felt by the chief writers, and especially by the editors, of the two principal reviews was coupled, in the realm of criticism, with a strong sense of their responsibility in maintaining what they considered to be high literary standards. The result was that both reviews tended to adopt a markedly judicial attitude towards literature;

[1] It is only modern scholars, working on the private papers of publishing houses, who have made such identifications of contributors as will be referred to below.

and this communicated itself to a number of the minor reviews and to some of the magazines and weeklies. Evaluation became the first and foremost order of the day. Now the evaluations made often contained a very fair measure of justice. But sometimes the rôle of judge was played at the expense of that of enlightened interpreter. Sometimes the criticism in the reviews completely failed to make contact with the really important features of the work before it. This was especially the case with criticism of Coleridge's poetry. It was not until Leigh Hunt wrote on *Christabel*, *Kubla Khan*, and *The Ancient Mariner* in 1821[1] that real insight into these poems began to appear in published criticism; and not until John Sterling published his analysis of *Christabel* in 1828[2] that anything approaching an adequate critique of any of these great poems reached the public. The finest appreciation of Coleridge's poetry appeared in the *Quarterly* in the year of his death (1834). It was written by Henry Nelson Coleridge.[3] Now, it is more than probable that Sterling's understanding of *Christabel*, and H. N. Coleridge's understanding of Coleridge's poetry in general, were both a result of listening long and intently to the poet's own explanations of his principal poems. If they were, then it was the listeners rather than the judges who eventually did proper *justice* to what really counts in Coleridge's poems. With all their culture and poise and wit and their frequent good sense, the critical experts sometimes badly failed to understand new things. They had too strong a faith in their infallibility as cultivated men, and also in the rigidity of specific critical standards. Two pronouncements by Jeffrey are of strong interest in this connexion. In reviewing Madame de Staël's *De la littérature* we

[1] *The Examiner*, 21 October, 1821, 664.

[2] *The Athenaeum*, No. 36, 2 July, 1828, reprinted in *Essays and Tales of John Sterling* (London, 1848). The article has the whimsical title "An Appeal from Philip Drunk to Philip Sober." An extract appears at p. 248 below.

[3] *QR*, LII, August 1834. Reprinted in the present anthology at p. 261.

find him laying down that "the artist should attempt to please especially those who from their rank and education are likely to regulate the judgment of the reader"—a maxim which is both attractive and perilous, for though such arbiters of taste may well more often be right than the unguided reader, yet, as we shall see, they may on occasion be lamentably insensitive to the merits of splendid poetry, in which case their pontifical reviews may simply act as barriers between the work of art and the public on whom it has a legitimate claim. Cultivated critics deserve respect, but the respect should often be seasoned by a grain or two of salty scepticism. The other pronouncement occurs in Jeffrey's critique of Southey's *Thalaba* in the *Edinburgh*'s very first number. It runs as follows: "Poetry has this much, at least, in common with religion, that its standards were fixed long ago by certain inspired writers, whose authority it is no longer lawful to call in question." A great danger in such a view is that the more specific the "standards" were taken to be, the more paralysing would be the effect on even valuable poetic innovation. On the other hand, the floodgates of literature must have seemed to be open, and it was possibly at least as important that really bad work should be damned, and weaknesses exposed, as that fully understanding criticism should be produced on work of real distinction. And certainly, on the whole, though sometimes too indulgent to rather timidly traditional work like that of Rogers, the *Edinburgh* followed well, in respect of work reviewed, the spirit of its motto: "Judex damnatur cum nocens absolvitur,"[1] though the number of works reviewed was small, and there was some ground for the denial by the editor of *The British Critic* that the *Edinburgh* really performed the functions of a review.[2] A similarly astringent spirit, however,

[1] 'The judge is condemned when a delinquent is acquitted.'

[2] *The British Critic*, XXXVII, January 1811, i–vi.

animated a number of the other reviews and magazines of repute, and it was quite hard for really bad work to escape sharp criticism from some quarter.

III

Some Leading Literary Periodicals and Reviewers and their Attitudes to the Work of Crabbe, Wordsworth, and Coleridge

Besides the two chief reviews, the *Edinburgh* and the *Quarterly*, and the chief magazine, *Blackwood's*, it will be worth giving attention to a few other representative periodicals: *The Monthly Review*, *The British Critic*, *The Eclectic Review*, *The London Magazine*, and *The Examiner*.[1]

The Edinburgh Review

The *Edinburgh* was founded in 1802 by three young men, Sydney Smith (1771–1845), Francis Jeffrey (1773–1850), and Francis Horner (1778–1817). Jeffrey was soon formally appointed editor, and ran the review until 1829. He is, for our purposes, the most important personality of the review, and, indeed, historically, the most important of the periodical critics of the time. Jeffrey had been a struggling lawyer. He was later to become a successful member of the Scottish Bar, later still Lord Advocate, then, after the Reform Act of 1832, M.P. for Edinburgh, and for the last sixteen years of his life a Judge of the Court of Session. Jeffrey was a highly intelligent man, of sound Scottish education, and an efficient

[1] *The Christian Observer*, representing Evangelical opinion, paid little attention to Wordsworth and Coleridge, and its two reviews of Crabbe do not entitle it to separate treatment.

administrator. He had also a genuine interest in literature, and, within limits, a fair literary sensibility. A number of his contemporaries, however, formed the impression that, despite his undoubted intellectual ability, Jeffrey was badly deficient in a sense for poetry. This was an exaggeration, but Jeffrey's range of sensibility was certainly somewhat restricted. It would be inaccurate to say that this restriction was due, throughout Jeffrey's career as a critic, to a belief in strict Augustan standards. Like most educated men of his time, Jeffrey had, indeed, been brought up on Virgil, Cicero, and Horace, and on Pope, Swift, and Addison; and there is little doubt that the literary values represented by these writers dominated Jeffrey in his early years. But during the first decade of the nineteenth century Jeffrey came to be more impressed by the Elizabethans than by the Augustans either of England or of Rome; and this change of attitude comes out clearly in his review of Weber's edition of John Ford (*ER*, August 1811), where he states categorically that he now thinks the Elizabethan age "by far the brightest in the history of English literature—or indeed of human intellect and capacity." He also detected a narrowing of the emotional range of poetry at the time of the Restoration, and attributed this largely to French influence. In Dryden, for instance, one could not, he thought, find a single line that was "pathetic," and very few that could be considered "sublime." Now, "pathos" and "sublimity" were certainly not among the typical Augustan values. Jeffrey also came to condemn Swift as vulgar and commonplace, and the serious styles of both Addison and Swift as tame and poor. Clearly, then, it would be absurd to think of Jeffrey as simply a hidebound Augustan critic. He did, indeed, still recognize the merits of those whom he now called "the Queen Anne wits," and particularly of Pope. Yet he thought even of Pope as "a satirist, and a moralist, and a wit, and a critic, and a fine writer" rather than as a poet.[1] "There are no pictures of nature or simple emotion in all his writings," wrote Jeffrey. We even find Jeffrey willing to admire a "strong spirit of originality, of pathos and natural feeling," in *Lyrical Ballads.*[2] Nevertheless, Jeffrey did certainly use, and continue to use, inexorably, some of the Augustan criteria of literary value, in his disparagement of what he took to be the weaknesses of much early Romantic poetry. He called, for instance, for polish, good sense, clarity, decorum, and economy; and he condemned homeliness, "mysticism," obscurity, eccentricity, and wordiness.

Jeffrey's chief targets were Wordsworth and Southey, and, to a lesser degree, Coleridge. Jeffrey's attitude to the work of Wordsworth is of particular interest and importance. *Lyrical Ballads* had been first published before the *Edinburgh* was founded. Not long after the publication of the second edition of *Lyrical Ballads* in 1800, however, Jeffrey fiercely attacked the whole 'Lake School,' and especially Wordsworth, in a review of Southey's *Thalaba.*[3] Jeffrey did not continue to maintain throughout his career as a reviewer all the positions he took up in that review (*e.g.*, about the value of poetry dealing with the poorer classes of society), but it is a key to a proper understanding of Jeffrey's attitude to the Lake Poets.

Jeffrey's first review of Wordsworth dealt with *Poems in Two Volumes* (1807).[4] Looking back on *Lyrical Ballads*, Jeffrey praises not only the poems' originality, pathos and natural feeling, but also "the clear impression which they bore of the amiable dispositions and virtuous principles of the author." But he found in them some instances of "vulgarity,

[1] "Weber's *Ford*" (*ER*, August 1811, 281).

[2] *ER*, XI, October 1807.

[3] *ER*, I, October 1802. A long extract from this review appears below at p. 163.

[4] *ER*, XI, October 1807.

affectation and silliness," which were, in his view, all the more dangerous as examples because of the genius of the poet. In the 1807 volumes Jeffrey found still more instances of these undesirable features. Wordsworth's diction seemed to him inelegant and undignified, and his versification slovenly and unmelodious. Furthermore, it was clear that Wordsworth had deliberately chosen to write in this way, and that he sometimes found it hard to keep to his system. But Wordsworth was also, in Jeffrey's view, an *eccentric* writer, who tied his deepest and loftiest feelings to insignificant objects, either through affectation or because he loved a lone, meditative life, and thought out-of-the-way thoughts which to most people would appear strange and unnatural. Jeffrey did, however, make an exception for the sonnets, which seemed to him to escape the trammels of Wordsworth's system by their strong connexions with the sonnets of Milton. Jeffrey's repudiation of the "eccentric" element in Wordsworth's work is of especial significance; for it is linked directly with Jeffrey's general presuppositions about poetry. These emerge fairly clearly from his "Essay on Beauty" (1811),[1] which was originally written as a review of Alison's *Essay on the Nature and Principles of Taste* (1790), but was republished in the *Encyclopaedia Britannica*, and continued to appear in it till 1875. The key statement there, for our purposes, is that the artist must be careful to employ

> only such objects as are the *natural* signs, or the inseparable concomitants of emotions of which the greater part of mankind are susceptible; and his taste will *then* deserve to be called bad or false, if he obtrude upon the public, as beautiful, objects that are not likely to be associated in common minds with any interesting impressions.

Wordsworth had evidently, in Jeffrey's eyes, been guilty of

[1] *ER*, XVIII, May 1811.

"bad or false taste." But it can be seen, without much difficulty, that the view maintained in this passage could easily lead to the repudiation of any poetry which did not keep close to the ground, and appeal by the "naturalness" of the associations called up, in "common minds," by the objects presented. Such a tendency appears, indeed, in the contrasts Jeffrey draws between the poetry of Wordsworth and that of Crabbe.[1] But the passage from the "Essay on Beauty" also contradicts some of Jeffrey's own preferences; for he could hardly have justifiably maintained that "common minds" could be expected to find "natural" many of the associations suggested in the poetry of what he considered the 'golden age' of Elizabeth. For his point to be valid Jeffrey would at least have had to assume that the "common minds" of which he wrote were those of highly educated readers. Jeffrey would, indeed, have contended that by "common minds" he did not necessarily mean uneducated minds, though he did not *demand* education either. What he objected to was what he considered to be oddity, affectation, and childishness. In an essay on Burns[2] he recommends to the Lake School, so keen on *simplicity*, the simplicity of Burns. That simplicity was, in Jeffrey's opinion, natural and manly; and Burns faithfully represented the spoken language of passion and affection, not debasing his work by "babyish interjections, and all the puling expletives of an old nurserymaid's vocabulary." Jeffrey also recommends the Lakers to

> contrast their own fantastical personages of hysterical schoolmasters and sententious leechgatherers, with the authentic rustics of Burns's "Cotter's Saturday Night," and his inimitable songs; and reflect on the different reception which these personifications have met with from the public. . . . Though [he suggests] they will not be reclaimed from their puny affectations by the example of their learned predecessors, they may,

[1] *ER*, XII, April 1808. [2] *ER*, XIII, January 1809.

> perhaps, submit to be admonished by a self-taught and illiterate poet, who drew from nature far more directly than they do, and produced something so much like the admired copies of the masters whom they have abjured.

There seems little doubt that Jeffrey's savage review of Wordsworth's 1807 volumes adversely affected sales. More than two years later the edition of five hundred copies was still not sold out. Still more important, however, is the distinct possibility that resultant worry over money, and a keen sense of discouragement, may actually have contributed to Wordsworth's well-known poetic decline. There was, indeed, some affectation and childishness in some of the incidents and language in Wordsworth's poems, but Jeffrey's concentration on these, and his failure to respond positively to the depth and importance of the "out-of-the-way" thoughts and feelings, and the superb spirit and language of the poetry at its finest, is a measure of some ultimate lack of depth and range in the man and in his critical attitudes.

Throughout his editorship of the *Edinburgh* Jeffrey continued to attack Wordsworth's poetry. His most famous review is that of *The Excursion*,[1] with its celebrated opening words: "This will never do!" He sums up the "absurdity" which "infects the whole substance of the work" as "a puerile ambition of singularity engrafted on an unlucky predilection for truisms; and an affected passion for simplicity and humble life, most awkwardly combined with a taste for mystical refinements and all the gorgeousness of obscure phraseology." *The Excursion* is, it must be admitted, a patchy poem, open to attack, but Jeffrey makes little attempt to understand it, though he does allow Wordsworth "great powers . . . and frequently a force in his moral declamations, and a tenderness in his pathetic narratives, which neither his

[1] *ER*, XXIV, November 1814. A long extract is printed below at pp. 185–188.

prolixity nor his affectation can altogether deprive of their effect."

The *Edinburgh*'s review of *The Excursion* was regarded by Jeffrey's partisans as "crushing," but the poem did bring Wordsworth in course of time a considerable band of admirers. Moreover, it was this review that provoked Coleridge to that balanced defence of Wordsworth in *Biographia Literaria* which is one of the classics of literary criticism.[1]

It is unnecessary to follow further the history of Jeffrey's criticism of Wordsworth, and Wordsworth's bitter reactions—for example, in his *Letter to a Friend of Robert Burns* (1816). Both became more and more personal. It is, however, worth drawing attention to the fact that Jeffrey gave some of his contemporaries the impression that he sometimes wrote maliciously with the object of increasing the sales of the review. It is also noteworthy that he told Crabb Robinson that he actually admired Wordsworth greatly, but, having set his course, was obliged to persist in it.

Jeffrey is probably at his best on Crabbe, whom he calls in one place the most original writer who had come before him. All Jeffrey's reviews of Crabbe are excellent.[2] He had very much admired *The Village* when it first appeared (1783), and when Crabbe's 1807 volume was published Jeffrey gave it a warm welcome,[3] holding that it was sufficient warrant for Crabbe to be considered "one of the most original, nervous, and pathetic poets of the present century." He has high praise for Crabbe's force and truth of description, "joined for the most part to great selection and condensation of exposition." He also draws attention to Crabbe's "gleams of gaiety and humour." He takes the opportunity,

[1] *Biographia Literaria* (1817), chapters xiv–xxii. Long extracts are printed below at pp. 194–208.

[2] Substantial extracts from Jeffrey's reviews of *The Borough* (1810) and *Tales of the Hall* (1819) are printed below at pp. 88–100 and 110–112.

[3] *ER*, XII, April 1808.

moreover, of contrasting Crabbe with Wordsworth, maintaining that, whereas Wordsworth invented "whimsical and unheard-of beings," with whom many readers found it impossible to sympathize, Crabbe exhibited the common people of England pretty much as they were, and brought their misfortunes home to readers with great force and pathos. Of the poems Jeffrey lays most stress on *The Parish Register*, but he also expresses admiration for *Sir Eustace Grey*, and still more for *The Hall of Justice*, which he considered to be written "with very unusual power of language," and to show that Crabbe had "great mastery over the tragic passions of pity and horror." Jeffrey ends his review by expressing the hope that Crabbe would soon "appear again among the worthy supporters of the old poetical establishment, and come in time to surpass the revolutionists in fast firing as well as in weight of metal."

Jeffrey also reviewed Crabbe's *Tales* (1812).[1] The review is a fine, detailed critique of the volume, but does not contain so many general observations on Crabbe's work as some of Jeffrey's other reviews. Those he does offer, however, are well worth attention. He expresses disappointment that the *Tales* did not contain more tragic poems like *Sir Eustace Grey* and *The Hall of Justice*. He would have liked less jocularity, rather more incidents, and rather fewer details. The *Tales* seemed to him "mere supplementary chapters" to *The Borough* or *The Parish Register*. They had, in his view,

> the same tone, subjects, style, measure, and versification, the same finished and minute delineation of things quite ordinary and common,—and generally very engaging when employed upon external objects, but often fatiguing when directed merely to insignificant characters and habits;—the same strange mixture too of feelings that tear the heart and darken the imagination, with starts of low humour and patches of ludi-

[1] *ER*, XX, November 1812.

> crous imagery;—the same kindly sympathy with the humble and innocent pleasures of the poor and inelegant, and the same indulgence for their venial offences, contrasted with a strong sense of their frequent depravity, and too constant a recollection of the sufferings it produces;—and, finally, the same honours paid to the delicate affections and ennobling passions of humble life, with the same generous testimony to their frequent existence, mixed up as before with a reprobation sufficiently rigid, and a ridicule sufficiently severe, of their excesses and affectations.

It would be hard to find elsewhere in criticism as compact and understanding a description of some of the chief features of Crabbe's work.

Jeffrey goes on to point out that the *Tales* depicted a larger share of generosity of heart and fineness of feeling in people of the middle and lower classes than Crabbe's earlier work had done; and he thought that this should make Crabbe's work still more popular with those classes. Jeffrey even gives it as his view (in contrast with what he had said in the *Thalaba* review) that their emotions were more powerful and better fitted for poetry than those of the upper classes. This should make it quite clear that it would be a great mistake to consider Jeffrey as simply a socially snobbish critic, and to try to account for his attitude to Wordsworth's work in those terms. In this connexion we should also remember Jeffrey's great admiration for the work of Burns.

Even when he is unjust Jeffrey is always worth reading. His reviews are clear and lively, and he had a genuine eye for weaknesses and strengths, when they fell within the range of his vision. His mind was also sensitive to many different kinds of features of poems, and took account of them in forming critical judgments. He was, however, an extravert and a humanist, with apparently little religious sense, and this deficiency must have made it very hard for him to understand Wordsworth.

One other review in the *Edinburgh* deserves passing mention: Hazlitt's review of *Christabel*, *Kubla Khan*, and *The Pains of Sleep*.[1] It is, in a way, amusing reading; but it is Hazlitt at his most cantankerous and critical worst. Coleridge's whole volume is dismissed as "utterly destitute of value." The review contains a satirical running commentary on *Christabel*, with many jibes both at its sense and at its sound. Hazlitt is completely deaf to the music both of *Christabel* and of *Kubla Khan*, and there is no attempt to enter into the spirit or atmosphere of either poem. It is a blatant instance of cocksure failure of comprehension.

The Quarterly Review

The *Quarterly* may have been first thought of by Stratford Canning—a cousin of George Canning, who later became Prime Minister; but prominent in its foundation (in 1809) were Sir Walter Scott and the publisher John Murray; and George Canning himself was politically a dominant figure behind the review, and actually wrote for it, though the fact that he did so was a closely guarded secret. William Gifford (1756–1826) was appointed editor, and remained so until 1824. John Taylor Coleridge, a nephew of the poet, then acted as editor for a year, after which John Gibson Lockhart (1794–1854), Scott's son-in-law and biographer, took on the post, and served until 1853.

For our purposes the most important period, on the whole, was that of Gifford's editorship (1809–24), though it was under Lockhart that Henry Nelson Coleridge wrote the admirable review of Coleridge's work already referred to.[2] During Gifford's editorship the most frequent contributors were Robert Southey, himself one of the Lake School of poets, and related to Coleridge by marriage; J. W. Croker,

[1] *ER*, XXVII, September 1816. [2] *QR*, LII, August 1834.

whose special province was recent French history, though he also wrote a slashing review of Keats; John Barrow, who wrote mainly on foreign countries, and did not write on literature; and Gifford himself, who, though he only wrote eight full articles, tinkered with many by other contributors, frequently altering them without permission from their writers, particularly where they deviated from Tory principles. Scott wrote a number of articles, but did not review any of our three poets. Three of the most interesting of the articles for our purposes are Robert Grant's article on Crabbe's *Borough* (November 1810),[1] Lamb's article on Wordsworth's *Excursion* (July 1814), of which unfortunately no manuscript version survives, and which was heavily modified by Gifford, and W. R. Lyall's review of Wordsworth's *White Doe of Rylstone* (October 1815), which contains much balanced and acute criticism. There is also an important appreciation of Wordsworth by Lockhart, written much later (November 1834).

The *Quarterly* was much kinder to Wordsworth than the *Edinburgh*. The explanation is, no doubt, partly political. The fact that Southey and Scott, both Tory Romantics, were so closely associated with the review may also have counted for much; probably in general counterbalancing the Augustan tendencies of Gifford, who was an expert on Roman satire, and had, as a young man, castigated the extravagancies of some innovating poetasters of the late eighteenth century in two satires written in Popean style (*The Baviad* (1794) and *The Maeviad* (1795)). On the other hand, the early *Quarterly* did not speak so highly of Crabbe as the early *Edinburgh* had done. It objected to the harshness of his realism, and to his "contempt for the *bienséances of life*." Possibly the *Quarterly* sensed that Crabbe's diagnosis of social abuses might offer ammunition to dangerous reformers.

[1] Reprinted at p. 100, below.

Though, however, the *Quarterly* was kinder to Wordsworth than the *Edinburgh*, Gifford's alteration of Lamb's enthusiastic review of *The Excursion*, which transformed Lamb's eulogies into something rather less warm, came at an unfortunate time for Wordsworth, who needed some financial success. One can therefore understand his complaint that the stupidity of Gifford combined with the impertinence of Jeffrey to destroy the profits he would otherwise have made. Nevertheless, even the modified review was still favourable; and there had also been some praise of the Lake Poets in general in an article published earlier the same year, though the article criticized them for associating too strong feelings with trifling causes.

Again, Lyall's review of the 1815 edition of Wordsworth's poems[1] spoke of them as exhibiting

> a mind richly stored with all the materials from which poetry is formed:—elevation of sentiment, tenderness of heart, the truest sensibility for the beauties of nature, combined with extraordinary fervour of imagination, and a most praiseworthy love of simplicity both in thought and language.

These are enthusiastic words, and that they were neither empty nor insincere is guaranteed by the discerning character of some adverse criticisms made in the same review, such as that Wordsworth lacked a "large and vigorous understanding," and that one found him sometimes ineffectually straining after something beyond plain good sense, and that his theory of diction contained defects which resulted in practice, paradoxically enough, in a kind of obscurity.

As to Coleridge, the early *Quarterly* paid no attention to his poetry. Though Scott thought well of Coleridge's poetry, Gifford did not, and he would not allow a review to be published of *Christabel*, *Kubla Khan*, and *The Pains of Sleep*,

[1] *QR*, XIV, October 1815. The same review dealt also, and chiefly, with *The White Doe of Rylstone* (see p. 35, above).

when they appeared in 1816, even though they were published by Murray, who also published the *Quarterly*.

After Lockhart became editor in 1826, however, the *Quarterly* eventually published fine appreciations both of Coleridge and of Wordsworth, and both poets were referred to as classics of our literature. Very high praise was also given to Crabbe, Croker going so far as to hold that Crabbe had exhibited the short and simple annals of the poor with such deep knowledge of human nature, with such general ease and simplicity, and with such accurate force of expression, whether gay or pathetic, as no poet except Shakespeare had excelled. Again, Lockhart pointed out that Crabbe did not write work of unrelieved gloom, and, indeed, that his "deep and dreadful pathos" fell on readers far more strongly because of the wit, humour, and playfulness with which he relieved it.

The literary attitudes of the *Quarterly* to the three poets were thus less clear-cut and consistent than those of the *Edinburgh*. Gifford was evidently favourable to neither of the poets, but he held a very different position in the hierarchy of the *Quarterly* from that held by Jeffrey in the hierarchy of the *Edinburgh*. Jeffrey was a co-founder of the periodical he edited. Gifford was not. He was only appointed to edit the *Quarterly* after Scott had declined to do so, and he had to fight hard for the editorial independence which he eventually to a considerable degree achieved. Again, though he was determined, Gifford never succeeded in imposing his literary opinions upon the review as a whole. The men with whom he was associated on the review had, in general, very different opinions of early Romantic poetry from his own. Gifford was, moreover, of weak health and uncertain vitality. Above all, he was not a critic of the stature of Jeffrey, and he wrote very few entire articles for the review. There is, indeed, no parallel in the *Quarterly* to the years-long series of criticisms which Jeffrey directed against the work of Wordsworth. Finally, after Lockhart took over, the general attitude to all three poets became, as we have seen, altogether more favourable. Gifford had to some extent succeeded in modifying or atrophying the expression of such favourable opinions during his editorship, but once his censoring influence had been removed, the flow of praise became free.

Blackwood's Edinburgh Magazine

After an undistinguished run of six numbers under weak editors, *Blackwood's* (established in 1817) was entrusted by its founder, William Blackwood, the Edinburgh publisher, to a lively triumvirate, John Wilson ("Christopher North") (1785–1854), James Hogg the Ettrick Shepherd (1770–1835), and John Gibson Lockhart (1794–1854), whom we have already mentioned in connexion with the *Quarterly*. Hogg was a rough, homespun genius, whereas Wilson and Lockhart had both been educated at Glasgow University and at Oxford. The spirit which animated them contrasted sharply with the purposes underlying the foundation of the two great reviews. They were out for some fun. Wilson, a remarkably high-spirited and unstable character, and perhaps the most brilliant personality of the three, was probably the ringleader in the early malpractices of the magazine. "*Maga*," as the periodical was soon nicknamed, was ostensibly started to provide a "nimbler and more familiar" kind of criticism in Edinburgh; but from the beginning of the régime of the triumvirate it was evident that to achieve an 'effect' its editors were prepared to go so far as to libel character and even to ridicule physical defects and infirmities. In the notorious "Chaldee Manuscript" they shocked many Edinburghers by using Biblical language as a medium for their satire on local personalities. It was at least ten years before

Maga thoroughly reformed her ways. Yet much reputable literary criticism appeared in her pages even during those early years.

Of the three editors Wilson is the most important for our consideration, for he knew both Wordsworth and Coleridge intimately, and wrote a good deal about them in *Maga*. Wilson's personal relations with them had important effects on his criticism of their work. As a boy of seventeen at school in Glasgow Wilson had written a long letter to Wordsworth, to whom he was a perfect stranger, expressing an enthusiastic and understanding admiration for *Lyrical Ballads*, but objecting that the poet had sometimes fallen into the error of writing on subjects which were improper for poetry because they would not interest people in general. The maternal affection described in *The Idiot Boy*, for instance, was, according to Wilson, merely animal, and so of no interest, and even disgusting. Wordsworth sent a reply which was probably the joint work of himself and his sister Dorothy. He was clearly gratified by Wilson's understanding appreciation, but maintained that a poet should try to *change* people's feelings. He should not simply write about what would naturally interest people. He should make people interested in things they were not interested in before. He said that writing *The Idiot Boy* had given him great pleasure, and that reading it did the same. He added that poor people easily forget their "natural disgust" towards idiots, who were actually worshipped in the East, and considered a blessing in the Alps!

A year later Wilson went up to Oxford, where he had a brilliant academic career, and also made a name for high spirits, personal charm, and unconventional behaviour. His pursuits included fisticuffs, jumping, and cock-fighting. His mother's opposition to his marrying a Glasgow girl he was in love with resulted in his taking drugs and threatening suicide, and also in restless activity of one kind and another. A little later, in 1807, he went to live in the Lake District, and got to know the Wordsworths well. His attitude to Wordsworth was at first one of rather bashful reverence, but he soon grew forward enough to play a practical joke or two on the poet, towards whom, however, he still remained basically respectful. In 1809 Wilson published in Coleridge's periodical *The Friend* a letter signed "Mathetes," in which he exhorted Wordsworth to rescue the young men of England from the "indifference" and "seduction" of the time, by leading them back, as only he could do, to the source of strength and wisdom in Nature. Wordsworth replied shortly after in the same periodical. He disclaimed an intention to lead people to escape from life. He maintained that they ought to think, and to apply their thinking to life. Contemplation must not be barren. The young men of the time would be saved by Nature and Reason together. Wordsworth even urged that the rewards of the world should not be scorned, though they should not take first place.

Wilson's friendship with the Wordsworths continued. In 1811 he married, and, needing to provide for a growing family, began before long to practise at the Scottish Bar. He also wrote some long but generally rather poor poems under strong Wordsworthian influence, and was soon considered one of the Lake School. Some reviewers even began to attack him in common with the other Lake Poets. Jeffrey, however, with whom he was friendly, praised his talent, compared him favourably with Wordsworth, and warned him against the Lakers' influence. This was in a review of Wilson's *The Isle of Palms* (1812). Wilson seemed to Jeffrey to show "open sociality," in contrast with the self-esteem and "offensive assumption of exclusive taste, judgment and morality" which Jeffrey thought pervaded the Lakers' work. Reaction among reviewers to Wilson's macabre poem *The City of the Plague* (1816) was generally that its subject was horrifying, that it contained powerful passages, and that it still showed strong Lakist influence. Jeffrey, however, denied this influence, and again contrasted the poem favourably with the work of Wordsworth. The *Edinburgh*'s preference of Wilson to Wordsworth was seen by the discerning observer Crabb Robinson to be a scandalous insult. Wordsworth felt the same. He considered Wilson's work entirely derivative from his own, and thought Wilson ought to have acknowledged as much publicly. Interestingly enough, Wilson said some years later that he did not think of his poetry as imitative of Wordsworth, and was galled at finding that the critics did.

In 1814 Wilson had invited Hogg to meet the Wordsworths, who were in Edinburgh. Wilson was apparently enthusiastic about *The Excursion*, which Hogg found heavy, though he admired many of Wordsworth's other poems. Hogg describes how they listened to Wordsworth that night "as to a superior being, far exalted above the common walks of life." Later the same year Hogg went to stay with Wilson at his house in the Lakes, partly in order to get to know the Wordsworths better. Hogg was upset when Wordsworth refused to partake of some rum punch he offered him, and "doubted if perfect sobriety and transcendent poetical genius can exist together"—an interesting sidelight both on Hogg and on Wordsworth. But, worst of all, Wordsworth offended Hogg by saying something which implied that he did not consider Hogg worthy to be considered a poet. There is little doubt that this put a permanent brake on Hogg's enthusiasm for the work of Wordsworth. As for Wilson, it seems that he was drifting somewhat away from Wordsworth and towards De Quincey, with whom his friendship lasted for life. Possibly, after a full taste of the world of Edinburgh, Wilson began to find Wordsworth limited and parochial. At all events, we soon find him referring to Wordsworth as "the stamp-master" and as "not a man of first-rate intellect." Wordsworth, on the other hand, was still writing kindly of Wilson in 1816.

This was all before the foundation of *Blackwood's* in 1817. Then, in one of the first numbers, Wilson attacked Wordsworth for his attack on Jeffrey in his *Letter to a Friend of Robert Burns*. Wilson's article was, like the rest, anonymous, and he himself replied to it in another article later the same year, in which he praised Wordsworth as

> a poet distinguished for the originality of his genius—for his profound knowledge of the human heart, for his spiritual insight into all the grandeur and magnificence of the external world, for a strain of the most serene, undisturbed, and lofty morality, within whose control no mind can come without being elevated, purified, and enlightened, for a religion partaking at once of all the solemnity of faith, and all the enthusiasm of poetry—and, to crown all with a perfect consummation, a poet who has realized, in a life of sublime solitude, the visions that have blessed the dreams of his inspiration.

It would be hard to praise Wordsworth more highly or more fulsomely. Yet in the very next number of *Maga* appeared another attack almost certainly also by Wilson. Wordsworth evidently read the articles, and, despite the eulogies of the second, refused to allow *Blackwood's* in his house for the future. Wilson had also referred to the Third Canto of *Childe Harold* as vanquishing Wordsworth as a descriptive poet, and as being alone "worth all the dull metaphysics of *The Excursion*." Yet the very next year he called such an opinion cold and unmeaning, and contended that what Byron really did was to follow Wordsworth "to the same eternal fountain of all beauty and all grandeur." It is hard to estimate how far these contradictions sprang from a journalistic desire of Wilson's to increase sales of the magazine by aggressive writing, how far from a wish to please both Jeffrey and Wordsworth, and both Byron and Wordsworth, and how far from temperamental instability and an ambivalent attitude to the object of his early hero-worship.

Most of Wilson's reviews of Wordsworth's poetry praise it. Perhaps most discerning is the second of his "Essays on the Lake School of Poetry," called "On the Habits of Thought inculcated by Wordsworth" (December 1818).[1] Another tribute occurs in a review of Crabbe's *Tales of the Hall* (July 1819), and yet another in a review of Wordsworth's *Sonnets and Memorials*[2] (August 1822), in which Wilson even praises his sonnet-sequence *Ecclesiastical Sketches*. Yet in October 1823 and September 1825 we find violent attacks on Wordsworth in two of Wilson's *Noctes Ambrosianae*,[3] and, though he praised Wordsworth in a number of other articles, we know that he intended to attack him virulently in the *Quarterly* not long after Wordsworth had been laid in his grave. It is a strange history.

Less strange, perhaps, but still curious enough, is the shorter and more scantily documented story of Wilson's relations with Coleridge. They met in 1808, and, though we have little information, they seem to have been on friendly terms until 1816. Yet in the very first number of *Blackwood's* published under the triumvirate (October 1817) Wilson wrote a review of Coleridge's *Biographia Literaria* in which he compared Coleridge unfavourably with other contemporary writers, and also attacked him personally. Scholars

[1] *B*, IV, December 1818.

[2] This volume consisted of: I. *Ecclesiastical Sketches*, and II. *Memorials of a Tour on the Continent*.

[3] Dialogues contributed to *Blackwood's* between 1822 and 1835, all except a few of the earliest being by Wilson. The characters were "Christopher North" (Wilson) and "The Ettrick Shepherd" (Hogg).

and biographers have found it hard to explain the disconcerting change. It seems that Wilson had already written one review of the *Biographia*, and lost it; which may have put him in a bad temper. There is also some evidence, of uncertain reliability, that Wilson had written an unflattering character-sketch of Coleridge on the fly-leaf of a book, that Coleridge had accidentally seen this, and that a quarrel had ensued. It is also possible that Coleridge's attack on Jeffrey in the *Biographia* was a part-cause, as Wilson was on very friendly terms with Jeffrey at the time. In another notorious attack in the same number of *Maga* whose target was Leigh Hunt and the Cockney School, probably mainly written by Lockhart, but in which Wilson may also have had a hand, Coleridge is incidentally attacked and Wordsworth praised, Coleridge being even referred to as a "greater quack" than Hunt. Coleridge actually thought of bringing a libel action, though he never did, and four years later even became a contributor to *Blackwood's*. Meanwhile in December 1817 the magazine had published a letter to the reviewer complaining at the unfair criticisms and personal attacks. This letter itself may well have been written either by Lockhart or by Wilson! In any case, in April 1818 Wilson attacked Jeffrey for having entrusted *Christabel* to the tender mercies of the "Jacobin" Hazlitt, whose review of the volume containing it was fiercely uncomprehending.[1] Wilson's references to Coleridge in ensuing numbers vary somewhat in tone; but in March 1819 Lockhart paid a signal tribute to Coleridge as a critic, and praised "the richness, and beauty, and wildness of his aerial and romantic imagination." The same month Blackwood called on Coleridge at Highgate and asked him to write for *Maga*, which Coleridge showed himself inclined to do, provided that *Maga* stopped "private slander and public malignity" and followed a policy oppo-

[1] See p. 34, above.

site to that of the *Edinburgh* in morals, politics, and religion. Other tributes from Lockhart followed in *Maga*, and then came a harmless and refreshing parody, apparently by "Delta" Moir, called *The Rime of the Auncient Waggonere*, which, with an inferior sequel on *Christabel*, Coleridge did not at all resent. The next important development was a highly appreciative essay on Coleridge's poetry in October 1819, probably by Lockhart, in which Coleridge is called "the prince of superstitious poets," and immortality is forecast for his few great poems, "in conception so original, and in execution so exquisite."

After Coleridge started to contribute, very irregularly, to *Maga*, the rate of praise was stepped up, and Coleridge continued to laud *Blackwood's* till the end of his life. Wilson's best contribution to Coleridgean criticism was published soon after Coleridge's death. It was his review of *Coleridge's Poetical Works* in October 1834.[1] While not so distinguished as that of H. N. Coleridge in the *Quarterly*, it offered, among much justifiable praise, a good analysis of Coleridge's cumulative creation of the character of Geraldine in *Christabel*, and contended that in the realm of the preternatural Coleridge surpassed all other poets except Shakespeare, whom he equalled. Finally, in 1838, Wilson brought out, in an analysis of Martin Tupper's inferior completion of *Christabel*, the immense superiority of Coleridge's work, with its "dim revelation, mysteriously diffused," of "a fearful being that all at once is present 'beyond the reaches of our souls'—something fiendish in what is most fair, and blasting in what is most beautiful." Wilson thought that Coleridge could never have put his conception of the rest of the poem into words adequate to it, and he hoped that it would for ever remain a fragment.

The mercurial Wilson, when he was in the right mood,

[1] An extract appears below at p. 257.

could pay eloquent and understanding tribute to features of the poetry of Wordsworth and Coleridge which would still be thought central now; but, as we have seen, his unstable personal relations with the poets, his temperamental vagaries, and his love for aggressive satire, sometimes led him to be flagrantly unjust.

Lockhart was a smoother, less self-assertive personality than Wilson, but he was inclined to snobbery, and he was a classical scholar who resented any mythologizing by those he considered ignoramuses. This made him harsh on Leigh Hunt and Keats. But he had no such grounds for attacking Wordsworth and Coleridge, nor did he have the close personal relations with either of them that affected Wilson's criticism. Lockhart left most of the reviewing of Wordsworth in *Maga* to Wilson, though he praised Wordsworth in his book *Peter's Letters to his Kinsfolk* (1819). He thought that to appreciate Wordsworth's poems properly one needed to pass through the same kind of sober discipline the poet himself had passed through in his quiet valleys. Lockhart even flayed the reading public of Edinburgh for the worldly complacency which prevented them, in his view, from being able to make contact with the poet's work. Lockhart recognized that Wordsworth had written far too much, and was far too often prosy and monotonous. Yet, in Lockhart's view, he had "cleared out for himself, by his own labour, a wide and magnificent path through the solitary forests of the human imagination." Wordsworth was no simple and touching pastoral poet, but something much grander. Yet Lockhart's final impression was that Wordsworth, though a great poet, had not made any great philosophical discovery, and that *The Excursion* was obscure, heavy, and unharmonious. Lockhart's criticism of Wordsworth, however, though on occasion felicitous, was far slighter and more impressionistic than Wilson's. Lockhart was more illuminating on

Coleridge. Though his main essay in the issue for October 1819 cannot compare for adequacy with the critiques by Sterling and H. N. Coleridge, it was quite good pioneering work, and even better were some remarks in *Peter's Letters to his Kinsfolk* praising Coleridge as "the most splendid versifier of our age" and "the most musical." Lockhart also commended Coleridge for not thrusting forward his psychological conceptions in his poetry, and for not adopting Wordsworth's practices in diction. He also contrasted Coleridge's love-poetry with Byron's, holding that it showed far more reverence for women, and "far deeper insight into the true grandeur of their gentleness." He considered Coleridge's love-poetry the finest produced in England since Shakespeare and the "old dramatists"—an unusual eulogy.

Neither Wilson nor Lockhart had personal contact with Crabbe. Both liked his poetry, but it was Wilson who reviewed Crabbe in *Blackwood's*. Crabbe's early poems, and *The Borough*, and *Tales* had appeared before *Maga* started. But Wilson gave a perceptive review to *Tales of the Hall* (July 1819).[1]

The reviews in *Blackwood's*, and especially those by Wilson, still make good reading; and, on the whole, they show more understanding of Wordsworth and of Coleridge than either the *Edinburgh* or the *Quarterly*, though exception must always be made of H. N. Coleridge's 1834 article on Coleridge in the *Quarterly*.

The Monthly Review

Unlike the Tory *Critical Review*, whose heyday was long past, the Whig *Monthly* still retained considerable vitality, especially until about 1816. Its contributors were able, and

[1] An extract from this review appears at p. 112 below.

remuneration was higher than with the *Critical*. But the *Monthly*'s pioneer editor, Ralph Griffiths, died in 1803 after fifty years of editorship, and his son, George Edward Griffiths, who conducted the review until 1825, had neither the ability nor the personality of his father. Inevitably the contributions appeared slight compared with those in the *Edinburgh* and *Quarterly*. Furthermore, George Griffiths required absolute consistency from review to review, and also proscribed "philosophical criticism." These policies were cramping, and undoubtedly they contributed, with the other factors, to the gradual supersession of the *Monthly* by the *Edinburgh* as the leading Whig review. Good reviewing continued in the *Monthly*, especially of works of science and of classical scholarship, but reviews of poetry were, with exceptions, inferior to those in most periodicals treated in this Introduction.

The *Monthly* was, on the whole, better and more sympathetic on Crabbe than on Wordsworth and Coleridge. Crabbe's first work, *The Library* (1781), had been very favourably received by Edmund Cartwright,[1] who later (1783) had given *The Village* a mixed reception,[2] casting doubt on whether Crabbe's grim picture of peasant life was really truer than the idealized picture drawn by the poets against whom he was reacting. Cartwright did acknowledge, however, that the poem contained many splendid lines and picturesque and original descriptions.

When, in 1807, after over twenty years' silence, Crabbe published a collected edition of his poems to date, the *Monthly* entrusted its review[3] to Thomas Denman, then a young barrister, but eventually, in 1832, Lord Chief Justice. Denman depreciated *The Village* in comparison with some of the other early work of Crabbe. He gave most attention,

[1] *MR*, LXVII, December 1781. [2] *MR*, LXIX, November 1783.
[3] *MR*, LVI, June 1808.

however, to *The Parish Register*, praising Crabbe's character-sketches, selection of incidents, "felicity of narration," natural pathos, and uncommon powers of satire. The only adverse criticism was of some prolixity and obscurity. Denman praised highly the tragic power of *Sir Eustace Grey* and *The Hall of Justice*, and commended the whole volume for "the flow of the verse," the "manly and powerful" language, and the "sterling poetry and original powers of thought."

Three years later *The Borough* appeared, and Denman wrote a full review,[1] criticizing the work as deficient both in composition and as a picture of man in society. The 'letters' were not really letters, and lacked liveliness and variety. And Crabbe had too low a view of humanity, and too austere a morality; and he was too touchy on behalf of the clergy. According to Denman, moreover, Crabbe often wasted his "nervous and powerful mind" on "useless and sometimes revolting details." Denman's own craving, which might well have originated in expectations set up by the poetry of Scott, was for some romantic details, for a monastery or towering castle as a setting for the borough!

Denman was more enthusiastic about Crabbe's *Tales* (1812),[2] which he welcomed as excelling Crabbe's early work "in grace and spirit, in copiousness, vigor, and sensibility," though he still objected to some useless and repellent details. He did not, however, demand any relation between the various tales (he had probably been disarmed by Crabbe's Preface).[3] In some of the tales Crabbe seemed to Denman to have united his "uncommon powers of searching into the mind of man" with "a remarkable power of affecting the feelings," whereas in most of the tales Crabbe had evidently been "satisfied with the former."

[1] *MR*, LXI, April 1810. [2] *MR*, LXIX, December 1812.
[3] See the extract from the Preface printed below at pp. 105–110.

It is uncertain who reviewed *Tales of the Hall* (1819) for the *Monthly*,[1] but the reviewer lamented that in the last few years poetic taste had grown vulgar. All people had come to want was energy in the leading action, or, perhaps, extravagant wickedness in the leading actor, with occasional felicity of expression. The reviewer was probably referring to the vogue for Byron's Eastern tales and imitations of them. He thought Crabbe had been affected by the pernicious influence. Crabbe had grown garrulous, though he still frequently showed a "vigour and correctness of description, a deep observation of the human heart, or a striking trait of manners" that put him "at the head of the moral painters of the age." He also excelled in "the humorous" as well as "the tender," and, in the reviewer's opinion, perhaps the humorous would have been Crabbe's true line. He was not delicate enough in touch and taste or skilful enough in selection to achieve a full effect in pathetic description, but he could yet turn his attention to satire and dispose of the "melancholy absurdity" of Methodism. Unfortunately, according to the reviewer, Crabbe showed in places—e.g., in "Ellen"—a propensity "to mix the most incongruous feelings together, and to excite in us the most genuine tears and the broadest grin at the same instant." The reviewer also questioned both the "moral use" and the "poetic probability" of investing such "rapscallions" as Crabbe's smugglers and poachers "with all the dignity of the loftiest passions," and of "setting them forth with all the eloquence of the most thrilling descriptions."

Finally, in 1834, long after George Griffiths, with his iron demand for consistency, had relinquished control of the periodical, the *Monthly* published a review[2] of Crabbe's son's edition of his father's Poetical Works, for which the son wrote a biography. The review dealt mainly with the Life,

[1] *MR*, XC, November 1819. [2] *MR* (N.S.), III, September 1834.

but it also briefly surveyed the poems, maintaining that the early work was more polished but less distinctive, and also artificially gloomy, whereas the later poems were more powerful because more detached. Crabbe, it held, was a master of everything related to human character and action, and no poet since Shakespeare had painted those diversities of character one meets in ordinary life with equal fidelity or effect. Again, before Crabbe poets had caricatured humble life, whereas he had painted it as it was, his work thereby contrasting also with the unreal pictures of "sentimental swains" offered by other contemporary poets (the reviewer was, no doubt, thinking chiefly of Wordsworth). Finally, the reviewer prophesied that when "all the exhalations of prejudice and fashion" passed away, "the simple truth and energy" of Crabbe would be more highly valued by the many than they had been. Crabbe's poetical abilities ensured him "a high and permanent rank among the poets of his country."

The history of the *Monthly*'s attitude to the work of Wordsworth and Coleridge is more complex. The *Monthly* was kinder to the early work of Coleridge than to that of Wordsworth.[1] It recognized Coleridge's "boldness and novelty of conception, strength of figure, and sublimity of sentiment," and also appreciated his range, and his ability to deal in "beauty and elegance" as well as in "the soft and tender emotions." In contrast it rapped Wordsworth over the knuckles for his frequent confusions of thought, though it granted that some passages showed imagination and afforded hope for his poetic future. The *Monthly* approved Coleridge's avoidance of exploded mythology, and his preference for originality to mere correctness. It also admired his repudiation of war, and his refusal to sing of "glory," and

[1] On Coleridge see *MR*, XX, June 1796; *MR*, XXII, March 1797; *MR*, XXIX, May 1799; on Wordsworth *MR*, XII, October 1793.

it enthused on the love of freedom and anti-Napoleonic patriotism in *Fears in Solitude* and *France: an Ode*. But it considered Coleridge careless about diction, and sometimes "very prosaic."

When *Lyrical Ballads* came out the *Monthly* gave the volume a mixed reception.[1] The reviewer was Dr Burney, the distinguished aesthetician and music historian, who had been a friend of Dr Johnson. Burney thought the poems "ingenious compositions," but regarded them as an inferior species of poetry, not comparable in quality with, for instance, the work of Milton. The "author" of *Lyrical Ballads* (like most reviewers, Burney thought there was only one author) certainly "had the art of pleasing and interesting in no common way by his delineation of human passions, human characters, and human incidents," but those effects were not produced by the poetry. "Pictures of misery and unmerited distress" were just as affecting in prose. "The elevation of soul, when it is lifted into the higher regions of imagination, affords us a delight of a different kind from the sensation which is produced by the detail of common incidents." Burney's differentiation is sound.

Burney's comments on individual poems are often interesting. *The Nightingale*, he wrote, "sings a strain of true and beautiful poetry; Miltonic yet original; reflective and interesting, in an uncommon degree." The poem "It is the first mild day of March" he wrote of as abounding "with beautiful sentiments from a polished mind." *The Idiot Boy* he found interesting and terrifying "almost to torture," and he recognized the depth and originality of *Tintern Abbey*, describing it as "the reflections of no common mind; poetical, beautiful, and philosophical." His criticism of it was that it over-valued solitariness and seclusion ("as if men were born to live in woods and wilds, unconnected with each

[1] *MR*, XXIX, May 1799.

other!"). His concluding words on the whole volume were these: "So much genius and originality are discovered in this publication, that we wish to see another from the same hand, written on more elevated subjects and in a more cheerful disposition."

This review was a remarkable performance. Burney had been brought up on a very different kind of poetry, yet, though he retained a number of prejudices, they did not prevent him from making intelligent and sensitive contact with the individual poems, or from according the volume the generous praise of his concluding words. Indeed, the review was, on the whole, more favourable than that written by Southey, the Romantic, in *The Critical Review*.[1]

On the 1802 edition of *Lyrical Ballads* the *Monthly* wrote only a short paragraph,[2] expressing the hope of encountering again "this natural, easy, sentimental Bard, in his pensive rambles through the hills and groves of his truly poetic, though somewhat peculiar imagination"—a curious description!

The *Monthly* did not review Wordsworth's 1807 volumes, but its critique of *The Excursion* was predominantly hostile.[3] The reviewer was J. H. Merivale. He allowed Wordsworth poetic genius, but he thought he weighed it down with "dark, heavy, confused heaps of nothingness." A "mysticism," out of the reach of any reader not similarly converted, pervaded the whole poem, and such mysticism was not the best conductor of misguided morals back to a calm and rational religion. Wordsworth's vaunted "originality" Merivale held to consist only in "a certain peculiarity of diction and manner," without which everything that was not "too mystical to be comprehended" would be "too commonplace to be tolerated." The poem, however, showed transient

[1] *CR*, XXIV, October 1798. [2] *MR*, XXXVIII, June 1802.
[3] *MR*, LXXVI, February 1815.

gleams of a powerful imagination, and an "ardent and devoted attachment" to nature, which could only exist in full force in a true poet. Merivale's review is shrewd, but his prejudice against the "mysticism" of the poem evidently prevented him from doing it real justice.

The *Monthly* also reviewed the 1815 edition of Wordsworth's *Poems*, and his new Preface and Supplementary Essay.[1] The review indicted Wordsworth for wasting his genius on unworthy subjects, and for showing "a whimsical and inveterately perverted taste." It considered his Preface "confused and arrogant," his classification of his poems "pompous and childish," and nine-tenths of the poems as silly and inharmonious. Among the few exceptions it made were the sonnets in honour of liberty.

The *Monthly*'s notice of the *Thanksgiving Ode*[2] was contemptuous, and so was its review of *Peter Bell*,[3] which it called an "infantine pamphlet," in which Wordsworth, in the reviewer's opinion, had shown himself "the buffoon of nature," who had "lowered her grand and general associations of physical and moral beauty into petty pastry-cook details of fruit and flowers." The hostility is petulant and uncharitable. *Peter Bell* is certainly not the best of Wordsworth's poems, but much can be said for it, and some of his contemporaries (*e.g.*, the reviewer in *The British Critic*[4]) were capable of saying it.

The *Monthly* liked Wordsworth's Duddon volume much better,[5] especially some of the miscellaneous poems and several of the Duddon sonnets. The volume seemed to the reviewer a recantation of all Wordsworth's "heresies" about poetic diction. Wordsworth's "ornamental" style was addressed to the "cultivated" imagination, whereas his plain

[1] *MR*, LXXVII, November 1815.
[2] *MR*, LXXXII, January 1817.
[3] *MR*, LXXXIX, August 1819.
[4] See p. 61, below.
[5] *MR*, XCIII, October 1820.

style was like addressing a child. Yet Wordsworthianisms remained in the volume—*e.g.*, the excessive use of the "old trick" (which Wordsworth, according to the reviewer, thought he had invented) of crediting plants and even inanimate objects with reason and emotion.

Even such reservations are absent from the *Monthly*'s review, fourteen years later (1835), of *Yarrow Revisited and other Poems.*[1] The tone is one of awestruck admiration. Wordsworth is spoken of as surpassing all living poets "for solemn, profound, and simple grandeur," and the volume reviewed is said to surpass in certain attributes all that Wordsworth had written before. He had "majestic knowledge, wisdom, and heaven-born benevolence." After all its past strictures the *Monthly* had now become uncritically idolatrous.

The *Monthly*'s reviews of Coleridge's poetry after *Lyrical Ballads* were unfavourable. That of *Christabel*, *Kubla Khan*, and *The Pains of Sleep*[2] was clearly intended to be crushing. It accused Coleridge of trying in *Christabel* to "dignify meanness of conception, to versify the flattest prose, and to teach the human ear a new and discordant system of harmony." *Kubla Khan* it regarded as "below criticism." *The Pains of Sleep* it thought contained some better lines. But, in the reviewer's opinion, it was lamentable that "so much superior genius should be corrupted and debased by such execrable taste."

The review of *Sibylline Leaves*[3] was not much more favourable. It asked why Coleridge, "gifted with much the strongest and most original powers of all the *Water Poets* of the day," was not even so popular as the other Lake Poets. Its answer was that this was partly due to the caprice and corruption of the national taste, and partly to Coleridge's

[1] *MR* (N.S.), 1835 (Vol. II), August 1835.
[2] *MR*, LXXXII, January 1817. [3] *MR*, LXXXVIII, January 1819.

abuse of his talents. Coleridge had "a more vigorous and distinguishing imagination," "a more condensed and vivid phraseology," and "deeper learning" than his poetical rivals. Perhaps he was too difficult, or perhaps his moral and political views may have repelled "a light and frivolous generation of readers." Yet he often dealt in "wonders and horrors" and "mysterious delineation of bad passions," which were, the reviewer affirmed, the exclusive fashion of the time. Coleridge, however, the reviewer thought, had overdone them, and even tried to mix in some Kantian "metaphysic mysticisms." He had also compressed *The Ancient Mariner* and *Christabel* too much, and he had dispersed many other poems in perishable newspapers and magazines. The reviewer had high praise for the "spirited" *France: an Ode*, for *Fears in Solitude*, for *Love*; and thought that Coleridge had made a gross mistake in forsaking their "old, established, classical style" for "meteors of prosaic expression." *Lines composed in a Concert-room*, however, seemed to the reviewer to show that Coleridge had satirical powers, while his lines on Mont Blanc could, the reviewer thought, have few rivals in English as descriptive or devotional blank verse. The reviewer praised a few other poems, including, except for its "cold metaphysical abstractions," *This Lime-tree Bower my Prison*; but in general he found many defects in Coleridge's diction, and he accused him of extreme digressiveness, and an excess of "minute Dutch painting."

The *Monthly*, then, except in Burney's striking review of *Lyrical Ballads*, failed as badly as the *Edinburgh* to respond to the values of the innovating poets Wordsworth and Coleridge. Moreover, its strictures on Wordsworth did not show the grasp of principle which we find in Jeffrey's reviews, however unjust they may be. However, like the *Edinburgh*, the *Monthly* showed discriminating appreciation of the work of Crabbe.

THE BRITISH CRITIC

The British Critic was founded in 1793 by William Beloe (1756–1817) and Robert Nares (1753–1829) to represent an anti-revolutionary standpoint in politics and an Anglican orthodoxy in religion. Beloe was a fair classical scholar who took orders in the Anglican Church. He became for a few years Keeper of Printed Books in the British Museum. Nares was a classical scholar of some distinction, though he is best known to-day as the compiler of a remarkable Glossary of Elizabethan Literature, still consulted by specialists. Nares also took Anglican orders, and eventually became an Archdeacon. He was Keeper of Manuscripts in the British Museum from 1799 until 1807. He was a Fellow of the Royal Society. Beloe and Nares edited the review jointly for nearly twenty years. It was then conducted for a time by Thomas Middleton (1769–1822), who became Bishop of Calcutta; and, later still, by William Rowe Lyall (1788–1857), already mentioned as the writer of a discerning review of Wordsworth in the *Quarterly*.[1] Lyall was also an Anglican priest, and became Dean of Canterbury. He was a classical scholar, and also had some philosophical ability.

For our purposes *The British Critic* is chiefly remarkable for some all too little-known reviews of Wordsworth's poetry, written by the Rev. Francis Wrangham (1769–1842), a man of brilliant academic ability and wide culture, who himself wrote poetry of some merit, and who was already on friendly terms with Wordsworth and Coleridge before the publication of *Lyrical Ballads*. Wrangham, while retaining critical independence, really tried to understand Wordsworth's poetic intentions and to assess his achievement and powers carefully and responsibly.

[1] See pp. 35, 36, above.

Wrangham cordially approved *Lyrical Ballads*,[1] for the poems' originality and animation. He contrasted their simple style favourably with the "meretricious frippery" of the then fashionable Erasmus Darwin and his imitators. He disliked in *Lyrical Ballads* the element of satire on the social order; but considered that all the poems had merit, and many a very high degree of merit. When the second edition appeared Wrangham defended the simple style of the poems as "infinitely more correspondent with true feeling" than what was usually called "poetic language."[2] He estimated the poems as outstanding, praising the originality of the thought, and the deep study of human nature from life. Wrangham also thought well of the Preface, which he considered often penetrating and judicious, and especially salutary at the time. He even accepted Wordsworth's sharply criticized tenet that prose and verse need only differ by metre. Wrangham analysed the appeal of particular kinds of poem in *Lyrical Ballads*, and attacked the habit, prevalent at the time, of trying to pigeon-hole every poem as "sublime" or "terrible" or "pathetic," and so on. This was pioneering critical work on Wrangham's part.

The review of Wordsworth's 1807 volumes[3] was entrusted to a far less sympathetic and understanding reviewer, who found the thoughts expressed "flimsy" and "puerile" and the verse "feeble" and "halting." The only exception made was the *Character of a Happy Warrior*.

With Wrangham's review of *The Excursion*,[4] however, *The British Critic* regained its sympathetic *rapport* with Wordsworth's work. Wrangham pointed out that, like the "Metaphysical" poets, Wordsworth roamed far from common associations of thought and language, but that, whereas they wanted to show their intellectual dexterity, he (and his

[1] *BC*, XIV, October 1799.
[2] *BC*, XVII, February 1801.
[3] *BC*, XXXIII, March 1809.
[4] *BC*, III (N.S.), May 1815.

fellow poets) were trying to instruct through the imagination and the emotions, and to use the knowledge obtained by analysis "to furnish a clue to the windings of the heart." Wordsworth deviated furthest and most frankly from the beaten track, and could hardly be universally popular. But his work followed what, in Wrangham's view, were the principles of "all true poetry": (1) that anything material or temporary is capable of being associated in human minds with something spiritual and eternal; (2) that such associations tend to ennoble and purify the heart; (3) that the purpose of descriptive verse is to make them habitual to our minds. Worldlings, who ridiculed Wordsworth's work, had not "learned the alphabet of his language." But people "with better and more honest feelings" were startled by Wordsworth's "new and abstruse combinations," and found his work "puerile" or "unintelligible." To indicate the drift of Wordsworth's poetry Wrangham quotes a passage from Bishop Hall's *Proeme to Occasionall Meditations*, some words of which may well have influenced the poet directly:

> Our active soul can no more forbear to think, than the eye can chuse but see when it is open. To doe well, no object should pass without use; every thing we see reads us new lectures of wisdom and piety. It is a shame for a man to be ignorant or godless under so many teachers.

In relation to this idea Wrangham outlined the history of descriptive poetry in Western Europe from Greek times until his own day, and maintained that the Lake Poets, and especially Wordsworth, had entered most profoundly of all into the idea of "deducing lessons from the works of Nature, such as Providence wanted them to convey." Nature had given Wordsworth feelings of exquisite delicacy, "fortune" had placed him "in the very palace of solitude and contemplation," education and habit had taught him to love what was lovely and revere what was sacred, and he had made it his daily and hourly business to spiritualize all sensible objects and had not been afraid or ashamed to reflect seriously and deeply on the humblest and most trivial incident of scenery and character. He had written, Wrangham admits, with too clear a disregard for common ideas about poetry; but he was not as heretical as some supposed. He only misapplied right principles, and, where he excelled, it was in the highest kind of poetry. Wrangham wrote a detailed appreciation of *The Excursion* as a poem joining "eternal things to perishable things." Deeply as he admired the poem, however, he despaired of its ever becoming popular. Wordsworth had, according to Wrangham, failed to realize how different his own habitual feelings and thoughts were from those of his readers. He left them to unravel utterly unfamiliar threads of ideas, and he occasionally lapsed into triviality or childishness when he left readers to use references to objects usually considered "low or uninteresting," for some purpose or feeling for which he used them habitually himself.

Wrangham thus regarded as exceptional lapses what Jeffrey had taken to be prevalent features of Wordsworth's poetry. Wrangham's view may, indeed, have been far too charitable to Wordsworth's poorer poems and passages; but he is by far the safer guide to the best of Wordsworth's work, on which Wordsworth's poetic reputation rests today. It is, however, interesting to find in Wrangham's review no objection or even reference to the theological status of Wordsworth's pantheism. *The Eclectic Review*, as we shall see, adopted a very different attitude. Whether Wrangham did not wish to urge theological considerations against a poem so clearly religious in spirit, or wished to capture it for orthodoxy, or whether he was motivated by personal friendship for the poet, it is hard to determine.

Perhaps Wrangham's most striking review of Wordsworth is his review of *Peter Bell*,[1] a poem which imposes a severe test on a Wordsworthian. Wrangham found faults in it, as who would not? He was very disappointed with it on a first reading. But on a careful rereading he considered it worthy of Wordsworth's fame, and thought that its "worthwhile beauties" more than counterbalanced its "staring defects." Wrangham appealed to readers to give the poem a chance. In his view, Wordsworth demanded from his readers not only "the sacrifice of many prejudices, and the conquest of some reasonable dispositions to laughter, or mortification, but also an open heart, and a patient exercise of his intellect." Some people might, Wrangham granted, question whether a poet had a right to demand all these, but he thought that whoever did accord them would derive from Wordsworth "nearly as high gratification as any poet is capable of bestowing." Wrangham's review was not only concerned directly with *Peter Bell*, however. The first part of it discussed Wordsworth's poetic achievement in general.[2] The actual critique of the poem is a piece of discriminating criticism, sympathetic and understanding, yet alert to absurdity or inferiority. It compares very favourably indeed with the unqualified dismissals the poem received from other, less charitable critics.

Wrangham's review of the Duddon volume[3] was another valuable appreciation. Wrangham offered a general estimate of Wordsworth's poetic gifts. He repudiated the view that Wordsworth was "a childish driveller," or "a writer of ballads too stiff for the nursery and too silly for the drawing-room," or even "a wild and unequal genius." Wordsworth, Wrangham maintained, was a systematic writer. He was

[1] *BC*, XI (N.S.), June 1819.

[2] A long extract from this part of the review is printed below at pp. 210–216.

[3] *BC*, XV (N.S.), February 1821.

generously endowed with moral feeling and intellectual power, which Wrangham considered the most important gifts of a poet. Wordsworth also argued well. As to his diction, it was, in general, "rather raised above than depressed below" the subject, and it was very English, very unaffected, while "lofty, ornate, and even gorgeous" where his subject allowed. Yet he was sometimes obscure, either through indistinctness in his idea, or the intrusion of irrelevant thoughts and images, or through imperfect description. As to metre, Wordsworth was, Wrangham thought, "in some respects the most practised and skilful metrist of the age." His blank verse was far better than his lyric measures. He was sometimes successful with these—for example, in the "Immortality Ode"—but in general he failed, probably, in Wrangham's view, because his subject-matter did not require the sweetness or rapidity of lyrics, and because he was deficient in both these characteristics, especially in rapidity. These are technical observations of considerable interest. In point of culture, Wrangham wrote, Wordsworth was less book-learned than any earlier great poet of England, but his strength lay in contemplation of external nature, and in meditation on the mysterious workings of his own heart, "and especially," Wrangham adds, most justly, "in the effects produced by the former on the latter." As an observer of inanimate nature Wordsworth seemed to Wrangham superior to all preceding poets. His scenery was, indeed, sometimes unlike anything one had ever seen, but one felt that Wordsworth had himself seen it, and that that was why he made us see it perfectly too. At other times the scenery was very ordinary, yet Wordsworth put in some individualizing touch that convinced us of its reality. He also kept perfect harmony of light and shade, time and season. This descriptive excellence sprang, Wrangham emphasized, from Wordsworth's *love* of nature. As to humanity, Wordsworth's theory of pre-existence, Wrangham frankly objected (without, however, labouring the theological point), was "unwarranted by Scripture, and contradicted by human experience," and also contravened the doctrines of original sin and of the Atonement. Yet, though wrong in his general theory, Wordsworth was an accurate observer of the human heart in every age and condition, and under an immense variety of circumstances. (Wrangham cites various poems, including *Michael*, *Ruth*, and *The Brothers*.) But Wordsworth, in Wrangham's opinion, had little dramatic skill, and also (Wrangham makes the point again) mistakenly assumed that his own reactions were a safe index to those of other people. On the other hand, he did have another gift, indispensable for poetic excellence—"an exalted and worthy notion of his art." Any faults of Wordsworth's poetry were not those of a weak or careless writer, Wrangham concluded. Moreover, it could give a pleasure higher in degree than that of any other modern poet, and almost different in kind. Wrangham allowed that there was, perhaps, a tendency to mysticism in the enthusiasm it excited, but the mysticism was "pure, meditative, and satisfactory." This was evidently Wrangham's considered answer to Jeffrey's harping charge of "mysticism."

Wrangham's series of reviews of Wordsworth's work, though little known to-day, were among the best contemporary criticism of Wordsworth's work, and do not deserve to be lost in the sands of time. Moreover, they may have contributed considerably to the firm establishment of Wordsworth's poetic reputation, and there is, in any case, direct evidence that the poet himself was deeply grateful to Wrangham for the understanding he showed.

The British Critic was far less interesting on Coleridge. Its review of *Sibylline Leaves* (1817)[1] contained little substantial

[1] *BC*, VIII (N.S.), November 1817.

criticism, and its estimate, published shortly after Coleridge's death (1834), of his poetic achievement,[1] though highly laudatory, was not very able.

On the other hand, *The British Critic* did have some interesting things to say about Crabbe, not so much in its reviews of his 1807 volume, or of *The Borough*, but in two later reviews. The first of these is the review of *Tales of the Hall* (1819).[2] The reviewer did not like Crabbe's matter or his manner. Crabbe's work was, the reviewer thought, far too gloomy about nature, which poetry, whose chief object is to give pleasure, should not be. Crabbe went out of his way to paint the offensive, just because it was natural. As to his verse, his couplets were "the most untunable in our language," though when he used other metres his verse became "rich music." On the other hand, the reviewer acknowledged Crabbe as unrivalled in "microscopic observation of certain peculiarities of the human heart." He was a skilful anatomist of a diseased patient, and his "preparations" from the dissected parts had an unrivalled freshness and life. That was Crabbe's originality. He had also a subdued humour, "more caustic than playful," "a melancholy for the most part bitter, but sometimes highly pathetic," "a facility for presenting reflections not the most obvious in very familiar forms," "a love of virtue, without any great willingness to believe in its prevalence." All this made Crabbe a very powerful, though not a very pleasing writer. The reviewer had certainly seized some of the salient features of Crabbe's work, and expressed them in well-weighed language.

The other interesting review was that by Hartley Coleridge, in 1834, of the posthumous edition of Crabbe's *Poetical Works*.[3] This contains a comparison of Crabbe and Wordsworth as poets of the poor. Wordsworth's peasants,

[1] *BC and Theol. Rev.*, July 1834. [2] *BC*, XII (N.S.), September 1819.
[3] *BC and Theol. Rev.*, XVI, July 1834.

according to the reviewer, were men into whom the music of nature had penetrated, purifying for them the atmosphere of life, and leading them up to God; whereas Crabbe's peasants had feelings as squalid as their dwellings. Yet Crabbe, Hartley Coleridge conceded, did present his readers here and there with "images of perfect beauty, innocence, and happiness," and he was right in thinking these rare in actual life, and in painting them as such. Crabbe did also dignify his peasants by the spirit of the Christian Gospel. Summing up Crabbe's status as a poet, however, Hartley Coleridge allowed him little poetic genius. His merits and defects were "those of a Dutch artist—vigour and coarseness." Moreover, many of his poems, without the metre, would have simply become very idiomatic prose. Hartley Coleridge seems to have wanted to 'place' Crabbe as a somewhat unimaginative poet of the second order, the great recommendation of whose work was its "truth." He did not discern the skilful construction of Crabbe's poems, or his talent as a story-teller in a tradition coming down from Boccaccio and Chaucer. But such an awareness was rarely shown in the periodical criticism of the time. Hartley Coleridge, however, failed even to notice a feature clearly recognized in Crabbe's work by some of the contemporary critics—the poignant sense of human pathos and tragedy.

The Eclectic Review

The Eclectic Review was started in 1805 by a group of men who wished to rescue English literature from "the dogmatism of superficial critics, and the irreligious influence of a semi-infidel party[1]." Its avowed object was "to unite the interests of Religion, Morality, and Literature, giving to each its respective importance, in a candid discussion of the

[1] Meaning the Whigs.

merits of living authors." In 1814 it was bought by Josiah Conder (1789–1855), who managed and eventually edited the periodical, retaining control until 1837, when he handed over the editorship to Dr Thomas Price. Conder was a remarkable personality and an indefatigable worker. Besides editing the *Eclectic* he found time to write many works, including an encyclopaedia of travel, a two-volume work on Protestant Nonconformity, and a number of other Nonconformist works on religion. He continued the original policy of the *Eclectic*, and its reviews of our poets often invoke religious criteria of value. Its literary reviewing maintained a Dissenting standpoint against adversaries such as Crabbe, but otherwise expressed what it considered broadly Christian views. This was Conder's deliberate policy.

The *Eclectic* first reviewed Crabbe in 1809.[1] It discussed the 1807 edition of his poems, estimating Crabbe's poetic qualities as limited. He had only a low degree of "fancy, fervour, grace, and feeling," though he had "strength, spirit, truth, and discrimination," and used them to the best advantage. His diction was "copious and energetic; though frequently hard and prosaic." His verse was very fluent, but very monotonous, though single lines were often excellent—sententious and epigrammatic. The reviewer acutely observed that a vein of peculiarly English humour permeated the poems, "a bitter pleasantry, a moody wit, a sarcastic sadness, that seems at once to frown and smile, to scorn and pity." The reviewer thought *The Village* (1783) Crabbe's masterpiece, and he also admired *Sir Eustace Grey* for its deep knowledge of human nature "in the unconverted state." *The Hall of Justice*, however, he found excessively horrible—vigorous, but not very poetical.

The *Eclectic*'s review of *The Borough*[2] attacked Crabbe's

[1] *Ecl.R.*, V, January 1809. [2] *Ecl.R.*, VI, i, June 1810.

strictures on Calvinism, and his satire on "the agency of evil spirits on the mind," and "the sinfulness of mental adultery," but maintained that Crabbe probably excelled all his contemporaries in the "impressive energy" of his narrative and the "striking exactness" of his description. It picked out *Peter Grimes* as the masterpiece of the volume.

The *Eclectic* thought less well of *Tales* (1812),[1] and compared Crabbe's poetic gifts unfavourably with those of Dryden and Pope. But it allowed him "originality." It considered Crabbe's great fault to be his choice of subjects. He wanted to substitute sober truth for imagination, whereas the end of poetry was "to relax and recreate the mind." His verse, moreover, was nothing but "prose measured, by ear or finger, into decasyllabic lines." And his descriptions were mostly wearisomely minute, and little relieved by simile, metaphor, or allusion. But he was powerful in "the pathetic," and his best descriptions were masterly. He was often successful in portrait-painting, especially of cases of madness. Yet the *Tales*, for the faults indicated, would not, the reviewer concluded, add to Crabbe's reputation. He was wrong.

The *Eclectic*'s best review of Crabbe, however, was of *Tales of the Hall*.[2] It took Crabbe to task for disclaiming the rôle of moralist, and also for satirizing Dissenters, and it even went so far as to maintain that Crabbe was utterly incapable of treating any subject connected with religion. He had even ridiculed "the cardinal doctrine of the Reformation, Justification by Faith." But the review allowed that he had an extraordinary power of describing every variety of moral morbidity. The review contains some illuminating phrases, as, for instance, its description of Crabbe's tales as "half elegy, half satire," which shows sensitive understanding. But

[1] *Ecl.R.*, VIII, ii, November 1812.
[2] *Ecl.R.* (N.S.), XIII, February 1820.

the reviewer did not approve of the dreariness of the prevailing atmosphere, or of Crabbe's evident demand that his readers should view the painful scenes and events calmly. Moreover, the reviewer noted with further disapproval that Crabbe did not offer his readers the consolations of faith.

Despite Crabbe's disclaimer, however, the reviewer considered him a didactic writer, and thought him, as such, "pointed, axiomatic, and often energetic, yet not infrequently trite and feeble." Crabbe's descriptions were generally accurate, in the reviewer's opinion, and sometimes strikingly picturesque and beautiful; but his great strength was delineation of character, and some of his narratives were unsurpassed. *Tales of the Hall*, the reviewer thought, was likely to obtain a permanent place in English literature, though it would only reinforce already anti-Christian tendencies. The reviewer also remarked, with acute perceptiveness, that the work of few poets showed less egotism or more individuality than Crabbe's. To have written those tales, moreover, he must, the reviewer affirmed, have "passed through a novitiate of no ordinary kind, and have lived long and seen much of life." Crabbe's work was original, in a substantial way, and so would live.

This able review shows great skill in distinguishing the religious from the more specifically literary aspects of Crabbe's work. Its religious comments were, besides, in fair measure justifiable from the Dissenting point of view; while the acuteness and fairness of the literary observations show the presence of a keen critical mind. I should not be surprised if Conder himself was the reviewer.

The *Eclectic* also showed appreciation of Wordsworth, though at first with many reservations.

Its first review of Wordsworth was of the 1807 volumes.[1] It recognized that Wordsworth was a bold innovator. To-

[1] *Ecl.R.*, IV, i, January 1808.

wards his theory of diction it adopted a moderate attitude, approving the pruning of epithets, but not the abolition of all embellishing words. Its view was that in dramatic verse a writer should speak "the truth of living nature," whereas in writing narrative poetry a writer should be allowed to exalt the language, in sound and structure, and also in "character and sentiment," above common speech.

The reviewer maintained that in some of his earlier poems, such as *The Old Cumberland Beggar*, and *Tintern Abbey*, Wordsworth had taught people "new sympathies, the existence of which in our nature had scarcely been intimated to us by any preceding poet" (a central and true appreciation). But, the reviewer pointed out, the language and thought of those poems were not ordinary. "Language more exquisitely elaborate, and thoughts more patiently worked out of the very marble of the mind we rarely met with in any writer either of verse or prose." The 1807 volumes were, in the reviewer's opinion, inferior to their predecessors. They contained no blank verse, "the glory" of Wordsworth's earlier volumes. Most of the poems were mere "reveries in rhyme," and the volumes were bound to be a failure. The Sonnets were, the reviewer thought, perhaps "in imagery and sentiment" the most poetical "of all these motley productions," but they were very unequal, often obscure, and generally heavy in the motion of the verse. Their lines were so frequently intertwined that if they had not been printed in lengths of ten syllables it would have been hard to break them into metre at all. The reviewer did, however, single out for high praise the sonnet on the Venetian Republic.

The reviewer rightly recognized as a special characteristic of Wordsworth's work that we find there images and feelings which we have "seen and felt a thousand times without particularly reflecting on them," and which, when presented by him, flash on us with all the delight and surprise of novelty.

The reviewer quotes "The cattle are grazing," "O Cuckoo!" and part of the first stanza of *Resolution and Independence*. But he took Wordsworth's "finest talent" to be "personal description," and quotes again from *Resolution and Independence*, which he much admired—in contrast to his reaction to the "Immortality Ode" which he considered a "wilderness of sublimity, tenderness, bombast, and absurdity," in which the reader was "turned loose" to find out the subject as well as he could.

It is not known who reviewed the 1807 poems, but it was certainly Conder himself who reviewed *The Excursion*.[1] He recognized that Wordsworth's earlier work had frequently been out of the range of "vulgar minds," so that superficial readers and even "self-constituted critics in the highest place" (the reference is certainly to Jeffrey among others) had scorned and censured him. In *The Excursion* Wordsworth had, in Conder's opinion, presented his system of ethics splendidly, if not clearly and fully; though Conder did not accept it. He maintained that, though there was some truth in the view that the soul could by mystic intercourse with Nature, "raise herself from profligacy and wretchedness to virtue and repose," it was certainly not the whole truth. Wordsworth had not insisted, as he ought to have done, on redemption by Christ as the only means of salvation. What was more, he had used about Nature words only appropriate to God. Yet no one, in Conder's view, had any right to recount the story of the poem so as to ridicule it. Wordsworth's imagination had ennobled the characters and incidents "far above the stalking heroes and monstrous adventures of romance." (The allusion was possibly pointed at such work as the Eastern tales of Byron.) In Conder's opinion, Wordsworth's style and thought were unique. He had invented a style more "intellectual" than that of any of his con-

[1] *Ecl.R.* (N.S.), III, January 1815. An extract appears below at p. 188.

temporaries, and in contradiction with his own theory. *The Excursion* was as distinguished by its "exquisite choice of ornament, and inevitably appropriate diction" as by its "depth, compass, and variety of speculation." Conder approved also of Wordsworth's "most daring experiment" in making his hero a pedlar, remarking, however, with a perceptiveness beyond the range of many of the reviewers, that the Wanderer was not a realistic portrait, but "as ideal as Homer's Achilles"—a compound of the working man, endowed with the sensibilities and made wise by the experience ascribed by Wordsworth to the Wanderer, with the learning and refinement of Wordsworth, the man of leisure. As to Wordsworth's villagers, Conder thought that, whereas Crabbe gave low life "with all its meanness and misery," Wordsworth "cast over it a pensive hue of thought," which softened its asperities and heightened its charms without diminishing its verisimilitude.

This review gave Wordsworth much pleasure, and he expressed to Southey[1] his admiration of "the very able manner" in which his poem had been treated in it.

Conder's review of *The White Doe of Rylstone*[2] again vigorously defended Wordsworth as a "man of genius," whose poetry was out of range for the great majority of people, with their "very low degree of mental cultivation." Wordsworth's intense cultivation of his imagination had made him prone to speculation, and had made his work unintelligible, and therefore uninteresting, to ordinary readers. He was a bold innovator, "a poetical schismatic," and his eccentricity would inevitably interfere with the impression which the excellences of his work were adapted to produce; though his mind "grasped the whole compass of poetry," and when he came in contact with ordinary human sympathies

[1] Letter from Southey to Conder, 29 March, 1815.
[2] *Ecl.R.* (N.S.), V, January 1816.

no living poet left such a strong impression of a "master-genius."

On the other hand, the *Eclectic* received *Peter Bell* and *The Waggoner* with contempt,[1] and only began to praise Wordsworth again when the Duddon volume appeared.[2] The reviewer was again Conder, and the interesting thing is that what he admired most in the volume was Wordsworth's prose memoir of the Rev. Robert Walker. Indeed, a comparison of the sonnet on Seathwaite Chapel with Wordsworth's note on it had suggested to Conder a remarkable thought—that Wordsworth was not so much to blame for the choice of his subjects as "for writing ballads and lyrical pieces about them, instead of throwing them into the form of honest prose." In free blank verse, however, Wordsworth had, Conder conceded, attained "a very unusual height of excellence." *The Excursion*, with all its faults, certainly contained, in Conder's opinion, some of the most exquisite blank verse in the language. Wordsworth's prose and blank verse were, indeed, Conder observed, generally quite free from the "puerilities and vulgarities" that disfigured many of his lyrical pieces. The diction of the prose and blank verse, and of the sonnets also, was often, Conder pointed out, in contradiction with Wordsworth's theory, "extremely elevated and richly figurative; sometimes to an excess bordering upon affectation." Conder still thought Wordsworth's talents to be of a very high order. In this volume there was, he thought, "a weight of sterling good poetry" that amply compensated for *Peter Bell* and *The Waggoner*. But Wordsworth had, in Conder's view, written too much for his permanent reputation. He ought to allow some competent friend to make a rigid selection of his work, and to "make a bonfire of the refuse—his potters, waggoners, and idiots, on the top of Skiddaw." After Wordsworth's death Matthew

[1] *Ecl.R.* (N.S.), XII, July 1819. [2] *Ecl.R.* (N.S.), XIV, August 1820.

Arnold was eventually to make a selection—though one which Conder himself might have found too "rigid."

Conder's reviews of Wordsworth, like Wrangham's, deserve recognition as among the best contemporary criticism of the poet's work. Both critics had a strong religious and moral sense which enabled them to realize and sympathize with some of the guiding impulses of Wordsworth's whole poetic achievement. Moreover, in more specifically 'literary' matters they were open-minded enough to see the value of Wordsworth's innovations, and they also had a feeling for verse which made them able to appreciate his finer verbal movements and harmonies.

On Coleridge, by contrast, the *Eclectic* was poor. Its review of *Christabel*, *Kubla Khan*, and *The Pains of Sleep*[1] was little better than that by Hazlitt in the *Edinburgh*.[2] It adopted a moral tone towards Coleridge's lack of productiveness, accusing him of desultory and luxurious habits, and admonishing him to brace his mind to mental exertion. It thought *Kubla Khan* and *The Pains of Sleep* ought never to have been published. As to *Christabel*, the poem's meaning was only half developed, though it was, the reviewer admitted, "gripping." Few readers, however, would, he thought, see its originality, because much verse in the same style and metre had recently appeared. Its "prevailing sentiment" was Horror—not that mixture of terror and disgust with which one listened to tales of crime and bloodshed, but the purely imaginative feeling, "the breathless thrill of indefinite emotion of which we are conscious when in the supposed presence of an unknown being, or acted upon by some influence mysteriously transcending the notice of the senses." As it stood, however, the poem was unintelligible.

[1] *Ecl.R.* (N.S.), V, June 1816. [2] See p. 34, above.

The London Magazine

The London Magazine, founded in 1820, set out to appreciate the work of the best contemporary writers. John Scott, who edited the magazine till his tragic death in 1821 in a duel caused by his attacks on the scandalous conduct of *Blackwood's*, had already written good criticism of Wordsworth in the weekly *Champion*. He now wrote another admirable appreciation of Wordsworth in a series on "Living Authors."[1] It is this and Hazlitt's somewhat adverse article on Crabbe in the same series that deserve our attention.

Scott singled out as an important feature of Wordsworth as a nature poet that he did not "disturb the august silence and secret influence of the spot or moment by officious interference," but seemed at once a fellow-worshipper of Nature and a superior being, whose more intimate communion with her glories only added to the simplicity of his zeal and the humility of his devotion. Scott considered that Wordsworth's lines connected themselves more permanently and easily with the scenery of nature and the workings of thought and passion than those of his contemporaries and rivals. Scott did not, however, place the value of Wordsworth's work in its literal truth. He maintained that its scenes and characters were only rendered interesting because the poet made them suggest and illuminate a certain system of thought and feeling which belonged to him rather than to them. Whenever Wordsworth tried to introduce realistic touches to make his humble characters more credible, the work seemed forced. Wordsworth's best[2] characters were impressed with his own personality. They were *Wordsworth's* beggar, *Wordsworth's* sailor, *Wordsworth's* schoolmaster, and

[1] *LM*, Vol. I, No. 3, March 1820.
[2] Scott evidently means 'best-drawn.'

so on. It was, Scott thought, a pity when Wordsworth attempted anything but poems in which this "impress" would be "the best of recommendations." "In spite of his familiarity of phrase, and long drawn-out minuteness of description," writes Scott, "his hedge-menders and ditch-cutters would be shyly looked at by the set at the Swan or the Red Lion, we fear." Wordsworth's intimacy with such people was, in Scott's view, not practical, but theoretical.

By this discriminating defence of Wordsworth, admitting the lack of realism in Wordsworth's best characterization, but maintaining that lack to be a strength, not a weakness, Scott completely turned the tables on Jeffrey's criticism.

Scott also held it a mistake to think that Wordsworth was a simple writer, or even that he aimed at simplicity. He could use familiar expressions and write fearlessly of familiar objects, because he was conscious of the "depth, grandeur and importance of his sentiments." People did not laugh at Newton for staring at flying soap-bubbles. No more, in Scott's view, should they laugh at Wordsworth for seeing "a vision of delight" in the bright blue eggs of a sparrow's nest. The "flippancy" of such criticisms as those in the *Edinburgh* were "infamous," in Scott's opinion. The chief offenders, however, were now beginning, Scott pointed out, to see that they had made a false move. But they had intervened between Wordsworth's poems and the public, who, despite the poems not being of a kind to gain popularity easily, might otherwise have learned to understand them sooner. In any case, Scott contended, most sanely and wisely, contemporary taste was not the standard of excellence, nor were the *Edinburgh*'s criticisms the voice even of contemporary taste. (By the early 'twenties the tide had certainly begun to turn in Wordsworth's favour.)

In spite of his admiration for Wordsworth's work, however, Scott criticized him for misconceiving, in some very important respects, the true nature and end of poetry, and for, still more often, perverting in practice the principles of his theory even where they were sound and valuable. Wordsworth's disdain of the "accidents and accessaries of grandeur" sometimes, Scott thought, caused him to try to make people admire not only what was humble but what was small, silly, vulgar, and weak. This led him into irrelevance, trifling, and incongruity with his deep moral and philosophical intentions. Scott cites *The Idiot Boy* and *The Sailor's Mother*, contrasting *The Old Cumberland Beggar* as free from such faults. In Scott's opinion, *bare* representation of common life could only be made pleasant in poetry in one of three ways: (1) by the poet creating a sense of delight in the accuracy of the description; (2) by his throwing the reader into another period or place where usual associations did not hold; (3) by exciting humour. Now, Wordsworth, Scott maintained, was a lamentable humorist; and he did not even attempt the first two methods. But (and this was the point Scott wished to emphasize) less than a quarter of Wordsworth's poetry was poetry of "bare representation." The great mass of his work was "high and pure poetry, majestic in expression, exquisite in sensibility, philosophic in thought, lofty in imagination, and splendid in imagery." He was the most powerful poet of the time.

Scott's review, though perhaps *too* laudatory, was a noble defence of Wordsworth's poetry against its traducers, and suggested a valuable way of looking at it.

Hazlitt's essay on Crabbe[1] was in a different tone. He found Crabbe's work depressing. He did not notice the touches of benignity and humour already pointed out by some of the other reviewers. The most interesting thing about Hazlitt's review is that it reveals a certain critical

[1] *LM*, III, May 1821. This review, slightly revised, was included by Hazlitt in *The Spirit of the Age* (1825). An extract appears below at p. 118.

obtuseness. Hazlitt asserted that poetry should contain charm and flights of imagination, but he also required "nature," in the sense of truth to reality, and he seems not to have realized that a serious demand for either might involve considerable forfeiture of the other. In any case, however, his essay, though lively, cannot be regarded as really fine-grained criticism.

The Examiner

A little must be said about one more periodical: *The Examiner* of John and Leigh Hunt. The avowed object of this weekly was "to assist in producing Reform in Parliament, liberality of opinion in general (especially freedom from superstition), and a fusion of literary taste into all subjects whatsoever." Its attacks on administrative abuses at home, and on attempts to create a hero-figure out of the sensual Prince Regent, involved its editors in indictments for libel. Both brothers were imprisoned for two years in 1813, and John Hunt was again imprisoned in 1821. In the same year Leigh Hunt went to Italy, only returning to England late in 1825. The brothers then quarrelled over Leigh Hunt's right to continue as editor, and the partnership broke up. *The Examiner*'s great days were over, though it continued to exist till 1881.

From a literary point of view *The Examiner*'s chief importance lies in its publication of some of the best essays of Hazlitt (from 1816) and Lamb (from 1819), and in its strong support for the work of Byron, Shelley, and Keats—none of which is our present concern. But its attitude to Wordsworth and Coleridge is of some interest.

In three numbers in 1814 (21, 28 August, 2 October) there appeared an important review, by Hazlitt, of *The Excursion.* It was one of the first reviews of the poem to appear. It gave high praise to the "power of intellect," "lofty conception," "depth of feeling, at once simple and sublime," the "vastness and magnificence, overwhelming, oppressive power" of the poem. The elemental character of the scenery depicted was well described by Hazlitt. And he also rightly stated that *The Excursion* was "not so much a description of natural objects as of the feelings associated with them; not an account of the manners of rural life, but the results of the poet's reflections on it." Again, Hazlitt thought, in describing human nature Wordsworth had avoided exciting incidents, and not described human vices in their full development, "but as lurking in embryo, the seeds of disorder inwoven with our very constitution." "He only sympathizes with those simple forms of feeling which mingle at once with his own identity, or with the stream of general humanity." All the characters and feelings Wordsworth described lost their individuality. "An intense intellectual egotism swallows up everything." Wordsworth's mind was the reverse of dramatic. It was as if there were nothing else but Wordsworth and the universe. (This was a criticism Hazlitt was to make far more sharply and unkindly two years later.) Hazlitt regretted that Wordsworth had not made *The Excursion* simply didactic, instead of including so much narrative and description. He also took issue with Wordsworth's view that philosophizing was egotistical, and maintained that such a condemnation could well recoil on the poet himself, since perhaps some of his love of nature was due to the opportunity it afforded him of analysing his own feelings and contemplating his own powers. Certainly Wordsworth's work exhibited "all the internal power without the external form of poetry"—by which Hazlitt meant that Wordsworth did not make use of pomp, decoration, or excitement for his poetic effects, but deliberately chose events and objects most simple and barren of effect, and made them "serious and even formidable" by the weight of interest he gave them from the resources of his own mind. Only the subject and style of Wordsworth's poetry were simple, the feelings and thoughts were "subtle and profound." But, though Hazlitt greatly admired these feelings and thoughts, he did not relish Wordsworth's so frequently attributing them to rustic characters. Hazlitt did not admire either rustic characters or country behaviour. He considered the inhabitants of the Lake District selfish. He thought Wordsworth's poetic power far superior to the subject-matter of *The Excursion*, and even wondered whether the weakness of the subject-matter might not prevent the poem from being, as Wordsworth hoped it would be, a "monument" worthy of him and of his country.

John Wilson used to tell the story that he started to read this review to a reluctant Wordsworth, who tried to deter him from continuing, speaking harshly of reviewers and reviews, but, yielding to Wilson's persistence, gradually warmed to admiration of the understanding shown—only to fall into a fury when Wilson revealed that the reviewer was Hazlitt, whom Wordsworth despised.

Wordsworth, who had met Leigh Hunt in London, started early in 1816 to send poems to *The Examiner*. But shortly afterwards Hunt began to attack the poet for political unreliability. Wordsworth had written some sonnets about Waterloo in *The Champion*, in which he had referred to the French armies as "that impious crew," and had depicted the angels as contributing to the cheering after Waterloo. Hunt took exception to this in a front-page article which closed with the hope that its writer would see many more of Mr Wordsworth's sonnets, but also that, "like his best ones," they would be "less Miltonic in one respect, and more so in another." Only one more poem by Wordsworth was ever printed in *The Examiner*.

Tendencies towards political reaction and religious superstition were the Hunts' prime bogeys, and the Lake Poets were roughly handled throughout 1816. Hazlitt slashed at *Christabel* and its mystery-mongering, and dismissed *Kubla Khan* as nonsense, adding: "It is not a poem, but a musical composition." (Here, in contrast with his review in the *Edinburgh*, he appears to recognize the poem's music.) He followed this with violent attacks on two of Coleridge's prose works. More venomous than all this, however, was Hazlitt's attack on Wordsworth at the end of the same year. The venom may perhaps be partly accounted for by Hazlitt's disgust at Wordsworth's political development, but the spite shown seems more personal. One wonders whether Hazlitt had been stung by some revelations of Wordsworth's attitude to him, such as those in Wilson's story.

In his attack Hazlitt wrote of the poet as "a person who founded a school of poetry on sheer humanity, on idiot boys and mad mothers, and on Simon Lee, the old huntsman." Hazlitt maintained that Wordsworth was concerned to bring everything down to a low level. In his poetry he wanted to level great people with small people; and in his politics he wanted to level the great Napoleon (one of Hazlitt's heroes) with kings and "hereditary imbecility." "This person," wrote Hazlitt, "admires nothing that is admirable, feels no interest in anything interesting, no grandeur in anything grand, no beauty in anything beautiful." And Hazlitt found the spring of all this in Wordsworth's egoism, in his intolerance for anything but what he himself created. Hazlitt had uncannily detected a great weakness in Wordsworth—his negative attitude towards so many worthwhile things, and the undoubted egoism closely connected with it. But the picture, though not without its point, was, of course, entirely one-sided. Wordsworth clearly loved Nature, and had positive attitudes towards many things and people apart from himself and his own creations. Besides, his own ideas and feelings were and are, in many cases, of considerable value, and continue to attract and delight many readers to-day, as does his memorable expression of them in the finely moving verse and superbly chosen diction of his best work.

IV

Summary Impressions of the Attitudes of the Leading Periodicals towards the Poetry of Wordsworth, Crabbe, and Coleridge

From our detailed examination of the reviews in Section III, and from the extracts printed later in this volume, it should be clear that it would be a great error to believe that the poetry of Wordsworth was badly received by all, or even by the majority, of the leading reviews and magazines. Substantially, among those periodicals we have considered, it was only the *Edinburgh* and the *Monthly* that set their faces against it; and even the *Monthly* gave a favourable reception to *Lyrical Ballads*. It is worth noting that both these periodicals were Whig and humanistic, and that Jeffrey had written for the *Monthly* before he helped to found the *Edinburgh*.[1] The greatest support for Wordsworth came from the Christian reviews, *The British Critic* and *The Eclectic Review*, though the Tory *Quarterly* and *Blackwood's* sometimes received his work favourably.

It should also emerge that the great challenge of Wordsworth's poetry, though it provoked much hostility at first,

[1] Indeed, Jeffrey had not counted on the remarkable success of the *Edinburgh* with the public, and for some time after its first appearance still thought of the *Monthly* as his chief permanent means of reaching the public.

eventually came to evoke from many of the reviewers an attitude not merely of admiration but of reverence. By way of counterpoise, however, we find that even his admirers had reservations towards some of his later work, though some of them approved his apparent capitulation on the issue of poetic diction.

The reputation of Crabbe during the period was evidently much steadier. Objection was made from early days to the harshness of his view of life, but his knowledge of human nature was always recognized. Moreover, he was never execrated as a poetic innovator, nor was he ever worshipped as a prophet. His work was, however, very popular from the start. The sanction of Dr Johnson and of Burke may have counted for much, but Crabbe's sombre strength was evident to his readers in its own right. If anything, he was less popular in 1830 than he had been twenty, or, again, forty, years earlier. His versification seemed to many old-fashioned and earth-bound, and his stories too painful and not steeped in the ether of idealism. They neither had glamour nor launched into bold speculation. It was left to an age setting a greater value on truth than on exaggeration to rediscover him.

As to Coleridge, though his early work was noticed appreciatively, it was a long time before the poems on which his poetic reputation now chiefly rests elicited more than bafflement, or even contempt, from the reviewers. This was partly a matter of personalities, but those poems offered a more elusive challenge than did the work of Wordsworth.

In the case of all three poets the best criticism of their work was written by the most sympathetic reviewers. The best criticism of Crabbe was Jeffrey's; the best of Wordsworth was Coleridge's, Wilson's, Wrangham's, and Conder's; the best of Coleridge was Sterling's and H. N. Coleridge's. Jeffrey's critiques of Wordsworth, however intelligent, lack a dimension. They are, in any case, the only possible exception to our generalization.

V

Other Expressions of Critical Opinion during the Period

The vast majority of the extant criticism of three of our poets by their contemporaries is in the form of reviews. For Blake, however, we have (for reasons mentioned on pp. 13, 14) only letters, records of conversations, and biography. Such sources, supplemented by essays such as those in Hazlitt's *Spirit of the Age*, by lectures, such as his *Lectures on the English Poets*, and by books with wider scope, such as Coleridge's *Biographia Literaria*, and also by poems, such as Shelley's *Peter Bell the Third*, are also available for our other three poets. Extracts from such sources are also printed in the present volume. Even very brief passages sometimes throw a valuable gleam, whether just or unjust, on the work of the poet concerned. They are, however, no substitute for the searching criticism offered by some of the reviewers.

As to the critical opinions of readers who did not express them in recorded conversation, it is clearly impossible to recapture them by any known technique. The nearest we can get to knowing the minds of those readers is to know how many copies they bought of the works concerned, and that is slender evidence of anything more than an interest which might have been hostile or favourable. Crabbe sold well until the 1820's, then less well. Wordsworth sold rather poorly between 1807 and 1820, but very well before and afterwards. Coleridge's early poems sold reasonably well, but his later poems did not sell well during his lifetime. But such facts are not of great significance. They do not tell us anything specific about what the readers thought and felt when they read the poems. That would be worth knowing, but we cannot ascertain it. It is better to turn our attention to recorded opinions, and of these the period has left us a rich harvest.

T.R.

George Crabbe
(1754–1832)

There be, who say, in these enlighten'd days,
That splendid lies are all the poet's praise;
That strain'd invention, ever on the wing,
Alone impels the modern bard to sing:
'Tis true, that all who rhyme—nay, all who write,
Shrink from that fatal word to genius—trite;
Yet Truth sometimes will lend her noblest fires,
And decorate the verse herself inspires:
This fact in Virtue's name let Crabbe attest;
Though nature's sternest painter, yet the best.

English Bards and Scotch Reviewers (1809)

BYRON, who found it "better to err with Pope than shine with Pye," and who considered the modern Romantic school of Lake Poets a worthless crew, gives epigrammatic force to an estimate of Crabbe which echoes through so many of the contemporary critics. Crabbe, to a critic like Jeffrey, was the true poet of Nature, a realist who approached his subject with decorum and correct moral seriousness, and who confined his formal skill to the couplet; he is the yardstick against which the Lake Poets are measured and found wanting. Jeffrey, reviewing his poems in *The Edinburgh Review* of April 1808, makes a devastating comparison between Crabbe, who "exhibits the common people of England pretty much as they are," and the Lake Poets, "the gentlemen of the new school," who "invent for themselves certain whimsical and unheard-of beings, to whom they impute some fantastical combination of feelings, and then labour to excite our sympathy for them."

From the beginning he was treated with respect. Jeffrey never missed an opportunity in *The Edinburgh Review* to eulogize him at great length; Grant, in the Tory *Quarterly*, reviews him with grudging admiration; while John Wilson, in *Blackwood's*, demonstrates a more interesting and complicated attitude. Whereas Jeffrey and Grant treat Crabbe as a realist of the mainstream tradition of the eighteenth century, Wilson (at heart an admirer of Wordsworth) lays more emphasis on his strange and melancholic aspects—in fact, he stresses what one might call the Romantic side of Crabbe. "The pleasure he excites," he says, "is almost always a troubled pleasure," and he chooses immensely long extracts from *Tales of the Hall* to illustrate his point that Crabbe is above all a poet of pathos, horror, and melancholy. It is a critical essay perhaps more illuminating about Wilson than about Crabbe, although it does draw attention to an aspect of Crabbe which had been missed by other critics.

The Romantic writers themselves regarded him with less reverence. It was impossible to discount the solid achievement of his work, but it was felt that he lacked the real and distinctive poetic gift of imagination which they valued above all else. In spite of the claims of John Wilson, Wordsworth could only remark that his poems were "mere matters of fact"; to Hazlitt, they want "an electric spark to kindle or expand," and to the new conception of poetry his works were alien. Coleridge is reported to have said, "In Crabbe there is an absolute defect of the high imagination; he gives me little or no pleasure" (*Table Talk*). But this must have caused Crabbe little dismay, since in his early years he had been praised by Dr Johnson himself, who in 1783 revised *The Village* before publication, with the comment, "It is original, vigorous, and elegant." Boswell tells us why Dr

Johnson liked it: "Its sentiments as to the false notions of rustick happiness and rustick virtue were quite congenial with his own." The poetic world inhabited by Crabbe was certainly more akin to *The Vanity of Human Wishes* than to the "Immortality Ode."

From most of the contemporary criticism of Crabbe a cold, stern, harshly moralizing figure seems to emerge. It is pleasantly corrective to turn to the *Life* written by his son in 1834, which is still the best memorial to the poet, and a work of scholarship and affection.

> As the chief characteristic of his heart was benevolence, so that of his mind was a buoyant exuberance of thought and perpetual exercise of intellect. Thus he had an inexhaustible resource within himself, and never for a moment, I may say, suffered under that *ennui* which drives so many from solitude to the busy search for notoriety.

The *Life* tells an illuminating story that should be read by all students of the poet's work.

P.H.

From a letter from Wordsworth to Samuel Rogers dated Grasmere, 29 September, 1808

I am happy to find that we coincide in opinion about Crabbe's *verses*; for *poetry* in no sense can they be called. . . . I remember that I mentioned in my last that there was nothing in the last publication so good as the description of the Parish workhouse, Apothecary, etc. This is true—and it is no less true that the passage which I commended is of no great merit, because the description, at the best of no high order, is in the instance of the apothecary, inconsistent, that is, false. It, no doubt, sometimes happens, but, as far as my experience goes, very rarely, that Country Practitioners neglect, and brutally treat, their Patients; but what kind of men are they who do so?—not Apothecaries like Crabbe's Professional, pragmatical Coxcombs, "generally neat, all pride, and business, bustle, and conceit," no, but drunken reprobates, frequenters of boxing matches, cock-fightings, and horse-races—these are the men who are hard-hearted with their Patients, but any man who attaches so much importance to his profession as to have strongly caught, in his dress and manner, the outward formalities of it, may easily indeed be much occupied with himself, but he will not behave towards his "Victims," as Mr Crabbe calls them, in the manner he has chosen to describe. After all, if the Picture were true to nature, what claim would it have to be called Poetry? At the best, it is the meanest kind of satire, except the merely personal. The sum of all is, that nineteen out of 20 of Crabbe's Pictures are mere matters of fact; with which the Muses have just about as much to do as they have with a Collection of medical reports, or of Law cases.

From Jeffrey's review of *The Borough*[1] in *The Edinburgh Review*, April 1810

We are very glad to meet with Mr Crabbe so soon again; and particularly glad to find, that his early return has been occasioned, in part, by the encouragement he received on his last appearance. This late spring of public favour, we hope,

[1] Jeffrey had reviewed *Poems* by Crabbe in April 1808, in *The Edinburgh Review*, in the famous critique in which he compares Crabbe and Wordsworth, to the considerable detriment of the latter.

he will yet live to see ripen into mature fame. We scarcely know any poet who deserves it better; and are quite certain there is none who is more secure of keeping with posterity whatever he may win from his contemporaries.

The present poem is precisely of the character of the *Village* and the *Parish Register*. It has the same peculiarities, and the same faults and beauties; though a severe critic might perhaps add, that its peculiarities are more obtrusive, its faults greater, and its beauties less. However that be, both faults and beauties are so plainly produced by the peculiarity, that it may be worth while, before giving any more particular account of it, to try if we can ascertain in what that consists.

And here we shall very speedily discover, that Mr Crabbe is distinguished, from all other poets, both by the choice of his subjects, and by his manner of treating them. All his persons are taken from the lower ranks of life; and all his scenery from the most ordinary and familiar objects of nature or art. His characters and incidents, too, are as common as the elements out of which they are compounded are humble; and not only has he nothing prodigious or astonishing in any of his representations, but he has not even attempted to impart any of the ordinary colours of poetry to those vulgar materials. He has no moralizing swains or sentimental tradesmen; and scarcely ever seeks to charm us by the artless manners or lowly virtues of his personages. On the contrary, he has represented his villagers and humble burghers as altogether as dissipated, and more dishonest and discontented, than the profligates of higher life; and, instead of conducting us through blooming groves and pastoral meadows, has led us along filthy lanes and crowded wharfs, to hospitals, almshouses, and gin-shops. In some of these delineations, he may be considered as the satirist of low life,—an occupation sufficiently arduous, and in a great degree new and original in our language. But by far the greater part of his poetry is of a different and a higher character; and aims at moving or delighting us by lively, touching, and finely contrasted representations of the dispositions, sufferings, and occupations of those ordinary persons who form the far greater part of our fellow-creatures. This, too, he has sought to effect, merely by placing before us the clearest, most brief, and most striking sketches of their external condition,—the most sagacious and unexpected strokes of character,—and the truest and most pathetic pictures of natural feeling and common suffering. By the mere force of his art, and the novelty of his style, he forces us to attend to objects that are usually neglected, and to enter into feelings from which we are in general but too eager to escape;—and then trusts to nature for the effect of the representation.

It is obvious, at first sight, that this is not a task for an ordinary hand; and that many ingenious writers, who make a very good figure with battles, nymphs, and moonlight landscapes, would find themselves quite helpless if set down among streets, harbours, and taverns. The difficulty of such subjects, in short, is sufficiently visible—and some of the causes of that difficulty: but they have their advantages also. . . .

. . . It appears to us to be certain, that where subjects taken from humble life can be made sufficiently interesting to overcome the distaste and the prejudices with which the usages of polished society too generally lead us to regard them, the interest which they excite will commonly be more profound and more lasting than any that can be raised upon loftier themes; and the poet of the *Village* and the *Borough* be oftener, and longer read, than the poet of the Court or the Camp. The most popular passages of Shakespeare and Cowper, we think, are of this description: and there is much, both in the volume before us, and in Mr Crabbe's former publications, to which we might now venture to refer, as proofs of the same doctrine. When such representations have once made an impression on the imagination, they are remembered daily, and for ever. We can neither look around, nor within us, without being reminded of their truth and their importance; and while the more brilliant effusions of romantic fancy are recalled only at long intervals, and in rare situations, we feel that we cannot walk a step from our own doors, nor cast a glance back on our departed years, without being indebted to the poet of vulgar life for some striking image or touching reflection, of which the occasions were always before us, but,—till he taught us how to improve them,—were almost always allowed to escape.

Such, we conceive, are some of the advantages of the subjects which Mr Crabbe has in a great measure introduced into modern poetry;—and such the grounds upon which we venture to predict the durability of the reputation which he has acquired. That they have their disadvantages also, is obvious; and it is no less obvious, that it is to these we must ascribe the greater part of the faults and deformities with which this author is fairly chargeable. The two great errors into which he has fallen, are—that he has described many things not worth describing;—and that he has frequently excited disgust, instead of pity or indignation, in the breasts of his readers. These faults are obvious,—and, we believe, are popularly laid to his charge; yet there is, in so far as we have observed, a degree of misconception as to the true grounds and limits of the charge, which we think it worth while to take this opportunity of correcting.

The poet of humble life *must* describe a great deal,—and must even describe, minutely, many things which possess in themselves no beauty or grandeur. The reader's fancy must be awaked,—and the power of his own pencil displayed:—a distinct locality and imaginary reality must be given to his characters and agents; and the ground colour of their common condition must be laid in, before his peculiar and selected groups can be presented with any effect or advantage. In the same way, he must study characters with a minute and anatomical precision; and must make both himself and his readers familiar with the ordinary traits and general family features of the beings among whom they are to move, before they can either understand, or take much interest in the individuals who are to engross their attention. Thus far, there is no excess or unnecessary minuteness. But this faculty of observation, and this power of description, hold out great temptations to go further. There is a pride and a delight in the exercise of all peculiar power; and the poet, who has learned to describe external objects exquisitely with a view to heighten the effect of his moral designs, and to draw characters with accuracy to help forward the interest or the pathos of the picture, will be in great danger of describing scenes, and drawing characters, for no other purpose, but to indulge his taste, and to display his talents. It cannot be denied, we think, that Mr Crabbe has, on many occasions, proved unequal to this temptation. He is led away, every now and then, by his lively conception of external objects, and by his nice and sagacious observation of human character; and wantons and luxuriates in descriptions and moral portrait-painting, while his readers are left to wonder to what end so much industry has been exerted.

His chief fault, however, is his frequent lapse into disgusting representations; and this, we confess, is an error for which we find it far more difficult either to account or to apologize. We are not, however, of the opinion which we have often heard stated, that he has represented human nature under too unfavourable an aspect, or that the distaste which his poetry sometimes produces, is owing merely to the painful nature of the scenes and subjects with which it abounds. On the contrary, we think he has given a juster, as well as a more striking picture, of the true character and situation of the lower orders of this country, than any other writer, whether in verse or in prose; and that he has made no more use of painful emotions than was necessary to the production of a pathetic effect . . .

. . . It is needless, we suppose, to explain what are the objects of disgust in physical or external existences. These are sufficiently plain and unequivocal; and it is universally admitted, that all mention of them must be carefully excluded from every poetical description. With regard again, to human character, action, and feeling, we should be inclined to term everything disgusting, which represented misery, without making any appeal to our love or our admiration. If the suffering person be amiable, the delightful feeling of love and affection tempers the pain which the contemplation of suffering has a tendency to excite, and enhances it into the stronger, and therefore more attractive, sensation of pity. If there be great power or energy, however united to guilt or wretchedness, the mixture of admiration exalts the emotion into something that is sublime and pleasing. Even in cases of mean and atrocious guilt, our sympathy with the victims upon whom it is practised, and our active indignation and desire of vengeance, reconcile us to the humiliating display, and make a compound that, upon the whole, is productive of pleasure.

The only sufferers, then, upon whom we cannot bear to look, are those that excite pain by their wretchedness, while they are too depraved to be the objects of affection, and too weak and insignificant to be the causes of misery to others, or consequently, of indignation to the spectators. Such are the depraved, abject, diseased and neglected poor,—creatures in whom everything amiable or respectable has been extinguished by sordid passions or brutal debauchery,—who have no means of doing the mischief of which they are capable,—whom every one despises, and no one can either love or fear. On the characters, the miseries, and the vices of such beings, we look with *disgust* merely: and, though it may perhaps serve some *moral* purpose, occasionally to set before us this humiliating spectacle of human nature sunk to utter worthlessness and insignificance, it is altogether in vain to think of exciting either pity or horror, by the truest and most forcible representations of their sufferings or of their enormities. They have no hold upon any of the feelings that lead us to take an interest in our fellow-creatures;—we turn away from them, therefore, with loathing and dispassionate aversion;—we feel our imaginations polluted by the intrusion of any images connected with them; and are offended and disgusted when we are forced to look closely upon those festering heaps of moral filth and corruption. It is with concern we add, that we know no writer who has sinned so deeply in this respect as Mr Crabbe, who has so often presented us with spectacles which it is purely painful and degrading to contemplate, and bestowed such powers of conception and expression in giving us distinct ideas of what we must abhor to remember. If Mr Crabbe had been a person of ordinary talents, we might have accounted for his error, in some degree, by supposing, that his frequent success in treating of subjects which had been usually rejected by other poets, had at length led him to disregard, altogether, the common impressions of mankind as to what was allowable and what inadmissible in poetry, and to reckon the unalterable laws by which nature has regulated our sympathies, among the prejudices by which they were shackled and impaired. It is difficult, however, to conceive how a writer of his quick and exact observation should have failed to perceive, that there is not a single instance of a serious interest being excited by an object of disgust; and that Shakespeare himself, who has ventured everything, has never ventured to shock our feelings with the crimes or the sufferings of beings absolutely without power or principle. Independent of universal practice, too, it is still more difficult to conceive how he should have overlooked the reason on which this practice is founded; for though it be generally true, that poetical representations of suffering and of guilt produce emotion, and consequently delight, yet it certainly did not require the penetration of Mr Crabbe to discover, that there is a degree of depravity which counteracts our sympathy with suffering, and a degree of insignificance which extinguishes our interest in guilt. We abstain from giving any extracts in support of this accusation; but those who have perused the volume before us, will have already recollected the story of Frederic Thompson, of Abel Keene, of Blaney, of Benbow, and a good part of those of Grimes and Ellen Orford,—besides many shorter passages. It is now time, however, to give the reader a more particular account of the work which contains them.

The Borough of Mr Crabbe, then, is a detailed and minute account of an antient English sea-port town, of the middling order; containing a series of pictures of its scenery, and of the different classes and occupations of its inhabitants. It is thrown into the form of letters, though without any attempt at the epistolary character; and treats of the vicar and curate —the sectaries—the attornies—the apothecaries; and the inns, clubs, and strolling-players, that make a figure in the place: but more particularly of the poor, and their characters and treatment; and of almshouses, prisons, and schools. There is, of course, no unity or method in the poem,—which consists altogether of a succession of unconnected descriptions, and is still more miscellaneous in reality, than would be conjectured from the titles of its twenty-four separate compartments.

. . . The style of this poem is distinguished, like all Mr Crabbe's other performances, by great force and compression of diction,—a sort of sententious brevity, once thought essential to poetical composition, but of which he is now the only living example. But though this is almost an unvarying characteristic of his style, it appears to us that there is great variety, and even some degree of unsteadiness and inconsistency in the tone of his expression and versification. His taste seems scarcely to be sufficiently fixed and settled as to these essential particulars: and along with a certain quaint, broken, and harsh manner of his own, we think we can trace very frequent imitations of poets of the most opposite character. The following antithetical and half-punning lines of Pope, for instance,—

> Sleepless himself, to give his readers sleep;[1]

and—

> Whose trifling pleases, and whom trifles please;

have evidently been copied by Mr Crabbe in the following, and many others,—

> And, in the restless ocean, seek for rest.
>
> Denying her who taught thee to deny.
>
> Scraping they liv'd, but not a scrap they gave.
>
> Bound for a friend, whom honour could not bind.
>
> Among the poor, for poor distinctions sigh'd.

[1] Jeffrey is obviously quoting from memory, because in each case he misquotes. "Sleepless themselves, to give their readers sleep," is from *The Dunciad*, Book I, line 94. The second quotation is from Pope's *Imitations of Horace* (the Second Epistle of the Second Book of Horace). The final lines are:

> Leave such to trifle with more grace and ease,
> Whom Folly pleases, and whose Follies please.

In the same way, the common, nicely balanced line of two members, which is so characteristic of the same author, has obviously been the model of our author in the following—

> That woe could wish, or vanity devise.
>
> Sick without pity, sorrowing without hope.
>
> Gloom to the night, and pressure to the chain.

—and a great multitude of others.

On the other hand, he appears to us to be frequently misled by Darwin[1] into a sort of mock-heroic magnificence, upon ordinary occasions. The poet of the *Garden*, for instance, makes his nymphs

> Present the fragrant quintessence of tea.

And the poet of the Dock-yards makes his carpenters

> Spread the warm pungence of o'erboiling tar.

Mr Crabbe, indeed, does not scruple, on some occasions, to adopt the mock-heroic in good earnest. When the landlord of the Griffin becomes bankrupt, he says—

> Th' insolvent Griffin struck her wings sublime.

—and introduces a very serious lamentation over the learned poverty of the curate, with this most misplaced piece of buffoonery—

> Oh! had he learn'd to make the wig he wears!

[1] Erasmus Darwin (1731–1802), author of *The Botanic Garden*, which came out in two parts, 1789 and 1791.

One of his letters, too, begins with this wretched quibble—

From Law to Physic stepping at our ease,
We find a way to finish—by *degrees*.

There are many imitations of the peculiar rhythm of Goldsmith and Campbell, too, as our readers must have observed in some of our longer specimens[1];—but these, though they do not always make a very harmonious combination, are better, at all events, than the tame heaviness and vulgarity of such verses as the following.

As soon
Could he have thought gold issued from the moon.

A seaman's body—*there'll be more* taught.[2]

Those who will not to any guide submit,
Nor find one creed to their conceptions fit—
True *Independents*: while they *Calvin* hate,
They heed as little what *Socinians* state.

Here pits of crag, with spongy, plashy base,
To some enrich th' uncultivated space. etc. etc.

Of the sudden, harsh turns, and broken conciseness which we think peculiar to himself, the reader may take the following specimens—

Has your wife's brother, or your uncle's son,
Done aught amiss; or is he thought t' have done?

Stepping from post to post he reach'd the chair;
And there he now reposes:—that's the Mayor.

[1] These are not included in the present extract.
[2] The *Edinburgh* printer's error for 'to-night.'

He has a sort of jingle, too, which we think is of his own invention; for instance—

> For forms and feasts that sundry times have past,
> And formal feasts that will for ever last.

> We term it free and easy; and yet we
> Find it no easy matter to be free.

We had more remarks to make upon the taste and diction of this author; and had noted several other little blemishes, which we meant to have pointed out for his correction: but we have no longer room for such minute criticism,—from which, indeed, neither the author nor the reader would be likely to derive any great benefit. We take our leave of Mr Crabbe, therefore, by expressing our hopes that, since it is proved that he *can* write fast, he will not allow his powers to languish for want of exercise; and that we shall soon see him again repaying the public approbation, by entitling himself to a still larger share of it. An author generally knows his own forte so much better than any of his readers, that it is commonly a very foolish kind of presumption to offer any advice as to the direction of his efforts; but we own we have a very strong desire to see Mr Crabbe apply his great powers to the construction of some interesting and connected story. He has great talents for narration; and that unrivalled gift in the delineation of character which is now used only for the creation of detached portraits, might be turned to admirable account in maintaining the interest, and enhancing the probability of an extended train of adventures. At present, it is impossible not to regret, that so much genius should be wasted in making us perfectly acquainted with individuals, of whom we are to know nothing but the characters. In such a poem, however, Mr Crabbe must entirely lay aside the sarcastic and jocose style to which he has rather too great a propensity; but which we know from what he has done in *Sir Eustace Grey*,[1] that he can, when he pleases, entirely relinquish. That very powerful and original performance, indeed, the chief fault of which is, to be set too thick with images,—to be too strong and undiluted, in short, for the digestion of common readers,—makes us regret that its author should ever have stooped to be trifling and ingenious, —or condescended to tickle the imaginations of his readers, instead of touching the higher passions of their nature.

From Robert Grant's review of *The Borough* in *The Quarterly Review*, November 1810

The history of Mr Crabbe as an author has been somewhat singular. He first appeared in that character in the year 1783, and was received in such a manner as might have warranted the hope that his second appearance would not be long delayed. But, too indolent or too unambitious, Mr Crabbe sunk back into privacy; and five and twenty years elapsed before he renewed his claims on the public notice. His increased success on this second occasion does not strike us as matter of surprise. We had become sick of the luscious monotony of Muses who seemed to have been fed only on flowers; and were therefore prepared to receive with indulgence even the rude efforts of a more firm and manly genius. At the same time it must be confessed, that the candidate was in no want of illustrious friends to bring him down (like the deductores of old) to the place of canvas, and to secure, by their in-

[1] In October 1807 appeared *Poems by the Revd. George Crabbe*, containing a reprint of *The Library*, *The Village*, and *The Newspaper*, and three new poems—*Sir Eustace Grey*, *The Hall of Justice*, and *Woman*. *Sir Eustace Grey* is a melodramatic poem, whose setting is a madhouse, in the form of a dramatic dialogue.

fluence, the favourable suffrages of his countrymen. Criticism itself could not refuse a smile to the verse which had early obtained the praise of Burke and Johnson, and more recently cheered the dying bed of Fox.

The first glow of admiration, however, is now gone; and sufficient time has since passed to allow of our ascertaining, pretty accurately, the final judgment of the public respecting the merits of Mr Crabbe. It is, if we are not mistaken, that he has greatly misapplied great powers; and that, although an able, he is not a pleasing poet. In this judgment we entirely acquiesce.

The peculiarity of this author is, that he wishes to discard every thing like illusion from poetry. He is the poet of reality, and of reality in low life. His opinions on this subject were announced in the opening of his first poem, *The Village*; and will be best explained by extracting from that work some lines which contain a general enunciation of his system.

> The village life, and ev'ry care that reigns
> O'er youthful peasants and declining swains;
> What labour yields, and what, that labour past,
> Age in its hour of languor finds at last;
> What form the real picture of the poor,
> Demand a song—the Muse can give no more.
>
> . . . .
>
> . . . .
>
> On Mincio's banks, in Caesar's bounteous reign,
> If Tityrus found the golden age again,
> Must sleepy bards the flatt'ring dreams prolong?
> Mechanic echoes of the Mantuan song?
> From Truth and Nature shall we widely stray
> Where Virgil, not where Fancy, leads the way?
> Yes, thus the Muses sing of happy swains,
> Because the Muses never knew their pains.
>
> . . . .
>
> . . . .

Then shall I dare these real ills to hide
In tinsel trappings of poetic pride?

. . . .

. . . .

By such examples taught, I paint the cot
As Truth will paint it, and as bards will not.

From these extracts, as well as from the constant tenor of his writings, it is clear, that Mr Crabbe condemns the common representations of rural life and manners as fictitious; that he is determined in his own sketches of them to confine himself, with more than ordinary rigour, to truth and nature;—to draw only "the real picture of the poor," which, be it remembered, must necessarily, according to his opinion, be a picture of sorrow and depravity. Now all this tends greatly to circumscribe, if not completely to destroy, the operation of illusion in poetry; and proceeds on what we conceive to be an entire misconception of the principles on which the pleasure of poetic reading depends. Notwithstanding the saving clause in favour of the privileges of Fancy, which is inserted in one of the preceding extracts, the doctrines of Mr Crabbe appear to us essentially hostile to the highest exercise of the imagination, and we cannot therefore help regarding them with considerable doubt and jealousy.

. . . The poetry, which speaks to the understanding alone, cannot permanently attract the mass of mankind; while that, which moves the passions and the heart, has already received the talisman of fame, and may securely commit itself to the affections of every coming age. It is very pleasing to perceive, that, in his best passages, Mr Crabbe is, practically at least, a convert to the good old principle of paying some regard to fancy and taste in poetry. In these passages he works expressly for the imagination; not perhaps awakening its loftiest exertions, yet studiously courting its assistance, and conciliating its good will. He now accommodates himself to the more delicate sympathies of our nature, and flatters our prejudices by attaching to his pictures agreable and interesting associations. Thus it is that, for his best success, he is indebted to something more than ungarnished reality. He is the Paladin, who on the day of decisive combat, laid aside his mortal arms, and took only the magic lance.

The remarks which we have made apply so generally to Mr Crabbe's writings, that little more remains for us now to do, than to exemplify them by extracts from the work to which they immediately owe their origin.

The Borough contains a description in twenty-four letters of a sea-port, under the following heads:

General Description—The Church—The Vicar, the Curate etc.,—Sects and Professions in Religion—Elections—Professions, Law, Physic — Trades — Amusements — Clubs and Social Meetings—Inns—Players—The Alms-House and Trustees—Inhabitants of the Alms-House, Blaney, Clelia, Benbow—The Hospital and Governors—The Poor and their Dwellings—The Poor of the Borough, the Parish Clerk, Ellen Orford, Abel Keene, Peter Grimes—Prisons—Schools.

A glance at the preceding table is sufficient to prove that our author is far from having abjured the system of delineating in verse subjects little grateful to poetry. No themes surely can be more untunable than those to which he has here attempered his lyre. It is observable too, that they are sought in a class of society yet lower than that which he has hitherto represented. The impurities of a rural hamlet were sufficiently repulsive;—what then must be those of a maritime borough? This gradual sinking in the scale of realities seems to us a direct consequence of that principle of Mr Crabbe, on which we have, in a former part of this article, hazarded some strictures. *The Borough* is purely the creature of that principle; the legitimate successor of the *Village* and the *Parish Register*. Indeed, if the checks of fancy and taste be removed from poetry, and admission be granted to images, of whatever description, provided they have the passport of reality, it is not easy to tell at what point the line of exclusion should be drawn, or why it should be drawn at all. No image of depravity, so long as it answers to some archetype in nature or art, can be refused the benefit of the general rule. The mind which has acquired a relish for such strong painting, is not likely to be made fastidious by indulgence. When it has exhausted one department of life, it will look for fresh materials in that which is more highly rather than in that which is more faintly coloured. From the haunts of rustic debauchery, the transition is natural to the purlieus of Wapping.

By the choice of this subject, Mr Crabbe has besides exposed himself to another inconvenience. It was the misfortune of his former poems that they were restricted to a narrow range. They treated of a particular class of men and manners, and therefore precluded those representations of general nature, which, it scarcely needs the authority of Johnson to convince us, are the only things that "can please many and please long." —But, with respect to the present poem, this circumstance prevails to a much greater degree. In the inhabitants of a sea-port there are obviously but few generic traces of nature to be detected. The mixed character of their pursuits, and their amphibious sort of life, throw their manners and customs into a striking cast of singularity, and make them almost a separate variety of the human race. Among the existing modifications of society, it may be questioned if there be one which is more distinctly specified, we might say individualized.

The volume before us exhibits all the characteristic qualities of its author; a genius of no common order, but impaired by system—a contempt for the *bienséances* of life, and a rage for its realities. The only "imaginary personage" (as Mr Crabbe is pleased to style him) introduced into this poem, is "a residing burgess in a large sea-port;" and this "ideal friend" is brought in for the purpose of describing the *Borough* to the inhabitant of a village in the centre of the kingdom. In other respects, the poem inherits the beauties and defects of its predecessors; but while the defects are more aggravated as well as more thickly sown, the beauties, though not less scantily doled out, are unquestionably touched with a more affecting grace and softness. Although, therefore, the effect of the whole may be far from lively, yet in the strength and pathos of single passages *The Borough* will not have many rivals.

From Crabbe's Preface to his *Tales* (1812)

There has been recommended to me, and from authority which neither inclination nor prudence leads me to resist, in any new work I might undertake, a unity of subject, and that arrangement of my materials which connects the whole and gives additional interest to every part; in fact, if not an Epic Poem, strictly so denominated, yet such composition as would possess a regular succession of events, and a catastrophe to which every incident should be subservient, and which every character, in a greater or less degree, should conspire to accomplish.

In a Poem of this nature, the principal and inferior characters in some degree resemble a general and his army, where no one pursues his peculiar objects and adventures, or pursues them in unison with the movements and grand purposes of the whole body; where there is a community of interests and a subordination of actors: and it was upon this view of the subject, and of the necessity for such distribution of persons and events, that I found myself obliged to relinquish an undertaking, for which the characters I could command, and the adventures I could describe, were altogether unfitted.

But if these characters which seemed to be at my disposal were not such as would coalesce into one body, nor were of a nature to be commanded by one mind, so neither on examination did they appear as an unconnected multitude, accidentally collected, to be suddenly dispersed; but rather beings of whom might be formed groups and smaller societies, the relations of whose adventures and pursuits might bear that kind of similitude to an Heroic Poem, which these minor associations of men (as pilgrims on the way to their saint, or parties in search of amusement, travellers excited by curiosity, or adventurers in pursuit of gain) have in points of connection and importance with a regular and disciplined army.

Allowing this comparison, it is manifest that, while much is lost for want of unity of subject and grandeur of design, something is gained by greater variety of incident and more minute display of character, by accuracy of description and diversity of scene: in these narratives we pass from gay to grave, from lively to severe, not only without impropriety, but with manifest advantage. In one continued and connected poem, the reader is, in general, highly gratified or severely disappointed; by many independent narratives, he has the renovation of hope, although he has been dissatisfied, and a prospect of reiterated pleasure, should he find himself entertained.

I mean not, however, to compare these different modes of writing as if I were balancing their advantages and defects before I could give preference to either; with me the way I take is not a matter of choice, but of necessity: I present not my Tales to the reader as if I had chosen the best method of ensuring his approbation, but as using the only means I possessed of engaging his attention. . . .

It has been already acknowledged, that these compositions have no pretensions to be estimated with the more lofty and heroic kind of poems; but I have great reluctance in admitting that they have not a fair and legitimate claim to the poetic character: in vulgar estimation, indeed, all that is not prose passes for poetry; but I have not ambition of so humble a kind as to be satisfied with a concession which requires nothing in the poet except his ability for counting syllables; and I trust something more of the poetic character will be allowed to the succeeding pages than what the heroes of *The Dunciad* might share with the author: nor was I aware that, by describing, as faithfully as I could, men, manners, and things, I was forfeiting a just title to a name which has been freely granted to many, whom to equal, and even to excel, is but very stinted commendation. . . .

Nevertheless, it must be granted that the pretensions of any composition to be regarded as poetry will depend upon that definition of the poetic character which he who undertakes to determine the question has considered as decisive; and it is confessed also, that one of great authority may be adopted, by which the verses now before the reader, and many others which have probably amused and delighted him, must be excluded: a definition like this will be found in the words which the greatest of poets, not divinely inspired, has given to the most noble and valiant Duke of Athens—

> The poet's eye, in a fine frenzy rolling,
> Doth glance from heaven to earth, from earth to heaven;
> And as imagination bodies forth
> The forms of things unknown, the poet's pen
> Turns them to shapes, and gives to airy nothing
> A local habitation and a name.

Hence we observe the Poet is one who, in the excursions

of his fancy between heaven and earth, lights upon a kind of fairyland, in which he places a creation of his own, where he embodies shapes, and gives action and adventure to his ideal offspring: taking captive the imagination of his readers, he elevates them above the grossness of actual being into the soothing and pleasant atmosphere of supramundane existence: there he obtains for his visionary inhabitants the interest that engages a reader's attention without ruffling his feelings, and excites that moderate kind of sympathy which the realities of nature oftentimes fail to produce, either because they are so familiar and insignificant that they excite no determinate emotion, or are so harsh and powerful that the feelings excited are grating and distasteful.

Be it then granted that (as Duke Theseus observes) "such tricks hath strong imagination," and that such poets "are of imagination all compact"; let it be further conceded, that theirs is a higher and more dignified kind of composition, nay, the only kind that has pretensions to inspiration; still, that these poets should so entirely engross the title as to exclude those who address their productions to the plain sense and sober judgment of their readers, rather than to their fancy and imagination, I must repeat that I am unwilling to admit—because I conceive that, by granting such right of exclusion, a vast deal of what has been hitherto received as genuine poetry would no longer be entitled to that appellation. . . .

But, in whatever degree I may venture to differ from any others in my notions of the qualifications and character of the true Poet, I most cordially assent to their opinion who assert, that his principal exertions must be made to engage the attention of his readers; and further, I must allow that the effect of poetry should be to lift the mind from the painful realities of actual existence, from its everyday concerns, and its perpetually recurring vexations, and to give it repose by substituting objects in their place which it may contemplate with some degree of interest and satisfaction: but, what is there in all this, which may not be effected by a fair representation of existing character? nay, by a faithful delineation of those painful realities, those every-day concerns, and those perpetually-recurring vexations themselves, provided they be not (which is hardly to be supposed) the very concerns and distresses of the reader? for when it is admitted that they have no particular relation to him, but are the troubles and anxieties of other men, they excite and interest his feelings as the imaginary exploits, adventures, and perils of romance;—they soothe his mind, and keep his curiosity pleasantly awake; they appear to have enough of reality to engage his sympathy, but possess not interest sufficient to create painful sensations. Fiction itself, we know, and every work of fancy, must for a time have the effect of realities; nay, the very enchanters, spirits, and monsters of Ariosto and Spenser must be present in the mind of the reader while he is engaged in their operations, or they would be as the objects and incidents of a nursery tale to a rational understanding, altogether despised and neglected: in truth, I can but consider this pleasant effect upon the mind of a reader as depending neither upon the events related (whether they be actual or imaginary), nor upon the characters introduced (whether taken from life or fancy), but upon the manner in which the poem itself is conducted; let that be judiciously managed, and the occurrences actually copied from life will have the same happy effect as the inventions of a creative fancy;—while, on the other hand, the imaginary persons and incidents to which the poet has given "a local habitation and a name," will make upon the concurring feelings of the reader the same impressions with those taken from truth and nature, because they will appear to be derived from that source, and therefore of necessity will have a similar effect.

Having thus far presumed to claim for the ensuing pages the rank and title of poetry, I attempt no more, nor venture to class or compare them with any other kinds of poetical composition; their place will doubtless be found for them.

From Jeffrey's review of *Tales of the Hall* in *The Edinburgh Review*, July 1819

["Our *fourth* article on Mr Crabbe's productions."]

There is, as everybody must have felt, a strange mixture of satire and sympathy in all his productions—a great kindliness and compassion for the errors and sufferings of our poor human nature—but a strong distrust of its heroic virtues and high pretensions. His heart is always open to pity, and all the milder emotions—but there is little aspiration after the grand and sublime of character, nor very much encouragement for raptures and ecstacies of any description. These, he seems to think, are things rather too fine for the said poor human nature—and that, in our low and erring condition, it is a little ridiculous to pretend, either to very exalted and immaculate virtue, or very pure and exquisite happiness. He not only never meddles, therefore, with the delicate distresses and noble fires of the heroes and heroines of tragic and epic fable, but may generally be detected indulging in a lurking sneer at the pomp and vanity of all such superfine imaginations—and turning to draw men in their true postures and dimensions, and with all the imperfections that actually belong to their condition:—the prosperous and happy overshadowed with passing clouds of *ennui*, and disturbed with little flaws of bad humour and discontent—the great and wise beset at times with strange weaknesses and meannesses and paltry vexations—and even the most virtuous and enlightened falling far below the standard of poetical perfection—and stooping every now and then to paltry jealousies and prejudices—or sinking into shabby sensualities,—or meditating on their own excellence and importance, with a ludicrous and lamentable anxiety.

This is one side of the picture; and characterizes sufficiently the satirical vein of our author: but the other is the most extensive and important. In rejecting the vulgar sources of interest in poetical narratives, and reducing his ideal persons to the standard of reality, Mr C. does by no means seek to extinguish the spark of human sympathy within us, or to throw any damp on the curiosity with which we naturally explore the characters of each other. On the contrary, he has afforded new and more wholesome food for all those propensities—and, by placing before us those details which our pride or fastidiousness is so apt to overlook, has disclosed in all their truth and simplicity, the native and unadulterated workings of those affections which are at the bottom of all social interest, and are really rendered less touching by the exaggerations of more ambitious artists—while he exhibits, with admirable force and endless variety, all those combinations of passions and opinions, and all that cross-play of selfishness and vanity, and indolence and ambition, and habit and reason, which make up the intellectual character of individuals, and present to every one an instructive picture of his neighbour or himself.

. . . Almost every human mind, he seems to think, may serve to display that fine and mysterious mechanism which it is his delight to explore and explain;—and almost every condition, and every history of life, afford occasions to show how it may be put into action, and pass through its various combinations. It seems, therefore, almost as if he had caught up the first dozen or two of persons that came across him in the ordinary walks of life,—and then opening up his little window in their breasts,—and applying his tests and instruments of observation, had set himself about such a minute and curious scrutiny of their whole habits, history, adventures and dispositions, as he thought must ultimately create not only a familiarity, but an interest, which the first aspect of the subject was far enough from leading any one to expect. That he succeeds more frequently than could have been anticipated, we are very willing to allow. But we cannot help feeling, also, that a little more pains bestowed in the selection of his characters, would have made his power of observation and description tell with tenfold effect; and that, in spite of the exquisite truth of his delineations, and the fineness of the perceptions by which he was enabled to make them, it is impossible to take any considerable interest in many of his personages, or to avoid feeling some degree of fatigue at the minute and patient exposition that is made of all that belongs to them.

From John Wilson's review of *Tales of the Hall* in *Blackwood's Magazine*, July 1819

Burns, Wordsworth, and Crabbe, are the three poets, who, in our days, have most successfully sought the subjects and scenes of their inspiration in the character and life of the People. While most of our other great poets have in imagination travelled into foreign countries, and endeavoured to add to those profounder emotions which all representations of human passion necessarily excite, that more lively impression of novelty and surprise produced by the difference of national manners, and all the varieties of external nature—or have restricted themselves, as, for example, in the splendid instance of Scott, to one romantic era of history—these Three have, in almost all of their noblest compositions, grappled closely with the feelings which at all times constitute the hearts and souls of our own Islanders, so that the haunt of their song may be said to have lain in the wide and magnificent regions of the British character. Accordingly, their poetry has been more deeply felt, where it has been felt at all, than that of any of their contemporaries. . . .

[Crabbe] delights to look over society with a keen, scrutinising, and somewhat stern eye, as if resolved that the human heart should not be suffered to conceal one single secret from his inquisitorial authority. He has evidently an intense satisfaction in moral anatomy; and in the course of his dissections, he lays bare, with an unshrinking hand, the very arteries of the heart. It will, we believe, be found, that he has always a humane purpose,—though conscious of our own frailties, as we all are, we cannot help sometimes accusing him of unrelenting severity. When he finds a wound, he never fails to probe it to the bottom.

Of all men of this age, he is the best portrait-painter. He is never contented with a single flowing sketch of a character —they must all be drawn full-length to the very life—and with all their most minute and characteristic features even of dress and manners. He seems to have known them all personally; and when he describes them, he does so as if he thought that he would be guilty of a kind of falsehood, in omitting the description of a single peculiarity. Accordingly, to make the picture in all things a perfect likeness, he very often enters into details that weary, nay, even disgust—and not unfrequently a character is forced, obtruded as it were on our acquaintance, of whose disagreable existence we were before happily ignorant. His observation of men and manners has been so extensive and so minute, that his power of raising up living characters is wholly without limitation; and Mr Crabbe has thrown open a gallery, in which single portraits and groups of figures follow each other in endless procession, habited in all the varieties of dress that distinguish the professions, orders, and occupations of the whole of human society.

Perhaps the very highest poetical enthusiasm is not compatible with such exquisite acuteness of discernment, or if it be, the continual exercise of that faculty must at least serve to abate it. Accordingly, the views which Mr Crabbe does in general take of human life, are not of a very lofty kind; and he rarely, if ever, either in principle or feeling, exhibits the idealism of nature. Accustomed thus to look on men as they exist and act, he not only does not fear, but he absolutely loves to view their vices and their miseries; and hence has his poetry been accused, and perhaps with some reason, of giving too dark a picture of life. But, at the same time, we must remember, what those haunts of life are into which his spirit has wandered. Throughout a great part of his poetry, he has chosen to describe certain kinds of society and people, of which no other poet we know could have made any thing at all. The power is almost miraculous with which he has stirred up human nature from its very dregs, and shewn working in them the common spirit of humanity. Human life becomes more various and wonderful in his hands, pregnant with passion as it seems to be, throughout the lowest debasement of profligacy and ignorance. He lays before us scenes and characters from which in real life we would turn our eyes with intolerant disgust; and yet he forces us to own, that on such scenes and by such characters much the same kind of part is played that ourselves, and others like us, play on another stage. He leaves it to other poets to carry us into the company of shepherds and dalesmen, in the heart of pastoral peace; and sets us down in crowds of fierce and sullen men, contending against each other, in lawful or in lawless life, with all the energies of exasperated passion. Mr

Hazlitt, in his *Lectures on English Poets*, has said, that in Crabbe we find the still life of tragedy. To us it appears, on the other hand, that till Crabbe wrote, we knew not what direful tragedies are for ever steeping in tears or in blood the footsteps of the humblest of our race; and that he has opened for us, as it were, a theatre on which the homely actors that pass before us assume no disguise—on which every catastrophe borrows its terror from truth, and every scene seems shifted by the very hands of nature.

In the poetry of this extraordinary man, we see a constant display of the passions as they are excited and exacerbated by the customs, and laws and institutions of society. Love, anger, hatred, melancholy, despair, and remorse in all their infinite modifications, as exhibited by different natures and under different circumstances, are rife throughout all his works; and a perpetual conflict is seen carried on among all the feelings and principles of our nature, that can render that nature happy or miserable. We see love breaking through in desperation, but never with impunity, the barriers of human laws; or in hopelessness dying beneath them, with or without its victim. The stream of life flows over a rugged and precipitous channel in the poetry of Crabbe, and we are rarely indeed allowed to sail down it in a reverie or a dream. The pleasure he excites is almost always a troubled pleasure, and accompanied with tears and sighs, or with the profounder agitation of a sorrow that springs out of the conviction forced upon us of the most imperfect nature, and therefore the most imperfect happiness of man.

Now, if all this were done in the mere pride of genius and power, we should look on Mr Crabbe in any other light than as the benefactor of his species. But in the midst of all his skill—all his art—we see often—indeed always—the tenderness of the man's heart; and we hear him, with a broken and melancholy voice, mourning over the woe and wickedness whose picture he has so faithfully drawn. Never in any one instance (and he claims this most boldly in his preface) has he sought to veil or to varnish vice—to confuse our notions of right and wrong—to depreciate moral worth, or exaggerate the value of worldly accomplishments—to cheat us out of our highest sympathies due to defeated or victorious virtue, or to induce us, in blindfolded folly, to bestow them on splendid guilt and dazzling crime. It is his to read aloud to us the records of our own hearts—the book of fate—and he does not close the leaves because too often stained with rueful tears. This world is a world of sin and sorrow, and he thinks, and thinks rightly, that it becomes him who has a gifted sight into its inmost heart, to speak of the triumphs of that sin, and the wretchedness of that sorrow, to beings who are all born to pass under that two-fold yoke. We do not believe that a bad or even an imperfect moral can be legitimately drawn from the spirit of any of Mr Crabbe's poetry.

We have said this now, because we know that he has been called a gloomy, which must mean, if any accusation is implied in the term, a false moralist. No doubt, to persons who read his poetry superficially and by snatches and glances, it may seem to give too dark a picture of life,—but this, we are convinced, is not the feeling which the study of the whole awakens. Here and there, he presents us with images of almost perfect beauty, innocence, and happiness—but as such things are seldom seen, and soon disappear in real life, it seems to be Mr Crabbe's opinion, that so likewise, ought they to start out with sudden and transitory smiles among the darker, the more solemn, or the gloomy pictures of his poetry. It is certain that there are, in this writer, passages of as pure and profound pathos as in any English poet—that he dwells with as holy a delight as any other on the settled countenance of peace, and that, in his wanderings through the mazes of human destiny, his heart burns within him, when his eyes are, at times, charmed away from the troubles and the wickedness of life to its repose and its virtue.

There is, however, one point on which we cannot agree with Mr Crabbe, and on which we feel that we may, without arrogance, affirm that he is wrong. He has not made use of religion in poetry which a poet, a philosopher, and a Christian such as he is, might—and ought to have made. On this subject, however, we intend to speak fully soon, and to shew that no poetry which aspires to the character of a picture of man and nature can be otherwise than imperfect from which are excluded, or but partially introduced, the consideration and illustration of the influence of religion on the whole structure of society and life.

From a letter from Robert Southey to his friend C. W. W. Wynn, dated 22 July, 1819, and written from Keswick

I was not disappointed with Crabbe's Tales. He is a decided mannerist, but so are all original writers in all ages; nor is it possible for a poet to avoid it if he writes much in the same key and upon the same class of subjects. Crabbe's poems will have a great and lasting value as pictures of domestic life, elucidating the moral history of these times,—times which must hold a most conspicuous place in history. He knows his own powers, and never aims above his reach. In this age, when the public are greedy for novelties, and abundantly supplied with them, an author may easily commit the error of giving them too much of the same kind of thing. But this will not be thought a fault hereafter, when the kind is good, or the thing good of its kind.

From Hazlitt's *The Spirit of the Age* (1825)

Mr Crabbe is one of the most popular and admired of our living authors. That he is so, can be accounted for on no other principle than the strong ties that bind us to the world about us and our involuntary yearnings after whatever in any manner powerfully and directly reminds us of it. His Muse is not one of *the Daughters of Memory*, but the old, toothless, mumbling dame herself, doling out the gossip and scandal of the neighbourhood, recounting *totidem verbis et literis* what happens in every place of the kingdom every hour in the year, and fastening always on the worst as the most palatable morsels. But she is a circumstantial old lady, communicative, scrupulous, leaving nothing to the imagination, harping on the smallest grievances, a village oracle and critic, most veritable, most identical, bringing us acquainted with persons and things just as they chanced to exist, and giving us a local interest in all she knows and tells.

Mr Crabbe's Helicon is choked up with weeds and corruption; it reflects no light from heaven; it emits no cheerful sound; no flowers of love, of hope, or joy spring up near it, or they bloom only to wither in a moment. Our poet's verse does not put a spirit of youth in everything, but a spirit of fear, despondency and decay. It is not an electric spark to kindle or expand, but acts like the torpedo's touch to deaden or contract. It lends no dazzling tints to fancy; it aids no soothing feelings in the heart; it gladdens no prospect, it stirs no wish; in its view the current of life runs slow, dull, cold, dispirited, half under ground, muddy, and clogged with all creeping things. The world is one vast infirmary; the hill of Parnassus is a penitentiary, of which our author is the overseer. To read him is a penance, yet we read on!

Mr Crabbe, it must be confessed, is a repulsive writer. He contrives to "turn diseases to commodities," and makes a virtue of necessity. He puts us out of conceit with this world, which perhaps a severe divine should do, yet does not, as a charitable divine ought, point to another. His morbid feelings droop and cling to the earth, grovel where they should soar, and throw a dead weight on every aspiration of the soul after the good or beautiful. By degrees we submit, and are reconciled to our fate, like patients to the physician, or prisoners in the condemned cell. We can only explain this by saying, as we said before, that Mr Crabbe gives us one part of nature: the mean, the little, the disgusting, the distressing, that he does this thoroughly and like a master; and we forgive all the rest.

. . . Painting is essentially an imitative art; it cannot subsist for a moment on empty generalities: the critic therefore, who had been used to this sort of substantial entertainment, would be disposed to read poetry with the eye of a connoisseur, would be little captivated with smooth, polished, unmeaning periods, and would turn with double eagerness and relish to the force and precision of individual details transferred, as it were, to the page from the canvas. Thus an admirer of Teniers or Hobbima might think little of the pastoral sketches of Pope or Goldsmith; even Thomson describes not so much the naked object as what he sees in his mind's eye, surrounded and glowing with the mild, bland, genial vapours of his brain. But the adept in Dutch interiors, hovels and pigsties must find in Mr Crabbe a man after his own heart. He is the very thing itself; he paints in words instead of colours: there is no other difference. As Mr Crabbe is not a painter, only because he does not use a brush and colours, so he is for the most part a poet, only because he writes in lines of ten syllables. All the rest might be found in a newspaper, an old magazine, or a county-register.

From the Journal of Sir Walter Scott, for the year 1827

Jan. 3rd: Talking of Wordsworth, he told Anne and I a story, the object of which was to show that Crabbe had not imagination. He, Sir George Beaumont and Wordsworth were sitting together in Murray the bookseller's back-room. Sir George after sealing a letter blew out the candle which had enabled him to do so, and exchanging a look with Wordsworth began to admire in silence the undulating thread of smoke which slowly arose from the expiring wick, when Crabbe put on the extinguisher.

From notes dictated by Wordsworth to Isabella Fenwick in 1843

[This is part of a note on Wordsworth's *Extempore Effusion upon the Death of James Hogg*, written in 1835, which mentions Crabbe among other poets who have recently died:

> Our haughty life is crowned with darkness,
> Like London with its own black wreath,
> On which with thee, O Crabbe! forth-looking,
> I gazed from Hampstead's breezy heath.]

Crabbe obviously for the most part preferred the company of women to that of men, for this among other reasons, that he did not like to be put upon the stretch in general conversation: accordingly in miscellaneous society his *talk* was so much below what might have been expected from a man so deservedly celebrated, that to me it seemed trifling. It must upon other occasions have been of a different character as I found in our rambles together on Hampstead Heath, and not so much from a readiness to communicate his knowledge of life and manners as of Natural History in all its branches. His mind was inquisitive, and he seems to have taken refuge from a remembrance of the distresses he had gone through, in these studies and employments to which they led. Moreover, such contemplations might tend profitably to counterbalance the painful truths which he had collected from his intercourse with mankind. Had I been more intimate with him, I should have ventured to touch upon his office as a Minister of the Gospel, and how far his heart and soul were in it so as to make him a zealous and diligent labourer. In poetry, though he wrote much, as we all know, he assuredly was not so. I happened once to speak of pains as necessary to produce merit of a certain kind which I highly valued: his observation was—"It is not worth while." You are right, thought I, if the labour encroaches upon the time due to teach truth as a steward of the mysteries of God: if there be cause to fear that, write less: but, if poetry is to be produced at all, make what you do produce as good as you can. Mr Rogers once told me that he expressed his regret to Crabbe that he wrote in his later works so much less correctly than in his earlier. "Yes," replied he, "but then I had a reputation to make; now I can afford to relax." Whether it was from a modest estimate of his own qualifications, or from causes less creditable, his motives for writing verse and his hopes and aims were not so high as is to be desired. After being silent for more than twenty years, he again applied himself to poetry, upon the spur of applause he received from the periodical publications of the day, as he himself tells us in one of his prefaces. Is it not to be lamented that a man who was so conversant with permanent truth, and whose writings are so valuable an acquisition to our country's literature, should have *required* an impulse from such a quarter?

From *A Life of the Rev. George Crabbe*, by his son (1834)

[Chapter vii ("1792–1804"), describing his residence at Glemham, in Suffolk.]

My brother says, in a memorandum now before me,

> While searching for and examining plants or insects, he was moulding verses into measure and smoothness. No one who observed him at these times could doubt that he enjoyed exquisite pleasure in composing. He had a degree of action while thus walking and versifying, which I hardly ever observed when he was preaching or reading. The hand was moved up and down; the pace quickened. He was, nevertheless, fond of considering poetical composition as a species of task and labour, and would say, "I have been hard at work, and have had a good morning."

My father had taught himself both French and Italian, so as to read and enjoy the best authors in either language, though he knew nothing of their pronunciation. He also continued all through his residence at Suffolk the botanical and entomological studies to which he had been so early devoted. I rather think, indeed, that this was, of his whole life, the period during which he carried the greatest and most indefatigable zeal into his researches in Natural History. There was, perhaps, no one of its departments to which he did not, at some time or other, turn with peculiar ardour; but, generally speaking, I should be inclined to say, that those usually considered as the least inviting had the highest attractions for him. In botany, grasses, the most useful, but the least ornamental, were his favourites; in minerals, the earths and sands; in entomology, the minuter insects. His devotion to these pursuits appeared to proceed purely from the love of science and the increase of knowledge—at all events, he never seemed to be captivated with the mere beauty of natural objects, or even to catch any taste for the arrangement of his own specimens. Within the house was a kind of scientific confusion; in the garden, the usual showy foreigners gave place to the most scarce flowers, and especially to the rarer weeds, of Britain; and these were scattered here and there only for preservation. In fact, he neither loved order for its own sake, nor had any very high opinion of that passion in others; witness his words, in the tale of Stephen Jones, the *Learned Boy*,—

> *The love of order*—I the thing receive
> From reverend men—and I in part believe—
> Shows a clear mind and clean, and whoso needs
> This love, but seldom in the world succeeds,
> Still has *the love of order* found a place
> With all that's low, degrading, mean, and base;
> With all that merits scorn, and all that meets disgrace.
> In the cold miser of all change afraid,
> In pompous men in public seats obeyed,
> In humble placemen, heralds, solemn drones,
> Fanciers of flowers, and lads like Stephen Jones;
> Order to these is armour and defence,
> And love of method serves for lack of sense.

Whatever truth there may be in these lines, it is certain that this insensibility to the beauty of order was a defect in his own mind; arising from what I must call his want of taste. There are, no doubt, very beautiful detached passages in his writings—passages apparently full of this very quality. It is not, however, in detached parts of a poem that the criterion of this principle properly lies, but in the conduct of the whole; in the selection of the subject and its amplifications;

in the relative disposition and comparative prominency of the parts, and in the contrasts afforded by bearing lightly or heavily on the pencil. In these things Mr Crabbe is generally admitted to be not a little deficient; and what can demonstrate the high rank of his other qualifications better than the fact, that he could acquire such a reputation in spite of so serious a disadvantage? This view of his mind, I must add, is confirmed by his remarkable indifference to almost all the proper objects of taste. He had no real love for painting, or music, or architecture, or for what a painter's eye considers as the beauties of landscape. But he had a passion for science—the science of the human mind, first; then, that of nature in general; and, lastly, that of abstract quantities. His powerful intellect did not seem to require the ideas of sense to move it to enjoyment, but he could at all times find luxury in the most dry and forbidding calculations.

William Blake

(1757–1827)

THE poetry of William Blake escaped the attention of contemporary critics for one very good reason: the only work printed during his lifetime was the early *Poetical Sketches* of 1783, and all his greatest poetry was known only to a few literary men and painters who were fortunate enough to know him or to see the hand-coloured engravings of his work. No formal recognition or criticism, therefore, is to be found at this period of Blake as a literary man, although a long study of him appears in Allan Cunningham's *Lives of the Most Eminent British Painters* (1829–33), which, as can be seen from the extract below, makes some attempt to analyse his genius. So remarkable is his absence from the critical scene that Alexander Gilchrist, who wrote the monumental *Life of William Blake* (1863), opens his first chapter with these words:

> From nearly all collections or beauties of 'The English Poets,' catholic to demerit as these are, tender of the expired and expiring reputations, one name has been hitherto perseveringly exiled. Encyclopaedias ignore it. The Biographical Dictionaries furtively pass it on with inaccurate despatch, as having had some connexion with the Arts. With critics it has had but little better fortune. The *Edinburgh Review*, twenty-seven years ago, specified as a characteristic sin of 'partiality' in Allan Cunningham's pleasant *Lives of British Artists*, that he should have ventured to include this name, since its possessor could (it seems) "scarcely be considered a painter" at all.

Apart from Cunningham's appraisal of Blake as a painter and craftsman, we have very few contemporary accounts of him. A description of him in his early years (1783–84), when he made a fleeting appearance in polite society, is given in two short extracts from the papers of J. T. Smith, Keeper of Prints and Drawings in the British Museum, and collector of literary and fashionable lions. It is as tantalizing to wonder about the tunes he composed and sang to his verses (these must have been *Songs of Innocence*) as it is to conjecture what song the Syrens sang, for no trace remains of his musical settings.

The fullest and most fascinating account of Blake appears in the papers of Henry Crabb Robinson (1775–1867), acute observer and recorder of famous men and their conversations. From the formidable mass of his private papers he put together his *Reminiscences of Blake*, an illuminating account of the occasions on which they met and the conversations they had. Of these I include Crabb Robinson's account of two interviews, both in 1825, together with a letter to Dorothy Wordsworth in which he gives her his impressions of "this very interesting man." Crabb Robinson is a reliable and sympathetic informant, always curious to observe genius at work, and undismayed by eccentricity. His *Reminiscences* are the best guide to Blake until the magnificent *Life* by Gilchrist, in which we have for the first time a full-length study of the life, together with an exhaustive treatment of the poetry and painting. This is the first, and in some ways still the best, critical estimate of the grandeur of Blake's genius, as well as the source of all our knowledge about his way of life and his character. Gilchrist, in this early attempt to relate the poetry to the designs which accompany the text, is a pioneer, and all modern critical work on Blake's iconography is indebted to his thorough scholarship.

Although most of his life was lived in retirement and

poverty, Blake's work was known and admired by other poets; Wordsworth[1] was of the opinion that, although mad, he was a genius, and Lamb, who dearly loved oddities and queer fish, recognized his quality. Of them all, Coleridge came the nearest to understanding him, since he shared Blake's knowledge of Swedenborgian philosophy; the extracts from his letters are characteristically obscure, but show an intense interest and the beginnings of an insight into Blake's extraordinary vision. Of particular interest is the letter in which we see Coleridge's personal choice of the *Songs*.

Our understanding of Blake would be incomplete without his letters, which have been collected and edited by Sir Geoffrey Keynes (1956). From this collection I include a very Blakeian declaration of faith in the power of the imagination, which echoes much of the style and sentiment of such works as *The Marriage of Heaven and Hell*. The recipient of the letter, the Reverend Dr Trusler, marked this letter, "Blake, dim'd with superstition."

P.H.

From *A Book for a Rainy Day, or Recollections of the Events of the Years 1766–1833* (1845),[2] by John Thomas Smith

[Smith was Keeper of Prints and Drawings in the British Museum.]

[1] In a conversation with Crabb Robinson he said, "There is something in the madness of this man which interests me more than the sanity of Lord Byron and Walter Scott."

[2] In the case of Blake it seems more illuminating not to arrange the passages strictly in the chronological order in which they were written.

At Mrs Mathew's[1] most agreable conversaziones I first met the late William Blake, the artist, to whom she and Mr Flaxman had been truly kind. There I have often heard him read and sing several of his poems. He was listened to by the company, with profound silence, and allowed by most of the visitors to possess original and extraordinary merit.

From *Nollekins and his Times*, Vol. 2 (1828), by John Thomas Smith

Much about this time,[2] Blake wrote many other songs, to which he also composed tunes. These he would occasionally sing to his friends; and though, according to his confession, he was entirely unacquainted with the science of music, his ear was so good, that his tunes were sometimes most singularly beautiful, and were noted down by musical professors. As for his later poetry, if it may be so called, attached to his plates, though it was certainly in some parts enigmatically curious as to its application, yet it was not always wholly uninteresting; and I have unspeakable pleasure in being able to state that though I admit he did not for the last forty years attend any place of Divine worship, yet he was not a Freethinker, as some invidious detractors have thought proper to assert, nor was he ever in any degree irreligious. Through life, his Bible was everything to him; and as a convincing proof how highly he reverenced the Almighty, I

[1] Mrs Mathew was a patron of artists and literary and musical figures of the period, and was famous for the soirées at her house at 27 Rathbone Place, Oxford Street. Blake was introduced to her by Flaxman; and her husband, the Rev. Henry Mathew, together with Flaxman, paid half the cost of printing the *Poetical Sketches* of 1783 (the only poems printed by Blake in his lifetime).

[2] *I.e.*, in 1784, after *Poetical Sketches* had been printed. The poems he would sing must have been some from *Songs of Innocence*.

shall introduce the following lines with which he concludes his address to the Deists.

For a tear is an intellectual thing;
And a sigh is the sword of an Angel-King;
And the bitter groan of a Martyr's woe
Is an arrow from the Almighty's bow.

From *The Lives of the Most Eminent British Painters* (1829–33), by Allan Cunningham

William Blake was of low stature and slender make, with a high pallid forehead, and eyes large, dark, and expressive. His temper was touchy, and when moved, he spoke with an indignant eloquence, which commanded respect. His voice, in general, was low and musical, his manners gentle and unassuming, his conversation a singular mixture of knowledge and enthusiasm. His whole life was one of labour and privation,—he had never tasted the luxury of that independence which comes from professional profit. This untoward fortune he endured with unshaken equanimity—offering himself, in imagination, as a martyr in the great cause of poetic art;—*pitying* some of his more fortunate brethren for their inordinate love of gain; and not doubting that whatever he might have won in gold by adopting other methods, would have been a poor compensation for the ultimate loss of fame. Under this agreable delusion he lived all his life—he was satisfied when his graver gained him a guinea a week—the greater the present denial, the surer the glory hereafter.

Though he was the companion of Flaxman[1] and Fuseli,[2]

[1] John Flaxman (1755–1826), sculptor and author of several works of outline drawings. A close friend of Blake.

[2] Henry Fuseli (1741–1825), the Swiss painter, who worked in England.

and sometimes their pupil, he never attained that professional skill, without which all genius is bestowed in vain. He was his own teacher chiefly; and self-instruction, the parent occasionally of great beauties, seldom fails to produce great deformities. He was a most splendid tinter, but no colourist, and his works were all of small dimensions, and therefore confined to the cabinet and the portfolio. His happiest flights, as well as his wildest, are thus likely to remain shut up from the world. If we look at the man through his best and most intelligible works, we shall find that he who could produce the *Songs of Innocence* and *Experience*, the *Gates of Paradise*,[1] and the *Inventions for Job*,[2] was the possessor of very lofty faculties, with no common skill in art, and moreover that, both in thought and mode of treatment, he was a decided original. But should we, shutting our eyes to the merits of those works, determine to weigh his worth by his *Urizen*, his *Prophecies of Europe and America*, and his *Jerusalem*,[3] our conclusion would be very unfavourable; we would say that, with much freedom of composition and boldness of posture, he was unmeaning, mystical, and extravagant, and that his original mode of working out his conceptions was little better than a brilliant way of animating absurdity. An overflow of imagination is a failing uncommon in this age, and has generally received of late little quarter from the critical portion of mankind. Yet imagination is the life and spirit of all great works of genius and

[1] *The Gates of Paradise* (1793), seventeen plates of designs, with verses. Cunningham writes: "The meaning of the artist is not a little obscure; it seems to have been his object to represent the innocence, the happiness, and the upward aspirations of man."

[2] *Inventions for Job* (1826), a series of engravings, which Gilchrist describes as "the best Blake ever did."

[3] *Urizen* (1794). (Gilchrist comments, "The poem is shapeless, unfathomable; but in the heaping up of gloomy and terrible images, the *America* and *Europe* are even exceeded.") *Prophecies of Europe and America* (1793–94). *erusalem* (1804).

taste; and indeed, without it, the head thinks and the hand labours in vain. Ten thousand authors and artists rise to the proper, the graceful, and the beautiful, for ten who ascend into "the heaven of invention." A work—whether from poet or painter—conceived in the fiery ecstasy of imagination, lives through every limb; while one elaborated out by skill and taste only will look, in comparison, like a withered and sapless tree beside one green and flourishing. Blake's misfortune was that of possessing this precious gift in excess. His fancy overmastered him—until he at length confounded "the mind's eye" with the corporeal organ, and dreamed himself out of the sympathies of actual life.

Postscript to a letter from S. T. Coleridge to the Rev. H. F. Cary, dated Highgate, 6 February, 1818

P.S. I have this morning been reading a strange publication—*viz*. Poems with very wild and interesting pictures, as swathing, etched (I suppose) but it is said printed and painted by the author, W. Blake. He is a man of Genius—and I apprehend a Swedenborgian[1]—certainly a mystic *emphatically*. You perhaps smile at *my* calling another poet a *Mystic*; but verily I am in the very mire of common-place common-place compared with Mr Blake, apo- or rather—ana-calyptic Poet, and Painter!

A letter from Coleridge to Charles Augustus Tulk, 1818

[Charles Augustus Tulk (1786–1849) was a Swedenborgian philosopher who had lent Coleridge a copy of *Songs of Innocence and Experience*.]

[1] Emanuel Swedenborg (1688–1772), the Swedish mystic, whose work had great influence on Blake.

Highgate, Thursday evening, 1818

. . . BLAKE'S POEMS. —I begin with my dyspathies that I may forget them, and have uninterrupted space for loves and sympathies. Title-page and the following emblem contain all the faults of the drawings with as few beauties as could be in the compositions of a man who was capable of such faults and such beauties. The faulty despotism in symbols amounting in the title-page to the μισητόν,[1] and occasionally, irregular unmodified lines of the inanimate, sometimes as the effect of rigidity and sometimes of exossation like a wet tendon. So likewise the ambiguity of the drapery. Is it a garment or the body incised and scored out? The lumpiness (the effect of vinegar on an egg) in the upper one of the two prostrate figures in the title-page, and the straight line down the waistcoat of pinky gold-beaters' skin in the next drawing, with the I don't-know-whatness of the countenance, as if the mouth had been formed by the habit of placing the tongue not contemptuously, but stupidly between the lower gums and the lower jaw—these are the only *repulsive* faults I have noticed. The figure, however, of the second leaf, abstracted from the *expression* of the countenance given it by something about the mouth, and the interspace from the lower lip to the chin, is such as only a master learned in his art could produce.

N.B. I signifies "It gave me great pleasure." +, "Still greater." ╫, "And greater still." ⊖, "In the highest degree." O, "In the lowest."

Shepherd, I; Spring, I (last stanza, +); Holy Thursday, ╫; Laughing Song, +; Nurse's Song, I; The Divine Image, ⊖; The Lamb, +; The little black Boy, ⊖, yea ⊖ + ⊖; Infant Joy, ╫ (N.B. For the three last lines I should write,

[1] μισητόν can be read as meaning 'loathsome,' 'hateful,' 'deformed,' or possibly as 'obscene.'

"When wilt thou smile," or "O smile, O smile! I'll sing the while." For a babe two days old does not, cannot smile, and innocence and the very truth of Nature must go together. Infancy is too holy a thing to be ornamented.) "The Echoing Green," I (the figures +, and of the second leaf, ++); "The Cradle Song," I; "The School Boy," ++; Night, ⊖; "On another's Sorrow," I; "A Dream," ?; "The little boy lost," I (the drawing, +); "The little boy found," I; "The Blossom," O; "The Chimney Sweeper," O; "The Voice of the Ancient Bard," O.

Introduction, +; Earth's Answer, +; Infant Sorrow, I; "The Clod and the Pebble," I; "The Garden of Love," +; "The Fly," I; "The Tyger," +; "A little boy lost," +; "Holy Thursday," I; "The little girl lost and found," (the ornaments most exquisite! the poem, I); "Chimney Sweeper in the Snow," O; "To Tirzah, and the Poison Tree," I—and yet O; "A little Girl lost," O. (I would have had it omitted, not for the want of innocence in the poem, but from the too probable want of it in many readers.) "London," I; "The Sick Rose," I; "The little Vagabond," O̲. Though I cannot approve altogether of this last poem, and have been inclined to think that the error which is most likely to beset the scholars of Emanuel Swedenborg is that of utterly demerging the tremendous incompatibilities with an evil will that arise out of the essential Holiness of the abysmal A-seity in the love of the eternal *Person*, and thus giving temptation to weak minds to sink this love itself into *Good Nature*, yet still I disapprove the mood of mind in this wild poem so much less than I do the servile blind-worm, wrap-rascal scurf-coat of *fear* of the *modern* Saint (whose whole being is a lie, to themselves as well as to their brethren), that I should laugh with good conscience in watching a Saint of the new stamp, one of the first stars of our eleemosynary advertisements, groaning in wind-pipe! and with the whites of his eyes upraised at the *audacity* of this poem! Anything rather than this degradation of Humanity, and therein of the Incarnate Divinity!

S.T.C.

O means that I am perplexed and have no opinion.
I, with which how can we utter "Our Father"?

From a letter from Henry Crabb Robinson to Dorothy Wordsworth, postmarked February 1826

. . . I have above mentioned *Blake*. I forget whether I ever mentioned to you this very interesting man, with whom I am now become acquainted. Were the 'memorials'[1] at my hand, I should quote a fine passage in the sonnet on the Cologne Cathedral as applicable to the contemplation of this singular being. I gave your brother some poems in M.S. by him & they interested him—as well they might, for there is an affinity between them as there is between the regulated imagination of a wise poet & the incoherent

[1] He refers to *Memorials of a Tour on the Continent, 1820*, by Wordsworth. It seems relevant to quote in full the sonnet "In the Cathedral at Cologne," in order to convey Crabb Robinson's meaning:

O for the help of Angels to complete
This Temple—Angels governed by a plan
Thus far pursued (how gloriously!) by Man,
Studious that *He* might not disdain the seat
Who dwells in heaven! But that aspiring heat
Hath failed; and now, ye Powers! whose gorgeous wings
And splendid aspect yon emblazonings
But faintly picture, 'twere an office meet
For you, on these unfinished shafts to try
The midnight virtues of your harmony:—
This vast design might tempt you to repeat
Strains that call forth upon empyreal ground
Immortal Fabrics, rising to the sound
Of penetrating harps and voices sweet!

dreams of a poet. Blake is an engraver by trade—a painter & a poet also whose works have been subject of derision to men in general, but he has a few admirers & some of eminence have eulogised his designs—he has lived in obscurity & poverty, to which the constant hallucinations in which he lives have doomed him. I do not mean to give you a detailed account of him. A few words will serve to inform you of what class he is. He is not so much a disciple of Jacob Böhmen[1] & Swedenborg as a fellow visionary. He lives as they did in a world of his own. Enjoying constant intercourse with a world of spirits, He receives visits from Shakespeare, Milton, Dante, Voltaire &c &c & has given me repeatedly their very words in their conversations. His paintings are copies of what he sees in his visions. His books (& his M.S.S. are immense in quantity) are dictated from the Spirits. He told me yesterday that when he writes, it is for the spirits only. —he sees the words fly about the room the moment he has put them on paper & his book is then published. A man so favoured of course has sources of wisdom & truth peculiar to himself—I will not pretend to give you an account of his religious & philosophical opinions. They are a strange compound of Christianity & Spinozaism & Platonism. I must confine myself to what he said about your brother's works & I fear this may lead me far enough to fatigue you in following me. After what I have said Mr W[ordsworth] will not be flattered by knowing that Blake deems him the *only poet* of the age. Nor much alarmed by hearing that like Muley Moloch[2] Blake thinks that he is often in his works an *Atheist*. Now according to Blake Atheism consists in worshipping the natural world, which same natural world properly speaking

[1] Jacob Boehme (1575–1624), German mystical writer, read not only by Blake but by Wordsworth and Coleridge. Sometimes spelt Behmen, or Böhmen, as here.

[2] Muley Moloch was Thomas Samuel Mulock (1789–1869), a well-known eccentric of the time, who engaged in religious controversy.

is nothing real, but a mere illusion produced by Satan. Milton was for a great part of his life an Atheist, & therefore has fatal errors in his Paradise Lost which he has often begged Blake to confute. Dante (tho' now with God) lived & died an Atheist. He was the slave of the world & time. But Dante & Wordsw. in spight of their Atheism were inspired by the Holy Ghost, & Wordsworth's poems, (a large proportion at least) are the work of divine inspiration. Unhappily he is left by God to his own illusions, & then the Atheism is apparent. I had the pleasure of reading to B. in my best style (& you know I am vain on that point & think I read W's poems peculiarly well) the Ode on Immortality. I never witnessed greater delight in any listener & in general B. loves the poems. What appears to have disturbed his mind, on the other hand, is the preface to the Excursion. He told me six months ago that it caused him a bowel complaint which nearly killed him. I have in his hand a copy of the extract & the following note . . .

When I first saw B. at Mr Aders's he very earnestly asked me: "Is Mr W. a sincere real Christian?" In reply to my answer he said, "If so, what does he mean by the worlds to which the heaven of heavens is but a veil & who is he that shall pass Jehovah unalarmed?"

I doubt whether what I have written will excite your & Mr W's curiosity, but there is something so delightful about the man—tho' in great poverty he is so perfect a gentleman with such genuine dignity & independence, scorning presents & of such native delicacy in words &c &c that I have not scrupled promising introducing him & Mr W. together. He expressed his thanks strongly, saying "You do me honour. Mr W. is a great man. Besides he may convince me I am wrong about him. I have been wrong before now," &c. Coleridge has visited B. & I am told talks finely about him. That I might not encroach on a 3d sheet I have compressed what I had to say about Blake. You must *see* him one of these days & he will interest you at all events, whatever character you give to his mind. . . .

From Henry Crabb Robinson's *Reminiscences of Blake*, collected, but not published, at the end of 1825

After my first evening with him [Blake] at Aders', I made the remark in my *Journal*, that his observations, apart from his visions and references to the spiritual world, were sensible and acute. In the sweetness of his countenance and gentility of his manner, he added an indescribable grace to his conversation. I added my regret, which I must now repeat, at my inability to give more than incoherent thoughts—not altogether my fault, perhaps.

On the 17th, I called on him at his house in Fountain Court in the Strand. The interview was a short one, and what I saw was more remarkable than what I heard. He was at work, engraving, in a small bedroom,—light, and looking out on a mean yard—everything in the room squalid and indicating poverty, except himself. There was a natural gentility about him, and an insensibility to the seeming poverty, which quite removed the impression. Besides, his linen was clean, his hand white, and his air quite unembarrassed when he begged me to sit down as if he were in a palace. There was but one chair in the room, besides that on which he sat. On my putting my hand to it, I found that it would have fallen to pieces if I had lifted it. So, as if I had been a Sybarite, I said, with a smile, "Will you let me indulge myself?" and sat on the bed near him. During my short stay there was nothing in him that betrayed that he was aware of what to other persons might have been even offensive,—not in his person, but in all about him. His wife I saw at this time, and she seemed to be the very woman to make him happy. She had been formed by him; indeed otherwise she could not have lived with him. Notwithstanding her dress, which was poor and dirty, she had a good expression in her countenance, and, with a dark eye, remains of beauty from her youth. She had an implicit reverence for her husband. It is quite certain that she believed in all his visions. On one occasion—not this day—speaking of his visions, she said: "You know, dear, the first time that you saw God was when you were four years old, and He put His head to the window, and set you screaming." . . .

. . . On the 24th December I called a second time on him. On this occasion it was that I read to him Wordsworth's *Ode* on the supposed pre-existent state (*Intimations of Immortality*). The subject of Wordsworth's religious character was discussed when we met on the 18th of February, and the 12th of May (1826). I will here bring together Blake's declarations concerning Wordsworth. I had been in the habit, when reading this marvellous Ode to friends, of omitting one or two passages, especially that—

> But there's a Tree, of many, one,
> A single Field which I have looked upon,
> Both of them speak of something that is gone:
>   The Pansy at my feet
>   Doth the same tale repeat:
> Whither is fled the visionary gleam?
> Where is it now, the glory and the dream?

lest I should be rendered ridiculous, being unable to explain precisely what I admired. Not that I acknowledged this to be a fair test. But with Blake I could fear nothing of the kind. And it was this very stanza which threw him almost into an hysterical rapture. His delight in Wordsworth's poetry was intense. Nor did it seem less, notwithstanding the reproaches he continually cast on his worship of nature; which, in the mind of Blake, constituted atheism. The combinations of the warmest praise with imputations which, from another, would assume the most serious character, and the liberty he took to interpret as he pleased, rendered it as difficult to be offended as to reason with him. The eloquent descriptions of nature in Wordsworth's poems were conclusive proofs of atheism: "For whoever believes in nature," said B., "disbelieves in God; for *Nature* is the work of the devil." On my obtaining from him the declaration that the Bible was the Word of God I referred to the commencement of *Genesis*. "In the beginning God created the heavens and the earth." But I gained nothing by this; for I was triumphantly told that this God was not Jehovah, but the Elohim; and the doctrine of the Gnostics was repeated with sufficient consistency to silence one so unlearned as myself. The *Preface* to *The Excursion*, especially the verses quoted from *Book I* of *The Recluse*, so troubled him as to bring on a fit of illness. These lines he singled out:—

> Jehovah—with His thunder, and the choir
> Of shouting angels, and the empyreal thrones—
> I pass them unalarmed.

"Does Mr W. think he can surpass Jehovah?" There was a copy of the whole passage in his own hand in the volume of Wordsworth's poems returned to my chambers after his death. There was this note at the end—"Solomon, when he married Pharaoh's daughter, and became a convert to the heathen mythology, talked exactly in this way of Jehovah—as a very inferior object of man's contemplations: he also passed Him 'unalarmed,' and was permitted. Jehovah dropped a tear and followed him by His spirit into the abstract void. It is called the Divine mercy. Sarah dwells in it, but mercy does not dwell in him." Some of the poems he maintained were from the Holy Ghost, others from the Devil. I lent him the 8vo edition, in two vols (1815) of W's poems, which he had in his possession at the time of his death. They were returned to me then. I did not recognise the pencil notes he had made in them to be his for some time, and was on the point of rubbing them out when I made the discovery; and they were preserved.

From *The Life of William Blake*, by Alexander Gilchrist (1863)

First of the Poems[1] let me speak, harsh as seems their divorce from the Design which blends with them, forming warp and woof in one texture. It is like pulling up a daisy by the roots from the green sward out of which it springs. To me many years ago, first reading these weird Songs in their appropriate environment of equally spiritual form and hue, the effect was as that of an angelic voice singing to oaten pipe, such as Arcadians tell of; or, as if a spiritual magician were summoning before human eyes, and through a human medium, images and scenes of divine loveliness; and in the pauses of the strain, we seem to catch the rustling of angelic wings. The Golden Age independent of Space or Time, object of vague sighs and dreams from many generations of struggling humanity—an Eden such as childhood sees, is brought nearer than ever poet brought it before. For this poet was in assured possession of the Golden Age, within the chambers of his own mind. As we read, fugitive glimpses open, clear as brief, of our buried childhood, of an unseen world present, past, to come; we are endowed with new spiritual sight, with unwonted intuitions, bright visitants

[1] He is writing about *Songs of Innocence*.

from finer realms of thought, which ever elude us, ever hover near. We encounter familiar objects, in unfamiliar, transfigured aspects, simple expression and deep meanings, type and antitype. True, there are palpable irregularities, metrical licence, lapse of grammar, and even of orthography; but often the sweetest melody, most daring eloquence of rhythm, and, what is more, appropriate rhythm. They are *unfinished* poems: yet would finish have bettered their bold and careless freedom? Would it not have brushed away the delicate bloom? that visible spontaneity, so rare and great a charm, the eloquent attribute of our old English Ballads and of the early Songs of all nations. The most deceptively perfect wax model is no substitute for the living flower. The form is, in these Songs, a transparent medium of the spiritual thought, not an opaque body. "He has dared to venture," writes Malkin, not irrelevantly, "on the ancient simplicity, and feeling it in his own character and manners, has succeeded better than those who have only seen it through a glass."

There is the same divine *afflatus* as in the Poetical Sketches, but fuller: a maturity of expression, despite surviving negligences, and of thought and motive. The "Child Angel," as we ventured to call the Poet in earlier years, no longer merely sportive and innocently wanton, wears a brow of thought; a glance of insight has passed into

a sense sublime
Of something far more deeply interfused

in Nature, a feeling of "the burthen of the mystery" of things; though still possessed by widest sympathies with all that is simple and innocent, with echoing laughter, little lamb, a flower's blossom, with "emmet wildered and forlorn."

These poems have a unity and mutual relationship, the

influence of which is much impaired if they be read otherwise than as a whole.

Who but Blake, with his pure heart, his simple exalted character, could have transfigured a commonplace meeting of Charity Children at St Paul's, as he has done in the *Holy Thursday*? a picture at once tender and grand. The bold images, by a wise instinct resorted to at the close of the first and second stanzas and opening of the third, are in the highest degree imaginative; they are true as only Poetry can be.

How vocal is the poem *Spring*, despite imperfect rhymes. From addressing the child, the poet, by a transition not infrequent with him, passes out of himself into the child's person, showing a chameleon sympathy with childlike feelings. Can we not see the little three-year-old prattler stroking the white lamb, her feelings made articulate for her?—Even more remarkable is the poem entitled *The Lamb*, sweet hymn of tender infantine sentiment appropriate to that perennial image of meekness; to which the fierce eloquence of *The Tiger*, in the *Songs of Experience*, is an antitype. In *The Lamb*, the poet again changes person to that of a child. Of lyrical beauty, take as a sample *The Laughing Song*, with its happy *ring* of merry innocent voices. This and *The Nurse's Song* are more in the style of his early poems, but, as we said, of far maturer execution. I scarcely need call attention to the delicate simplicity of the little pastoral, entitled *The Shepherd*: to the picturesqueness in a warmer hue, the delightful domesticity, the expressive melody of *The Echoing Green*: or to the lovely sympathy and piety which irradiate the touching *Cradle Song*. More enchanting still is the stir of fancy and sympathy which animates *The Dream*, that

> Did weave a shade o'er my angel guarded bed;

of an emmet that had

Lost her way,
Where on grass methought I lay.

Few are the readers, I should think, who can fail to appreciate the symbolic grandeur of *The Little Boy Lost* and *The Little Boy Found*, or the enigmatic tenderness of the *Blossom* and the *Divine Image*; and the verses *On Another's Sorrow* express some of Blake's favourite religious ideas, his abiding notions on the subject of the Godhead, which surely suggest the kernel of Christian feeling. A similar tinge of the divine, colours the lines called *Night*, with its revelation of angelic guardians, believed in with unquestioning piety by Blake, who makes us in our turn conscious, as we read, of angelic noiseless footsteps. For a nobler depth of religious beauty, with accordant grandeur of sentiment and language, I know no parallel nor hint elsewhere of such a poem as *The Little Black Boy*—

My mother bore me in the southern wild.

We may read these poems again and again, and they continue fresh as at first. There is something unsating in them, a perfume as of a growing violet, which renews itself as fast as it is inhaled.

One poem, *The Chimney Sweeper*, still calls for special notice. This and *Holy Thursday* are remarkable as an anticipation of the daring choice of homely subject, of the yet more daringly familiar manner, nay, of the very metre and trick of style adopted by Wordsworth in a portion of those memorable "experiments in Poetry,"—the *Lyrical Ballads*:—in *The Reverie of Poor Susan*, for instance (not written till 1797), the *Star Gazers*, and *The Power of Music* (both 1806). The little Sweep's dream has the spiritual touch peculiar to Blake's hand. This poem, I may add, was extracted thirty-five years later in a curious little volume (1824), of James

Montgomery's editing, as friend of the then unprotected Climbing-Boys. It was entitled *The Chimney Sweeper's Friend, and Climbing-Boy's Album*: a miscellany of verse and prose, original and borrowed, with illustrations by Robert Cruikshank. Charles Lamb, one of the living authors applied to by the kind-hearted Sheffield poet, while declining the task of rhyming on such a subject, sent a copy of this poem from the *Songs of Innocence*, communicating it as "from a very rare and curious little work." At line five, "Little Tom Dacre" is transformed by a sly blunder of Lamb's into "little Tom Toddy." The poem on the same subject in the *Songs of Experience*, inferior poetically, but in an accordant key of gloom, would have been the more apposite to Montgomery's volume.

The tender loveliness of these poems will hardly reappear in Blake's subsequent writing. Darker phases of feeling, more sombre colours, profounder meanings, ruder eloquence, characterise the *Songs of Experience* of five years later.

In 1789, the year in which Blake's hand engraved the *Songs of Innocence*, Wordsworth was finishing his versified *Evening Walk* on the Goldsmith model; Crabbe ("Pope in worsted stockings," as Hazlitt christened him), famous six years before by his *Village*, was publishing one of his minor quartos, *The Newspaper*. . . .

. . . The designs, simultaneous offspring with the poems, which in the most literal sense illuminate the *Songs of Innocence*, consist of poetized domestic scenes. The drawing and draperies are grand in style as graceful, though covering few inches' space; the colour pure, delicate, yet in effect rich and full. The mere tinting of the text and of the free ornamental border often makes a refined picture. The costumes of the period are idealized, the landscapes given in pastoral and symbolic hints. Sometimes these drawings almost suffer from being looked at as a book and held close, instead of at due distance as pictures, where they become more effective. In composition, colour, pervading feeling, they are lyrical to the eye, as the *Songs* to the ear.

On the whole, the designs to the *Songs of Innocence* are finer as well as more pertinent to the poems; more closely interwoven with them, than those which accompany the *Songs of Experience*.

A letter from Blake to Dr Trusler[1] (1799)

REVD SIR,

I really am sorry that you are fall'n out with the Spiritual World, Especially if I should have to answer for it. I feel very sorry that your Ideas & Mine on Moral Painting differ so much as to have made you angry with my method of Study. If I am wrong, I am wrong in good company. I had hoped your plan comprehended All Species of this Art, & Expecially that you would not regret that Species which gives Existence to Every other, namely, Visions of Eternity. You say that I want somebody to Elucidate my Ideas. But you ought to know that What is Grand is necessarily obscure to Weak men. That which can be made Explicit to the Idiot is not worth my care. The wisest of the Ancients consider'd what is not too Explicit as the fittest for Instruction, because it rouzes the faculties to act. I name Moses, Solomon, Esop, Homer, Plato.

But as you have favor'd me with your remarks on my Design, permit me in return to defend it against a mistaken

[1] The Rev. Dr Trusler (1735–1820), who lived near Egham, at Englefield Green, was an eccentric clergyman who studied medicine, cultivated the arts, and established a business as a bookseller. This letter is reprinted with permission from *The Letters of William Blake*, edited by Sir Geoffrey Keynes (Hart-Davis, 1956).

one, which is, That I have supposed Malevolence without a Cause. Is not Merit in one a Cause of Envy in another, & Serenity & Happiness & Beauty a Cause of Malevolence? But Want of Money & the Distress of A Thief can never be alledged as the Cause of his Thieving, for many honest people endure greater hardships with Fortitude. We must therefore seek the Cause elsewhere than in want of Money, for that is the Miser's passion, not the Thief's.

I have therefore proved your Reasonings Ill proportion'd, which you can never prove my figures to be; they are those of Michael Angelo, Rafael & the Antique, & of the best living Models. I percieve that your Eye is perverted by Caricature Prints, which ought not to abound so much as they do. Fun I love, but too much Fun is of all things the most loathsom. Mirth is better than Fun, & Happiness is better than Mirth. I feel that a Man may be happy in this World. And I know that This World Is a World of imagination & Vision. I see Every thing I paint in This World, but Every body does not see alike. To the Eyes of a Miser a Guinea is more beautiful than the Sun, & a bag worn with the use of Money has more beautiful proportions than a Vine filled with Grapes. The tree which moves some to tears of joy is in the Eyes of others only a Green thing that stands in the way. Some See Nature all Ridicule & Deformity, & by these I shall not regulate my proportions; & Some Scarce see Nature at all. But to the Eyes of the Man of Imagination, Nature is Imagination itself. As a man is, So he Sees. As the Eye is formed, such are its Powers. You certainly Mistake, when you say that the Visions of Fancy are not to be found in This World. To Me This World is all One continued Vision of Fancy or Imagination, & I feel Flatter'd when I am told so. What is it sets Homer, Virgil, & Milton in so high a rank of Art? Why is the Bible more Entertaining & Instructive than any other book? Is it not because they are addressed to the

Imagination, which is Spiritual Sensation, & but mediately to the Understanding or Reason? Such is True Painting, and such was alone valued by the Greeks & the best modern Artists. Consider what Lord Bacon says: "Sense sends over to Imagination before Reason have judged, & Reason sends over to Imagination before the Decree can be acted." See Advancemt of Learning, Part 2, P. 47 of first Edition.

But I am happy to find a Great Majority of Fellow Mortals who can Elucidate My Visions, & Particularly they have been Elucidated by Children, who have taken a greater delight in contemplating my Pictures than I even hoped. Neither Youth nor Childhood is Folly or Incapacity. Some Children are Fools & so are some Old Men. But There is a vast Majority on the side of Imagination or Spiritual Sensation.

To Engrave after another Painter is infinitely more laborious than to Engrave one's own Inventions. And of the size you require my price has been Thirty Guineas, & I cannot afford to do it for less. I had Twelve for the Head I sent you as a Specimen, but after my own designs I could do at least Six times the quantity of labour in the same time, which will account for the difference in price as also that Chalk Engraving is at least six times as laborious as Aqua tinta. I have no objection to Engraving after another Artist. Engraving is the profession I was apprenticed to, & should never have attempted to live by any thing else. If orders had not come in for my Designs & Paintings, which I have the pleasure to tell you are Increasing Every Day. Thus If I am a Painter it is not to be attributed to Seeking after. But I am contented whether I live by Painting or Engraving.

I am, Revd. Sir, your very obedient servant,

WILLIAM BLAKE.

13 HERCULES BUILDINGS
LAMBETH
August 23, 1799

From a letter from Charles Lamb to his friend Bernard Barton, postmarked 15 May, 1824

Blake is a real name, I assure you, and a most extraordinary man, if he is still living. He is the Robert[1] Blake, whose wild designs accompany a splendid folio edition of the "Night Thoughts,"[2] which you may have seen, in one of which he pictures the parting of soul and body by a solid mass of human form floating off, God knows how, from a lumpish mass (fac Simile to itself) left behind on the dying bed. He paints in water colours marvellous strange pictures, visions of his brain, which he asserts that he has seen. They have great merit. He has *seen* the old Welsh bards on Snowdon—he has seen the Beautifullest, the strongest, & the Ugliest Man, left alone from the Massacre of the Britons by the Romans, and has painted them from memory (I have seen his paintings), and asserts them to be as good as the figures of Raphael & Angelo, but not better, as they had precisely the same retro-visions & prophetic visions with themself [himself]. The painters in oil (which he will have it that neither of them practised) he affirms to have been the ruin of art, and affirms that all the while he was engaged in his Water paintings, Titian was disturbing him, Titian the Ill Genius of Oil Painting. His Pictures—one in particular, the Canterbury

[1] Lamb knows so little about Blake that he makes an error over his Christian name.

[2] "Edwards of New Bond Street, at that day a leading bookseller, engaged Blake in 1796 to illustrate an expensive edition, emulating Boydell's Shakespere and Milton, of Young's *Night Thoughts*. The *Night Thoughts* was then, as it had been for more than half a century, a living classic, which rival booksellers delighted to re-publish." (Gilchrist.) But Lamb's memory plays him false. He is in fact thinking of a plate in an edition of Blair's *Grave* for which Blake composed twelve "Inventions."

Pilgrims (far above Stothard)—have great merit, but hard, dry, yet with grace. He has written a Catalogue[1] of them with a most spirited criticism on Chaucer, but mystical and full of Vision. His poems have been sold hitherto only in Manuscript. I never read them; but a friend[2] at my desire procured the 'Sweep Song.' There is one to a tiger, which I have heard recited, beginning—

> Tiger, Tiger, burning bright,
> Thro' the desarts of the night,

which is glorious, but alas! I have not the book; for the man is flown, whither I know not—to Hades or a Madhouse. But I must look on him as one of the most extraordinary persons of the age.

[1] *A Descriptive Catalogue of Pictures* (1809), to describe an exhibition of Blake's work which was held in May 1809 on the first floor of his brother the hosier's house in Broad Street, London. Lamb is speaking of pictures which were exhibited on this occasion—*The Canterbury Pilgrims* and *The Ancient Britons* (No. V in the Catalogue. Blake writes, "In the last Battle of King Arthur only Three Britons escaped; these were the Strongest Man, the Beautifullest Man, and the Ugliest Man.")

[2] James Montgomery, who was compiling a book about chimney-sweepers. Lamb sent him Blake's poem, and Bernard Barton liked it so much that he asked Lamb for more information about the author. The letter above is Lamb's reply. See above, p. 144.

William Wordsworth

(1770–1850)

WHATEVER is too original will be hated at the first," writes De Quincey in his essay on Wordsworth's poetry; and on another occasion he surveys the poet's career: "Up to 1820 the name of Wordsworth was trampled under foot; from 1820 to 1830 it was militant; from 1830 to 1835 it has been triumphant." These remarks serve as an admirable commentary on Wordsworth's treatment at the hands of his critics and his public. As we see from his letters, he expected little or nothing from them; and very early on he spiked their guns by a description of the ideal critic, to be found in the "Essay, Supplementary to the Preface" of 1800:

> Whither then shall we turn for that union of qualifications which must necessarily exist before the decisions of a critic can be of absolute value? For a mind at once poetical and philosophical; for a critic whose affections are as free and kindly as the spirit of society, and whose understanding is severe as that of dispassionate government? Where are we to look for that initiatory composure of mind which no selfishness can disturb? For a natural sensibility that has been tutored into correctness without losing anything of its quickness; and for active faculties, capable of answering the demands which an Author of original imagination shall make upon them, associated with a judgment that cannot be duped into admiration by aught that is unworthy of it?—among those and those only, who, never having suffered their youthful love of poetry to remit much of its force, have applied to the consideration of the laws of this art the best power of their understandings.

Since no such ideal creatures were in existence, his early poems were at the mercy of reviewers who regarded this "Author of original imagination" with dismay and derision. The first edition of the *Lyrical Ballads* of 1798 was received not too unkindly. *The Monthly Review* of June 1799, although upset by the prevailing gloominess of the subject matter ("Each ballad is a tale of woe") was judicious and encouraging; although Southey, writing in *The Critical Review* of October 1798 (the article in which he dismissed *The Ancient Mariner* as "a poem of little merit," assuming all the poems to be the work of the same author), seemed not over-enthusiastic.

> The experiment [he says in conclusion], we think, has failed, not because the language of conversation is little adapted to "the purposes of poetic pleasure" but because it has been tried upon uninteresting subjects. Yet every piece discovers genius; and ill as the author has frequently employed his talents, they certainly rank him with the best of living poets.

The appearance of the 1800 edition, with prefaces, seems to have been the signal for the more damaging attacks. Coleridge has some very shrewd things to say about this in *Biographia Literaria* (Chapter IV):

> In the critical remarks . . . prefixed and annexed to the Lyrical Ballads, I believe, we may safely rest, as the true origin of the unexampled opposition which Mr Wordsworth's writings have been since doomed to encounter. The humbler passages in the poems themselves were dwelt on and cited to justify the rejection of the theory. What in and for themselves would have been either forgotten or forgiven as imperfections, or at least comparative failures, provoked direct hostility when announced as intentional, as the result of choice after full deliberation. Thus the poems, admitted by all as excellent, joined with those which had pleased the far greater number, though they formed two-thirds of the whole work, instead of

being deemed (as in all right they should have been, even if we take for granted that the reader judged aright) an atonement for the few exceptions, gave wind and fuel to the animosity against both the poems and the poet. In all perplexity there is a portion of fear, which predisposes the mind to anger. Not able to deny that the author possessed both genius and a powerful intellect, they felt *very positive*,—but yet were not *quite certain* that he might not be in the right, and they themselves in the wrong; an unquiet state of mind, which seeks alleviation by quarrelling with the occasion of it, and by wondering at the perverseness of the man, who had written a long and argumentative essay to persuade them, that

Fair is foul, and foul is fair;

in other words, that they had been all their lives admiring without judgment, and were now about to censure without reason.

Wordsworth's high and uncompromising claims, and more particularly his new theories on diction and literary 'artlessness,' irritated the reviewers and at the same time provided them with ready-made weapons for ridicule. Jeffrey, who could never come to terms with Wordsworth's mystical outlook, was his cruellest critic. Reviewing the *Poems* of 1807, and again in a review of Crabbe's *Poems* in 1808, in which he contrasts Crabbe's faithful realism with what he feels to be the bogus simplicity of Wordsworth, he never ceases to be hostile to the whole of the Lake School. Even as late as 1814, he begins his review of *The Excursion* with the famous words, "This will never do!"

Wilson, whose opinions changed with bewildering perverseness (as we see in his attitudes to Coleridge), was on the whole by temperament a supporter of Wordsworth. In his essays in *Blackwood's*, "On the Lake School of Poetry," in 1818 he comes near to understanding:

> Two things may be chiefly observed in Mr Wordsworth's poetry; namely, first, an attempt to awaken in the minds of his countrymen certain *lumières* which they do not generally possess, and certain convictions of moral laws existing silently in the universe, and actually modifying events; . . . and secondly, a thorough knowledge of all the beauties of the human affections, and of their mutual harmonies and dependencies.

But, in general, De Quincey was right. Wordsworth was too original for the public, as he himself realized after the first shock of pained surprise. He had warned his readers that they would have to "struggle with feelings of strangeness and awkwardness," and in his letter to Lady Beaumont (part of which is printed below), he reasserts his belief that "every great and original writer . . . must himself create the taste by which he is to be relished." Indeed, his life was devoted to this task; not only in the "Preface" to *Lyrical Ballads*, which is the fullest statement of his poetic aims, but in his letters and conversation, he tried to explain and elucidate his work. His attitude inclined to the severe, even to friends and family. To Sara Hutchinson, who had had the temerity to say that she was not entirely charmed by *Resolution and Independence*, he writes rather sharply:

> My dear Sara, it is not a matter of indifference whether you are pleased with this figure and his employment; it may be comparatively so, whether you are pleased or not with *this Poem*; but it is of the utmost importance that you should have had pleasure from contemplating the fortitude, independence, persevering spirit, and the general moral dignity of this old man's character. Your feelings upon the Mother, and the Boys with the Butterfly, were not indifferent: it was an affair of whole continents of moral sympathy. I will talk more with you on this when we meet. . . .

Crabb Robinson catches him in a characteristic moment, as

Wordsworth loftily says of some of his own lines "They *ought* to be liked."

Whether he was understood or not, Wordsworth survived his critics to become Poet Laureate in 1843, after Southey. The *nouvelle vague* of Romantic writers had been irreverent and disrespectful to him, largely because of his political change of heart. The bitterness of Byron, Shelley, and Peacock springs from their contempt at his betrayal of the ideals of the French Revolution, and his final transformation into an Establishment bore is cruelly sketched by Browning. Keats, less politically involved, was more sympathetic, and his letters are full of references and quotations from Wordsworth's poems, especially from the Immortality Ode, which he found deeply moving. Although he disapproved of the "wordsworthian or egotistical sublime"[1] type of poetry and "poetry that has a palpable design upon us—and if we do not agree, seems to put its hand in its breeches pocket,"[2] he nevertheless could see the distinctive quality of Wordsworth's vision.

Contemporary criticism of Wordsworth is mostly not very rewarding, except to show the critical attitudes against which he was trying to justify himself. The only man to measure up to Wordsworth's definition of the ideal critic—"a mind at once poetical and philosophical"—was Coleridge, the greatest critic of the age, and in *Biographia Literaria* we are fortunate enough to have a long analysis by him of the defects and beauties of Wordsworth's poetry. For reasons of space, it is only possible to print excerpts here, but it should be read in full as the most profound and penetrating commentary of the period.

P.H.

[1] Letter to Richard Woodhouse, 27 October, 1818.
[2] Letter to John Hamilton Reynolds, 3 February, 1818.

From the Preface to *Lyrical Ballads*, second edition (1800)

The first volume of these Poems has already been submitted to general perusal. It was published, as an experiment, which, I hoped, might be of some use to ascertain, how far, by fitting to metrical arrangement a selection of the real language of men in a state of vivid sensation, that sort of pleasure and that quantity of pleasure may be imparted, which a Poet may rationally endeavour to impart.

I had formed no very inaccurate estimate of the probable effect of those Poems: I flattered myself that they who should be pleased with them would read them with more than common pleasure: and, on the other hand, I was well aware, that by those who should dislike them they would be read with more than common dislike. The result has differed from my expectation in this only, that a greater number have been pleased than I ventured to hope I should please.

Several of my Friends are anxious for the success of these Poems, from a belief, that, if the views with which they were composed were indeed realized, a class of Poetry would be produced, well adapted to interest mankind permanently, and not unimportant in the quality, and in the multiplicity of its moral relations: and on this account they have advised me to prefix a systematic defence of the theory upon which the Poems were written. But I was unwilling to undertake the task, knowing that on this occasion the Reader would look coldly upon my arguments, since I might be suspected of having been principally influenced by the selfish and foolish hope of *reasoning* him into an approbation of these particular Poems: and I was still more unwilling to undertake the task, because adequately to display the opinions, and fully to enforce the arguments, would require a space wholly disproportionate to a preface. For, to treat the subject with the clearness and coherence of which it is susceptible, it would be necessary to give a full account of the present state of the public taste in this country, and to determine how far this taste is healthy or depraved; which, again, could not be determined, without pointing out in what manner language and the human mind act and re-act on each other, and without retracing the revolutions, not of literature alone, but likewise of society itself. I have therefore altogether declined to enter regularly upon this defence; yet I am sensible, that there would be something like impropriety in abruptly obtruding upon the Public, without a few words of introduction, Poems so materially different from those upon which general approbation is at present bestowed.

It is supposed, that by the act of writing in verse an Author makes a formal engagement that he will gratify certain known habits of association; that he not only thus apprises the Reader that certain classes of ideas and expressions will be found in his book, but that others will be carefully excluded. This exponent or symbol held forth by metrical language must in different eras of literature have excited very different expectations: for example, in the age of Catullus, Terence, and Lucretius, and that of Statius or Claudian; and in our own country, in the age of Shakespeare and Beaumont and Fletcher, and that of Donne and Cowley, or Dryden, or Pope. I will not take upon me to determine the exact import of the promise which, by the act of writing in verse, an Author in the present day makes to his Reader: but it will undoubtedly appear to many persons that I have not fulfilled the terms of an engagement thus voluntarily contracted. They who have been accustomed to the gaudiness and inane phraseology of many modern writers, if they persist in reading this book to its conclusion, will, no doubt, frequently have to struggle with feelings of strangeness and awkwardness: they will look round for poetry, and will be induced to inquire by what species of courtesy these attempts can be permitted to assume that title. I hope therefore the Reader will not censure me for attempting to state what I have proposed to myself to perform; and also (as far as the limits of a preface will permit) to explain some of the chief reasons which have determined me in the choice of my purpose: that at least he may be spared any unpleasant feeling of disappointment, and that I myself may be protected from one of the most dishonourable accusations which can be brought against an Author; namely, that of an indolence which prevents him from endeavouring to ascertain what is his duty, or, when his duty is ascertained, prevents him from performing it.

The principal object, then, proposed in these Poems was to choose incidents and situations from common life, and to relate or describe them, throughout, as far as was possible in a selection of language really used by men, and, at the same time, to throw over them a certain colouring of imagination, whereby ordinary things should be presented to the mind in an unusual aspect; and, further, and above all, to make these incidents and situations interesting by tracing in them, truly though not ostentatiously, the primary laws of our nature: chiefly, as far as regards the manner in which we associate ideas in a state of excitement. Humble and rustic life was generally chosen, because, in that condition, the essential passions of the heart find a better soil in which they can attain their maturity, are less under restraint, and speak a plainer and more emphatic language; because in that condition of life our elementary feelings coexist in a state of greater simplicity, and, consequently, may be more accurately contemplated, and more forcibly communicated;

because the manners of rural life germinate from those elementary feelings, and, from the necessary character of rural occupations, are more easily comprehended, and are more durable; and, lastly, because in that condition the passions of men are incorporated with the beautiful and permanent forms of nature. The language, too, of these men has been adopted (purified indeed from what appear to be its real defects, from all lasting and rational causes of dislike or disgust) because such men hourly communicate with the best objects from which the best part of language is originally derived; and because, from their rank in society and the sameness and narrow circle of their intercourse, being less under the influence of social vanity, they convey their feelings and notions in simple and unelaborated expressions. Accordingly, such a language, arising out of repeated experience and regular feelings, is a more permanent, and a far more philosophical language, than that which is frequently substituted for it by Poets, who think that they are conferring honour upon themselves and their art, in proportion as they separate themselves from the sympathies of men, and indulge in arbitrary and capricious habits of expression, in order to furnish food for fickle tastes, and fickle appetites, of their own creation.[1]

I cannot, however, be insensible to the present outcry against the triviality and meanness, both of thought and language, which some of my contemporaries have occasionally introduced into their metrical compositions; and I acknowledge that this defect, where it exists, is more dishonourable to the Writer's own character than false refinement or arbitrary innovation, though I should contend at the same time, that it is far less pernicious in the sum of its consequences.

[1] It is worth while here to observe, that the affecting parts of Chaucer are almost always expressed in language pure and universally intelligible even to this day. [W.W.]

From such verses the Poems in these volumes will be found distinguished at least by one mark of difference, that each of them has a worthy *purpose*. Not that I always began to write with a distinct purpose formally conceived; but habits of meditation have, I trust, so prompted and regulated my feelings, that my descriptions of such objects as strongly excite those feelings, will be found to carry along with them a *purpose*. If this opinion be erroneous, I can have little right to the name of a Poet. For all good poetry is the spontaneous overflow of powerful feelings: and though this be true, Poems to which any value can be attached were never produced on any variety of subjects but by a man who, being possessed of more than usual organic sensibility, had also thought long and deeply. For our continued influxes of feeling are modified and directed by our thoughts, which are indeed the representatives of all our past feelings; and, as by contemplating the relation of these general representatives to each other, we discover what is really important to men, so, by the repetition and continuance of this act, our feelings will be connected with important subjects, till at length, if we be originally possessed of much sensibility, such habits of mind will be produced, that, by obeying blindly and mechanically the impulses of those habits, we shall describe objects, and utter sentiments, of such a nature, and in such connexion with each other, that the understanding of the Reader must necessarily be in some degree enlightened, and his affections strengthened and purified.

. . . . . .

Taking up the subject, then, upon general grounds, let me ask, what is meant by the word Poet? What is a Poet? To whom does he address himself? And what language is to be expected from him?—He is a man speaking to men: a man, it is true, endowed with more lively sensibility, more enthusiasm and tenderness, who has a greater knowledge of human nature, and a more comprehensive soul, than are supposed to be common among mankind; a man pleased with his own passions and volitions, and who rejoices more than other men in the spirit of life that is in him; delighting to contemplate similar volitions and passions as manifested in the goings-on of the Universe, and habitually impelled to create them where he does not find them. To these qualities he has added a disposition to be affected more than other men by absent things as if they were present; an ability of conjuring up in himself passions, which are indeed far from being the same as those produced by real events, yet (especially in those parts of the general sympathy which are pleasing and delightful) do more nearly resemble the passions produced by real events, than anything which, from the motions of their own minds merely, other men are accustomed to feel in themselves:—whence, and from practice, he has acquired a greater readiness and power in expressing what he thinks and feels, and especially those thoughts and feelings which, by his own choice, or from the structure of his own mind, arise in him without immediate external excitement.

But whatever portion of this faculty we may suppose even the greatest Poet to possess, there cannot be a doubt that the language which it will suggest to him, must often, in liveliness and truth, fall short of that which is uttered by men in real life, under the actual pressure of those passions, certain shadows of which the Poet thus produces, or feels to be produced, in himself.

However exalted a notion we would wish to cherish of the character of a Poet, it is obvious, that while he describes and imitates passions, his employment is in some degree mechanical, compared with the freedom and power of real and substantial action and suffering. So that it will be the wish of the Poet to bring his feelings near to those of the persons whose feelings he describes, nay, for short spaces of time, perhaps, to let himself slip into an entire delusion, and even confound and identify his own feelings with theirs; modifying only the language which is thus suggested to him by a consideration that he describes for a particular purpose, that of giving pleasure. Here, then, he will apply the principle of selection which has been already insisted upon. He will depend upon this for removing what would otherwise be painful or disgusting in the passion; he will feel that there is no necessity to trick out or to elevate nature: and, the more industriously he applies this principle, the deeper will be his faith that no words, which *his* fancy or imagination can suggest, will be to be compared with those which are the emanations of reality and truth.

But it may be said by those who do not object to the general spirit of these remarks, that, as it is impossible for the Poet to produce upon all occasions language as exquisitely fitted for the passion as that which the real passion itself suggests, it is proper that he should consider himself as in the situation of a translator, who does not scruple to substitute excellencies of another kind for those which are unattainable by him; and endeavours occasionally to surpass his original, in order to make some amends for the general inferiority to which he feels that he must submit. But this would be to encourage idleness and unmanly despair. Further, it is the language of men who speak of what they do not understand; who talk of Poetry as of a matter of amusement and idle pleasure; who will converse with us as gravely about a *taste* for Poetry, as they express it, as if it were a thing as indifferent as a taste for rope-dancing, or Frontiniac or Sherry. Aristotle, I have been told, has said, that Poetry is the most philosophic of all writing: it is so: its object is truth, not individual and local, but general, and operative; not standing upon external testimony, but carried alive into the heart by passion; truth which is its own testimony, which gives competence and confidence to the tribunal to which it appeals, and receives them from the same tribunal. Poetry is the image of man and nature. The obstacles which stand in the way of the fidelity of the Biographer and Historian, and of their consequent utility, are incalculably greater than those which are to be encountered by the Poet who comprehends the dignity of his art. The Poet writes under one restriction only, namely, the necessity of giving immediate pleasure to a human Being possessed of that information which may be expected from him, not as a lawyer, a physician, a mariner, an astronomer, or a natural philosopher, but as a Man. Except this one restriction, there is no object standing between the Poet and the image of things; between this, and the Biographer and Historian, there are a thousand.

From Jeffrey's review of Southey's *Thalaba*, in *The Edinburgh Review*, October 1802

[An attack on the "Lake School of Poetry," and especially on Wordsworth.]

Poetry has this much, at least, in common with religion, that its standards were fixed long ago, by certain inspired writers, whose authority it is no longer lawful to call in question. . . .

The author who is now before us belongs to a *sect* of poets, that has established itself in this country within these ten or twelve years, and is looked upon, we believe, as one of its chief champions and apostles. The peculiar doctrines of this sect, it would not, perhaps, be very easy to explain; but, that they are *dissenters* from the established systems in poetry and criticism is admitted, and proved, indeed, by the whole tenor of their compositions. Though they lay claim, we believe, to a creed and a revelation of their own, there can be little doubt, that their doctrines are of *German* origin, and have been derived from some of the great modern reformers in that country. Some of their leading principles, indeed, are probably of an earlier date, and seem to have been borrowed from the great apostle of Geneva.[1] . . .

The disciples of this school boast much of its originality, and seem to value themselves very highly, for having broken loose from the bondage of ancient authority, and re-asserted the independence of genius. Originality, however, we are persuaded, is rarer than mere alteration; and a man may change a good master for a bad one, without finding himself at all nearer to independence. That our new poets have abandoned the old models, may certainly be admitted; but we have not been able to discover that they have yet created any models of their own; and are very much inclined to call in question the worthiness of those to which they have transferred their admiration. The productions of this school, we conceive, are so far from being entitled to the praise of originality, that they cannot be better characterized than by an enumeration of the sources from which their materials have been derived. The greatest part of them, we apprehend, will be found to be composed of the following elements: 1. The antisocial principles, and distempered sensibility of Rousseau—his discontent with the present constitution of society—his paradoxical morality, and his perpetual hankerings after some unattainable state of voluptuous virtue and perfection. 2. The simplicity and energy (*horresco referens*) of Kotzebue and Schiller. 3. The homeliness and harshness of some of Cowper's language and versification, interchanged occasionally with the *innocence* of Ambrose Philips, or the quaintness of Quarles and Dr Donne. . . .

The authors of whom we are now speaking have, among

[1] Jean-Jacques Rousseau.

them, unquestionably, a very considerable portion of poetical talent, and have, consequently, been enabled to seduce many into an admiration of the false taste (as it appears to us) in which most of these productions are composed. They constitute, at present, the most formidable conspiracy that has lately been formed against sound judgment in matters poetical. . . .

Their most distinguishing symbol is undoubtedly an affectation of great simplicity and familiarity of language. They disdain to make use of the common poetical phraseology, or to ennoble their diction by a selection of fine or dignified expressions. There would be too much *art* in this, for that great love of nature with which they are all of them inspired; and their sentiments, they are determined, shall be indebted, for their effect, to nothing but their intrinsic tenderness or elevation. There is something very noble and conscientious, we will confess, in this plan of composition; but the misfortune is, that there are passages in all poems that can neither be pathetic nor sublime; and that, on these occasions, a neglect of the establishments of language is very apt to produce absolute meanness and insipidity. The language of passion, indeed, can scarcely be deficient in elevation; and when an author is wanting in that particular, he may commonly be presumed to have failed in the truth, as well as in the dignity of his expression. The case, however, is extremely different with the subordinate parts of composition; with the narrative and description, that are necessary to preserve its connection; and the explanation, that must frequently prepare us for the great scenes and splendid passages. In these, all the requisite ideas may be conveyed, with sufficient clearness, by the meanest and most negligent expressions; and if magnificence or beauty is ever to be observed in them, it must have been introduced from some other motive than that of adapting the style to the subject.

It is in such passages, accordingly, that we are most frequently offended with low and inelegant expressions; and that the language, which was intended to be simple and natural, is found oftenest to degenerate into mere slovenliness and vulgarity. It is in vain, too, to expect that the meanness of those parts may be redeemed by the excellence of others. A poet who aims at all at sublimity or pathos, is like an actor in a high tragic character, and must sustain his dignity throughout, or become altogether ridiculous. . . .

The followers of simplicity are, therefore, at all times in danger of occasional degradation; but the simplicity of this new school seems intended to ensure it. *Their* simplicity does not consist, by any means, in the rejection of glaring or superfluous ornament,—in the substitution of elegance to splendour,—or in that refinement of art which seeks concealment in its own perfection. It consists, on the contrary, in a very great degree, in the positive and *bona fide* rejection of art altogether, and in the bold use of those rude and negligent expressions, which would be banished by a little discrimination. One of these authors, indeed, has very ingeniously set forth, (in a kind of manifesto,[1] that preceded one of their most flagrant acts of hostility,) that it was their capital object "to adapt to the uses of poetry the ordinary language of conversation among the middling and lower orders of the people." What advantages are to be gained by the success of this project, we confess ourselves unable to conjecture. The language of the higher and more cultivated orders may fairly be presumed to be better than that of their inferiors; at any rate, it has all those associations in its favour, by means of which a style can ever appear beautiful or exalted, and is adapted to the purposes of poetry, by having been long consecrated to its use. The language of the vulgar, on the other hand, has all the opposite associations to contend with; and

[1] Wordsworth's Preface to the Second Edition of *Lyrical Ballads*, 1800.

must seem unfit for poetry, (if there were no other reason,) merely because it has scarcely ever been employed in it. A great genius may indeed overcome these disadvantages; but we scarcely conceive that he should court them. We may excuse a certain homeliness of language in the productions of a ploughman or a milkwoman; but we cannot bring ourselves to admire it in an author, who has had occasion to indite odes to his college-bell, and inscribe hymns to the Penates.

But the mischief of this new system is not confined to the depravation of language only; it extends to the sentiments and emotions, and leads to the debasement of all those feelings which poetry is designed to communicate. It is absurd to suppose, that an author should make use of the language of the vulgar, to express the sentiments of the refined. His professed object, in employing that language, is to bring his compositions nearer to the true standard of nature; and his intention to copy the sentiments of the lower orders, is implied in his resolution to make use of their style. Now, the different classes of society have each of them a distinct character, as well as a separate idiom; and the names of the various passions to which they are subject respectively have a signification that varies essentially, according to the condition of the persons to whom they are applied. The love or grief, or indignation of an enlightened and refined character, is not only expressed in a different language, but is in itself a different emotion from the love, or grief, or anger of a clown, a tradesman or a market-wench. . . . The question, therefore, comes simply to be—Which of them is the most proper object for poetical imitation? It is needless for us to answer a question, which the practice of all the world has long ago decided irrevocably. The poor and vulgar may interest us, in poetry, by their *situation*; but never, we apprehend, by any sentiments that are peculiar to their condition, and still less by any language that is characteristic of it. The truth is, that it is impossible to copy their diction or their sentiments correctly, in a serious composition; and this, not merely because poverty makes men ridiculous, but because just taste and refined sentiment are rarely to be met with among the uncultivated part of mankind; and a language fitted for their expression, can still more rarely form any part of their "ordinary conversation."

The low-bred heroes, and interesting rustics of poetry, have no sort of affinity to the real vulgar of this world; they are imaginary beings, whose characters and language are in contrast with their situation; and please those who can be pleased with them, by the marvellous, and not by the nature of such a combination. In serious poetry, a man of the middling or lower order *must necessarily* lay aside a great deal of his ordinary language; he must avoid errors in grammar and orthography; and steer clear of the cant of particular professions, and of every impropriety that is ludicrous or disgusting; nay, he must speak in good verse, and observe all the graces in prosody and collocation. After all this, it may not be very easy to say how we are to find him out to be a low man, or what marks can remain of the ordinary language of conversation in the inferior orders of society. If there be any phrases that are not used in good society, they will appear as blemishes in the composition, no less palpably than errors in syntax or quantity; and if there be no such phrases, that style cannot be characteristic of that condition of life, the language of which it professes to have adopted. . . .

It has been argued, indeed, (for men will argue in support of what they do not venture to practise,) that, as the middling and lower orders of society constitute by far the greater part of mankind, so their feelings and expressions should interest more extensively, and may be taken, more fairly than any other, for the standards of what is natural and true. To this it seems obvious to answer, that the arts that aim at exciting admiration and delight, do not take their models from what is ordinary, but from what is excellent; and that our interest in the representation of any event does not depend upon our familiarity with the original, but on its intrinsic importance, and the celebrity of the parties it concerns. The sculptor employs his art in delineating the graces of Antinous or Apollo, and not in the representation of those ordinary forms that belong to the crowd of his admirers. When a chieftain perishes in battle, his followers mourn more for him than for thousands of their equals that may have fallen around him. . . .

In making these strictures on the perverted taste for simplicity, that seems to distinguish our modern school of poetry, we have no particular allusion to Mr Southey, or the production now before us: On the contrary, he appears to us to be less addicted to this fault than most of his fraternity; and if we were in want of examples to illustrate the preceding observations, we should certainly look for them in the effusions of that poet who commemorates with so much effect, the chattering of Harry Gill's teeth, tells the tale of the one-eyed huntsman, "who had a cheek like a cherry," and beautifully warns his studious friend of the risk he ran of "growing double." . . .

Our new school of poetry has a moral character also; though it may not be possible, perhaps, to delineate it quite so concisely.

A splenetic and idle discontent with the existing institutions of society, seems to be at the bottom of all their serious and peculiar sentiments. Instead of contemplating the wonders and pleasures which civilization has created for mankind, they are perpetually brooding over the disorders by which its progress has been attended. They are filled with horror and compassion at the sight of poor men spending their blood in the quarrels of princes, and brutifying their sublime capabilities in the drudgery of unremitting labour. For all sorts of vice in the lower orders of society they have the same virtuous horror, and the same tender compassion. While the existence of these offences overpowers them with grief and confusion, they never permit themselves to feel the smallest indignation or dislike towards the offenders. The present vicious constitution of society alone is responsible for all these enormities; the poor sinners are but the helpless victims or instruments of its disorders, and could not possibly have avoided the errors into which they have been betrayed. Though they can bear with crimes, therefore, they cannot reconcile themselves to punishments; and have an unconquerable antipathy to prisons, gibbets, and houses of correction, as engines of oppression, and instruments of atrocious injustice. While the plea of moral necessity is thus artfully brought forward to convert all the excesses of the poor into innocent misfortunes, no sort of indulgence is shown to the offences of the powerful and rich. Their oppressions, and seductions, and debaucheries, are the theme of many an angry verse; and the indignation and abhorrence of the readers is relentlessly conjured up against those perturbators of society and scourges of mankind.

From a letter from Coleridge to Thomas Poole, 14 October, 1803, from Greta Hall, Keswick

The habit of writing such a multitude of small Poems was in this instance hurtful to him—such Things as that Sonnet of his in Monday's Morning Post,[1] about Simonides & the

[1] In 1803 Wordsworth printed seven sonnets in *The Morning Post* with the signature W.L.D. The initials, Thomas Hutchinson suggests, stand for "Wordsworthius Libertati dedicavit."

Ghost—I rejoice therefore with a deep & true Joy, that he has at length yielded to my urgent & repeated—almost unremitting—requests & remonstrances & will go on with the Recluse exclusively. A Great Work, in which he will sail; on an open Ocean, & a steady wind; unfretted by short tacks, reefing, & hawling & disentangling the ropes—great work necessarily comprehending his attention & Feelings within the circle of great objects & elevated Conceptions—this is his natural Element—the having been out of it has been his Disease—to return into it is the specific Remedy, both Remedy & Health. It is what Food is to Famine. I have seen enough, positively to give me feelings of hostility towards the plan of several of the poems in the L. Ballads: & I really consider it as a misfortune, that Wordsworth ever deserted his former mountain Track to wander in Lanes & allies; tho' in the event it may prove to have been a great Benefit to him. He will steer, I trust, the middle course.—But he found himself to be, or rather to be called, the Head & founder of a *Sect* in Poetry; & assuredly he has written—& published in the M. Post, as W.L.D. & sometimes with no signature—poems written with a *sectarian* spirit, & in a sort of Bravado.

From a letter from Coleridge to Richard Sharp, dated 15 January, 1804

W. Wordsworth does not excite that almost painfully profound moral admiration which the sense of the exceeding difficulty of a given virtue can alone call forth, and which therefore I feel exclusively towards T. Wedgwood; but, on the other hand, he is an object to be contemplated with greater complacency, because he both deserves to be, and *is*, a happy man; and a happy man, not from natural temperament, for therein lies his main obstacle, not by enjoyment of the good things of this world—for even to this day, from the first dawn of his manhood, he has purchased independence and leisure for great and good pursuits by austere frugality and daily self-denials; nor yet by an accidental confluence of amiable and happy-making friends and relatives, for every one near to his heart has been placed there by choice and after knowledge and deliberation; but he is a happy man, because he is a Philosopher, because he knows the intrinsic value of the different objects of human pursuit, and regulates his wishes in strict subordination to that knowledge; because he feels, and with a *practical* faith, the truth of that which you, more than once, my dear sir, have with equal good sense and kindness pressed upon me, that we can do but one thing well, and that therefore we must make a choice. He has made that choice from his early youth, has pursued and is pursuing it; and certainly no small part of his happiness is owing to this unity of interest and that homogeneity of character which is the natural consequence of it, and which that excellent man, the poet Sotheby,[1] noticed to me as the characteristic of Wordsworth.

Wordsworth is a poet, a most original poet. He no more resembles Milton than Milton resembles Shakspere—no more resembles Shakspere than Shakspere resembles Milton. He is himself, and, I dare affirm that, he will hereafter be admitted as the first and greatest philosophical poet, the only man who has effected a complete and constant synthesis of thought and feeling and combined them with poetic forms, with the music of pleasurable passion, and with Imagination or the *modifying* power in that highest sense of the word, in which I have ventured to oppose it to Fancy, or the *aggregating*

[1] William Sotheby (1757–1833), poet, dramatist, and friend of Sir Walter Scott.

power—in that sense in which it is a dim analogue of creation, —not all that we can *believe*, but all that we can *conceive* of creation.—Wordsworth is a poet, and I feel myself a better poet, in knowing how to honour *him* than in all my own poetic compositions, all I have done or hope to do; and I prophesy immortality to his "Recluse," as the first and finest philosophical poem, if only it be (as it undoubtedly will be) a faithful transcript of his own most august and innocent life, of his own habitual feelings and modes of seeing and hearing.

From a letter from Wordsworth to Lady Beaumont from Coleorton, dated 21 May, 1807

[Wordsworth's *Poems in Two Volumes* had just been published.]

. . . It is impossible that any expectations can be lower than mine concerning the immediate effect of this little work upon what is called the Public. I do not here take into consideration the envy and malevolence, and all the bad passions which always stand in the way of a work of any merit from a living Poet; but merely think of the pure absolute honest ignorance, in which all worldlings of every rank and situation must be enveloped, with respect to the thoughts, feelings, and images, on which the life of my Poems depends. The things which I have taken, whether from within or without,—what have they to do with routs, dinners, morning calls, hurry from door to door, from street to street, on foot or in Carriage; with Mr Pitt or Mr Fox, Mr Paul or Sir Francis Burdett, the Westminster Election, or the Borough of Honiton; in a word, for I cannot stop to make my way through the hurry of images that present themselves to me, what have they to do with endless talking about things nobody cares anything for except as far as their own vanity is concerned, and this with persons they care nothing for but as their vanity or *selfishness* is concerned; what have they to do (to say all at once) with a life without love? in such a life there can be no thought; for we have no thought (save thoughts of pain) but as far as we have love and admiration. It is an awful truth, that there neither is, nor can be, any genuine enjoyment of Poetry among nineteen out of twenty of those persons who live, or wish to live, in the broad light of the world—among those who either are, or are striving to make themselves, people of consideration in society. This is a truth, and an awful one, because to be incapable of a feeling of Poetry in my sense of the word is to be without love of human nature and reverence for God.

Upon this I shall insist elsewhere; at present let me confine myself to my object, which is to make you, my dear friend, as easy-hearted as myself with respect to these poems. Trouble not yourself upon their present reception; of what moment is that compared with what I trust is their destiny? —to console the afflicted; to add sunshine to daylight, by making the happy happier; to teach the young and the gracious of every age to see, to think, and feel, and, therefore, to become more actively and securely virtuous; this is their office, which I trust they will faithfully perform, long after we (that is, all that is mortal of us) are mouldered in our graves. I am well aware how far it would seem to many I overrate my own exertions, when I speak in this way, in direct connexion with the volume I have just made public.

I am not, however, afraid of such censure, insignificant as probably the majority of those poems would appear to very respectable persons; I do not mean London wits and witlings, for these have too many bad passions about them to be respectable even if they had more intellect than the benign laws of providence will allow to such a heartless existence as theirs is; but grave, kindly-natured, worthy persons, who would be pleased if they could. I hope that these Volumes are not without some recommendations, even for Readers of this class, but their imagination has slept; and the voice which is the voice of my Poetry without Imagination cannot be heard.

. . . Never forget what I believe was observed to you by Coleridge, that every great and original writer, in proportion as he is great or original, must himself create the taste by which he is to be relished; he must teach the art by which he is to be seen; this, in a certain degree, even to all persons, however wise and pure may be their lives, and however unvitiated their taste; but for those who dip into books in order to give an opinion of them, or talk about them to take up an opinion—for this multitude of unhappy, and misguided, and misguiding beings, an entire regeneration must be produced; and if this be possible, it must be a work *of time*. To conclude, my ears are stone-dead to this idle buzz, and my flesh as insensible as iron to these petty stings; and after what I have said I am sure yours will be the same. I doubt not that you will share with me an invincible confidence that my writings (and among them these little Poems) will co-operate with the benign tendencies in human nature and society, wherever found; and that they will, in their degree, be efficacious in making men wiser, better and happier.

From Jeffrey's review of Wordsworth's *Poems in Two Volumes* (1807) in *The Edinburgh Review*, October 1807

This author is known to belong to a certain brotherhood of poets, who have haunted for some years about the Lakes of Cumberland; and is generally looked upon, we believe, as the purest model of the excellences and peculiarities of the school which they have been labouring to establish. Of the general merits of that school, we have had occasion to express our opinions pretty fully, in more places than one, and even to make some allusion to the former publications of the writer now before us. We are glad, however, to have found an opportunity of attending somewhat more particularly to his pretensions.

The Lyrical Ballads were unquestionably popular; and, we have no hesitation in saying, deservedly popular; for, in spite of their occasional vulgarity, affectation, and silliness, they were undoubtedly characterised by a strong spirit of originality, of pathos, and natural feeling; and recommended to all good minds by the clear impression which they bore of the amiable dispositions and virtuous principles of the author. By the help of these qualities, they were enabled, not only to recommend themselves to the indulgence of many judicious readers, but even to beget among a pretty numerous class of persons, a sort of admiration of the very defects by which they were attended. It was upon this account chiefly, that we thought it necessary to set ourselves against this alarming innovation. Childishness, conceit, and affectation, are not of themselves very popular or attractive; and though mere novelty has sometimes been found sufficient to give them a temporary currency, we should have had no fear of their prevailing to any dangerous extent, if they had been graced with no more seductive accompaniments. It was precisely because the perverseness and bad taste of this new school was combined with a great deal of genius and of laudable feeling, that we were afraid of their spreading and gaining ground among us, and that we entered[1] into the dis-

[1] This refers to Jeffrey's review of Southey's *Thalaba* in the first number of *The Edinburgh Review* (October 1802). An extract is printed at p. 163, above.

cussion with a degree of zeal and animosity which some might think unreasonable towards authors, to whom so much merit had been conceded. There were times and moods indeed, in which we were led to suspect ourselves of unjustifiable severity, and to doubt whether a sense of public duty had not carried us rather too far in reprobation of errors, that seemed to be atoned for by excellences of no vulgar description. . . .

. . . Mr Wordsworth, we think, has now brought the question, as to the merit of his new school of poetry, to a very fair and decisive issue. The volumes before us are much more strongly marked by all its peculiarities than any former publication of the fraternity. In our apprehension, they are, on this very account, infinitely less interesting or meritorious; but it belongs to the public, and not to us, to decide upon their merit, and we will confess, that so strong is our conviction of their obvious inferiority, and the grounds of it, that we are willing for once to waive our right of appealing to posterity, and to take the judgment of the present generation of readers, and even of Mr Wordsworth's former admirers, as conclusive on this occasion. If these volumes, which have all the benefit of the author's former popularity, turn out to be nearly as popular as the lyrical ballads—if they sell nearly to the same extent—or are quoted and imitated among half as many individuals, we shall admit that Mr Wordsworth has come much nearer the truth in his judgment of what constitutes the charm of poetry, than we had previously imagined—and shall institute a more serious and respectful inquiry into his principles of composition than we have yet thought necessary. . . .

. . . The end of poetry, we take it, is to please—and the name, we think, is strictly applicable to every metrical composition from which we receive pleasure, without any laborious exercise of the understanding. This pleasure may, in general, be analyzed into three parts—that which we receive from the excitement of Passion or emotion—that which is derived from the play of Imagination, or the easy exercise of Reason—and that which depends on the character and qualities of the Diction. The two first are the vital and primary springs of poetical delight, and can scarcely require explanation to any one. The last has been alternately over-rated and under-valued by the professors of the poetical art, and is in such low estimation with the author now before us and his associates, that it is necessary to say a few words in explanation of it.

One great beauty of diction exists only for those who have some degree of scholarship or critical skill. This is what depends on the exquisite *propriety* of the words employed, and the delicacy with which they are adapted to the meaning which is to be expressed. Many of the finest passages in Virgil and Pope derive their principal charm from the fine propriety of their diction. Another source of beauty, which extends only to the more instructed class of readers, is that which consists in the judicious or happy application of expressions which have been sanctified by the use of famous writers, or which bear the stamp of a simple or venerable antiquity. There are other beauties of diction, however, which are perceptible by all—the beauties of sweet sound and pleasant associations. The melody of words and verses is indifferent to no reader of poetry; but the chief recommendation of poetical language is certainly derived from those general associations, which give it a character of dignity or elegance, sublimity or tenderness. Every one knows that there are low and mean expressions, as well as lofty and grave ones; and that some words bear the impression of coarseness and vulgarity, as clearly as others do of refinement and affection. We do not mean, of course, to say any thing in defence of the hackneyed common-places of ordinary versemen. Whatever might have been the original character of these unlucky phrases, they are now associated with nothing but ideas of schoolboy imbecility and vulgar affectation. But what we do maintain is, that much of the most popular poetry in the world owes its celebrity chiefly to the beauty of its diction; and that no poetry can be long or generally acceptable, the language of which is coarse, inelegant or infantine.

From this great source of pleasure, we think the readers of Mr Wordsworth are in a great measure cut off. His diction has nowhere any pretensions to elegance or dignity; and he has scarcely ever condescended to give the grace of correctness or melody to his versification. If it were merely slovenly and neglected, however, all this might be endured. Strong sense and powerful feeling will ennoble any expressions; or, at least, no one who is capable of estimating those higher merits, will be disposed to mark these little defects. But, in good truth, no man, now-a-days, composes verses for publication with a slovenly neglect of their language. It is a fine and laborious manufacture, which can scarcely ever be made in a hurry; and the faults which it has, may, for the most part, be set down to bad taste or incapacity, rather than to carelessness or oversight. With Mr Wordsworth and his friends, it is plain that their peculiarities of diction are things of choice, and not of accident. They write as they do, upon principle and system; and it evidently costs them much pains to keep *down* to the standard which they have proposed to themselves. They are, to the full, as much mannerists, too, as the poetasters who ring changes on the commonplaces of magazine versification; and all the difference between them is, that they borrow their phrases from a different and a scantier *gradus ad Parnassum.* If they were, indeed, to discard all imitation and set phraseology, and to bring in no words merely for show or for metre—as much, perhaps, might be gained in freedom and originality, as would infallibly be lost in allusion and authority; but, in point of fact, the new poets are just as great borrowers as the old; only that, instead of borrowing from the more popular passages of their illustrious predecessors, they have preferred furnishing themselves from vulgar ballads and plebeian nurseries.

Their peculiarities of diction alone, are enough, perhaps, to render them ridiculous; but the author before us really seems anxious to court this literary martyrdom by a device still more infallible,—we mean, that of connecting his most lofty, tender, or impassioned conceptions, with objects and incidents, which the greater part of his readers will probably persist in thinking low, silly, or uninteresting. Whether this is done from affectation and conceit alone, or whether it may not arise, in some measure, from the self-illusion of a mind of extraordinary sensibility, habituated to solitary meditation, we cannot undertake to determine. It is possible enough, we allow, that the sight of a friend's garden spade, or a sparrow's nest, or a man gathering leeches, might really have suggested to such a mind a train of powerful impressions and interesting reflections; but it is certain, that, to most minds, such associations will always appear forced, strained, and unnatural; and that the composition in which it is attempted to exhibit them will always have the air of parody, or ludicrous and affected singularity. All the world laughs at Elegiac stanzas to a sucking-pig—a Hymn on Washing-day—Sonnets to one's grandmother—or Pindarics on gooseberry-pie; and yet, we are afraid, it will not be quite easy to convince Mr Wordsworth, that the same ridicule must infallibly attach to most of the pathetic pieces in these volumes.

[These general observations are followed by a long, detailed review of the poems, which consists of long quotations with sneering and largely unconstructive comments. For example, *Beggars* is described as "a very paragon of silliness and affectation," and the Immortality Ode is dismissed as "the most illegible and unintelligible part of the publication." Of *Resolution and Independence* Jeffrey says, "We defy the bitterest enemy of Mr Wordsworth to produce anything at all parallel to this from any collection of English poetry." He praises the sonnets, but ends with the typical remark, "We venture to hope, that there is now an end of this folly."]

From a letter from Wordsworth to Sir George Beaumont, dated January or February 1808

MY DEAR SIR GEORGE,

I am quite delighted to hear of your Picture for Peter Bell; I was much pleased with the Sketch, and I have no doubt that the picture will surpass it as far as a picture ought to do. I long much to see it. I should approve of any Engraver approved of by you. But remember that no Poem of mine will ever be popular; and I am afraid that the sale of Peter would not carry the expense of the Engraving, and that the Poem, in the estimation of the public, would be a weight upon the Print. I say not this in modest disparagement of the Poem, but in sorrow for the sickly taste of the Public in verse. The *People* would love the Poem of Peter Bell, but the *Public* (a very different Being) will never love it. Thanks for dear Lady B's transcript from your Friend's Letter; it is written with candour, but I must say a word or two not in praise of it. "Instances of what I mean," says your Friend, "are to be found in a poem on a Daisy" (by the bye, it is on *the* Daisy, a mighty difference!) "and on Daffodils *reflected in the Water*!" Is this accurately transcribed by Lady

Beaumont? If it be, what shall we think of criticism or judgement founded upon, and exemplified by, a Poem which must have been so inattentively perused? My Language is precise; and, therefore, it would be false modesty to charge myself with blame.

> Beneath the trees,
> Ten thousand dancing in the *breeze*.
> The *waves beside* them danced, but they
> Outdid the *sparkling waves* in glee.

Can expression be more distinct? And let me ask your Friend how it is possible for flowers to be *reflected* in water where there are *waves*? They may indeed in *still* water; but the very object of my poem is the trouble or agitation, both of the flowers and the Water. I must needs respect the understanding of every one honoured by your friendship; but sincerity compels me to say that my Poems must be more nearly looked at before they can give rise to any remarks of much value, even from the strongest minds. . . . A Letter was also sent to me, addressed to a friend of mine, and by him communicated to me, in which this identical poem was singled out for fervent approbation. What then shall we say? Why, let the Poet first consult his own heart, as I have done and leave the rest to posterity; to, I hope, an improving posterity. The fact is, the English *Public* are at this moment in the same state of mind with respect to my Poems, if small things may be compared with great, as the French are in respect to Shakespear; and not the French alone, but almost the whole Continent. In short, in your Friend's Letter, I am condemned for the very thing for which I ought to have been praised; viz., that I have not written down to the level of superficial observers and unthinking minds. Every great Poet is a Teacher: I wish either to be considered as a Teacher, or as nothing.

The concluding stanzas of Shelley's *Peter Bell the Third* (1819)

A printer's boy, folding those pages,
  Fell slumbrously upon one side,
Like those famed Seven who slept three ages.
To wakeful frenzy's vigil-rages,
  As opiates, were the same applied.

Even the Reviewers who were hired
  To do the work of his reviewing,
With adamantine nerves, grew tired;—
Gaping and torpid they retired,
  To dream of what they should be doing.

And worse and worse, the drowsy curse
  Yawned in him till it grew a pest;
A wide contagious atmosphere
Creeping like cold through all things near;
  A power to infect and to infest.

His servant-maids and dogs grew dull;
  His kitten, late a sportive elf;
The woods and lakes so beautiful,
Of dim stupidity were full;
  All grew dull as Peter's self.

The earth under his feet, the springs
  Which lived within it a quick life—
The air, the winds of many wings
That fan it with new murmurings—
  Were dead to their harmonious strife.

The birds and beasts within the wood,
  The insects and each creeping thing,
Were now a silent multitude;
Love's work was left unwrought—no brood
  Near Peter's house took wing.

And every neighbouring cottager
  Stupidly yawned upon the other;
No jackass brayed, no little cur
Cocked up his ears; no man would stir
  To save a dying mother.

Yet all from that charmed district went
  But some half-idiot and half-knave,
Who, rather than pay any rent,
Would live with marvellous content
  Over his father's grave.

No bailiff dared within that space,
  For fear of the dull charm, to enter;
A man would bear upon his face,
For fifteen months, in any case,
  The yawn of such a venture.

Seven miles above—below—around—
  This pest of dulness holds its sway;
A ghastly life without a sound;
To Peter's soul the spell is bound—
  How should it ever pass away?

From Jeffrey's review of *The Excursion* in *The Edinburgh Review*, November 1814

The case of Mr Wordsworth, we perceive, is now manifestly hopeless; and we give him up as altogether incurable, and beyond the power of criticism. We cannot indeed altogether omit taking precautions now and then against the spreading of the malady;—but for himself, though we shall watch the progress of his symptoms as a matter of professional curiosity and instruction, we really think it right not to harass him any longer with nauseous remedies,—but rather to throw in cordials and lenitives, and wait in patience for the natural termination of the disorder. In order to justify this desertion of our patient, however, it is proper to state why we despair of the success of a more active practice.

A man who has been for twenty years at work on such matter as is now before us, and who comes complacently forward with a whole quarto of it, after all the admonitions he has received, cannot reasonably be expected to "change his hand, or check his pride," upon the suggestion of far weightier monitors than we can pretend to be. Inveterate habit must now have given a kind of sanctity to the errors of early taste; and the very powers of which we lament the perversion, have probably become incapable of any other application. The very quantity, too, that he has written, and is at this moment working up for publication upon the old pattern, makes it almost hopeless to look for any change of it. All this is so much capital already sunk in the concern; which must be sacrificed if it be abandoned: and no man likes to give up for lost the time and talent and labour which he has embodied in any permanent production. We were not previously aware of these obstacles to Mr Wordsworth's conversion; and, considering the peculiarities of his former writings merely as the result of certain wanton and capricious experiments on public taste and indulgence, conceived it to be our duty to discourage their repetition by all the means in our power. We now see clearly, however, how the case stands;—and, making up our minds, though with the most sincere pain and reluctance, to consider him as finally lost to the good cause of poetry, shall endeavour to be thankful for the occasional gleams of tenderness and beauty which the natural force of his imagination and affections must still shed over all his productions,—and to which we shall ever turn with delight, in spite of the affectation and mysticism and prolixity, with which they are so abundantly contrasted.

Long habits of seclusion, and an excessive ambition of originality, can alone account for the disproportion which seems to exist between this author's taste and his genius; or for the devotion with which he has sacrificed so many precious gifts at the shrine of those paltry idols which he has set up for himself among his lakes and his mountains. Solitary musings, amidst such scenes, might no doubt be expected to nurse up the mind to the majesty of poetical conception,—(though it is remarkable, that all the greater poets lived, or had lived, in the full current of society):—But the collision of equal minds—the admonition of prevailing impressions—seems necessary to reduce its redundancies, and repress that tendency to extravagance or puerility, into which the self-indulgence and self-admiration of genius is so apt to be betrayed, when it is allowed to wanton, without awe or restraint, in the triumph and delight of its own intoxication. That its flights should be graceful and glorious in the eyes of men, it seems almost to be necessary that they should be made in the consciousness that men's eyes are to behold them,—and that the inward transport and vigour by which they are inspired, should be tempered by an occasional reference to what will be thought of them by those ultimate dispensers of glory. An habitual and general knowledge of the few settled and permanent maxims, which form the canon of general taste in all large and polished societies—a certain tact, which informs us at once that many things, which we still love and are moved by in secret, must necessarily be despised as childish, or derided as absurd, in all such societies—though it will not stand in the place of genius, seems necessary to the success of its exertions; and though it will never enable anyone to produce the higher beauties of art, can alone secure the talent which does produce them, from errors that must render it useless. Those who have most of the talent, however, commonly acquire this knowledge with the greatest facility;—and if Mr Wordsworth, instead of confining himself almost entirely to the society of the dalesmen and cottagers and little children, who form the subjects of his book, had condescended to mingle a little more with the people that were to read and judge of it, we cannot help thinking that its texture might have been considerably improved: at least it appears to us to be absolutely impossible, that anyone who had lived or mixed familiarly with men of literature and ordinary judgment in poetry, (of course we exclude the coadjutors and disciples of his own school) could ever have fallen into such gross faults, or so long mistaken them for beauties. His first essays we looked upon in a good degree as poetical paradoxes—maintained experimentally, in order to display talent, and court notoriety;—and so maintained, with no more serious belief in their truth, than is usually generated by an ingenious and animated defence of other paradoxes. But when we find that he has been for twenty years exclusively employed upon articles of this very fabric, and that he has still enough of raw material on hand to keep him so employed for twenty years to come, we cannot refuse him the justice of believing that he is a sincere convert to his own system, and must ascribe the peculiarities of his composition, not to any transient affectation, or accidental caprice of imagination, but to a settled perversity of taste or understanding, which has been fostered, if not altogether created, by the circumstances to which we have already alluded.

From Josiah Conder's review of *The Excursion* in *The Eclectic Review*, January 1815

It was one of the most captivating dreams of ancient philosophy, one of its infant dreams, for the earliest idolatry sprang from this source,—that there was a living Spirit in every orb of the universe; the sun, the moon, the stars, the earth itself, were conscious beings, acting and re-acting one on another by their respective influences. Superstition afterwards multiplied intelligences through the minor forms of nature, and turned them all into divinities. Hence the sympathetic intercourse, which exalted understandings may hold with animate and inanimate things, as the effects of one great cause, was debased into a false religion, in which the devotees, by a direct inversion of what reason would teach on such a subject, worshipped objects inferior to themselves, creatures of God, or creatures of the imagination. Language itself in its origin was composed of pictures in words; things that *were* representing things that *were not*; and men spoke, as well as wrote, in hieroglyphics, before abstract terms and letters were invented. Poetry in all ages has retained the figures of primitive speech as its most graceful and venerable ornaments: hence its professors have invariably realized the dream of philosophy, and given souls, not only to the host of heaven, but to all the shapes and substances on earth. Mountains, trees, rivers, elements, &c. are personified, apostrophisized, and made both the subjects and the objects of hope, fear, love, anger, revenge, and every human affection. With the multitude of poets these are only technical modes of expression employed to charm or astonish their readers; but with Mr Wordsworth, the Author of the extraordinary volume before us, they are far otherwise. Common place prosopopoeias he disdains to use; he has a poetical mythology of his own. He loves nature with a passion amounting almost to devotion; and he discovers throughout her works an omnipresent spirit, which so nearly resembles God in power and goodness, that it is sometimes difficult to distinguish the reverence which he pays to it, from the homage due to the Supreme alone. In proportion, all subordinate identities and phenomena, whether on the earth or in the sky, excite in him joy or wonder, corresponding to the character of simplicity or complexity, beauty or sublimity, inherent in them, and holding mysterious affinity with congenial qualities in the Poet's own soul. Hence, in the poems formerly published, he frequently divulged sensations of rapture, surprise, or admiration, unintelligible to vulgar minds; and avowed sympathies too profound for utterance, in the contemplation of every-day objects, which ordinary eyes pass over as mere matters of fact, no more demanding attention than a truism requires demonstration. Consequently, such passages provoked the scorn of superficial readers, and even incurred the heaviest censure of self-constituted critics in the highest place, solely because the poet, when most solemnly touched, either awakened ludicrous associations, or failed to present his peculiar ideas in such colours as to excite answering emotions in bosoms unaccustomed to feel and reflect after his manner. Few people would be sentimentally struck by the unexpected appearance "of a host of dancing daffodils" on the margin of a lake, "whose sparkling waves danced beside them;" and still fewer would carry away the image and treasure it up in memory for the occasional exhilaration of their private thoughts; yet Mr Wordsworth, after fancifully describing such a merry dance of flowers and sunbeams on the waters, says,

> Oft when on my couch I lie,
> In vacant or in pensive mood,
> They flash upon that inward eye,
> Which is the bliss of solitude,
> And then my heart with pleasure fills,
> And dances with the daffodils.

From Henry Crabb Robinson's Diary, entry for 9 May, 1815

May 9th. Took tea with the Lambs. Mr and Mrs Wordsworth were there. We had a long chat, of which, however, I can relate but little. Wordsworth, in answer to the common reproach that his sensibility is excited by objects which produce no effect on others, admits the fact, and is proud of it. He says that he cannot be accused of being insensible to the real concerns of life. He does not waste his feelings on unworthy objects, for he is alive to the actual interests of society. I think the justification is complete. If Wordsworth expected immediate popularity, he would betray an ignorance of public taste impossible in a man of observation.

He spoke of the changes in his new poems. He has substituted *ebullient* for *fiery*, speaking of the nightingale, and *jocund* for *laughing*, applied to the daffodils; but he will probably restore the original epithets. We agreed in preferring the original reading. But on my alluding to the lines—

Three feet long and two feet wide,

and confessing that I dared not read them aloud in company, he said, "They ought to be liked."

Wordsworth particularly recommended to me, among his Poems of Imagination, "Yew Trees," and a description of Night. These he says are among the best for the imaginative power displayed in them. They are fine, but I believe I do not understand in what their excellence consists. The poet himself, as Hazlitt has well observed, has a pride in deriving no aid from his subject. It is the mere power which he is conscious of exerting in which he delights, not the production of a work in which men rejoice on account of the sympathies and sensibilities it excites in them. Hence he does not much esteem his "Laodamia," as it belongs to the inferior class of poems founded on the affections. In this, as in other peculiarities of Wordsworth, there is a German bent in his mind.

From Henry Crabb Robinson's Diary, entry for 10 September, 1816

If this were the place, and if my memory were good, I could enrich my journal by retailing Wordsworth's conversation. He is an eloquent speaker, and he talked upon his own art, and his own works, very feelingly and very profoundly; but I cannot venture to state more than a few intelligible results, for I own that much of what he said was above my comprehension.

He stated, what I had before taken for granted, that most of his lyrical ballads were founded on some incident he had witnessed, or heard of. He mentioned the origin of several poems.

"Lucy Gray," that tender and pathetic narrative of a child mysteriously lost on a common, was occasioned by the death of a child who fell into the lock of a canal. His object was to exhibit poetically entire *solitude*, and he represents the child as observing the day-moon, which no town or village girl would even notice.

The "Leech-Gatherer" he did actually meet near Grasmere, except that he gave to his poetic character powers of mind which his original did not possess.

The fable of "The Oak and the Broom" proceeded from his beholding a rose in just such a situation as he described the broom to be in. Perhaps, however, all poets have had their works suggested in like manner. What I wish I could venture to state after Wordsworth, is his conception of the manner in which the mere fact is converted into poetry by the power of imagination.

He represented, however, much as, unknown to him, the German philosophers have done, that by the imagination the mere fact is exhibited as connected with that infinity without which there is no poetry.

He spoke of his tale of the dog, called "Fidelity." He says he purposely made the narrative as prosaic as possible, in order that no discredit might be thrown on the truth of the incident. In the description at the beginning, and in the moral at the end, he has alone indulged in a poetic vein; and these parts, he thinks, he has peculiarly succeeded in.

He quoted some of the latter poem, and also from "The Kitten and the Falling Leaves," to show he had connected even the kitten with the great, awful, and mysterious powers of nature. But neither now, nor in reading the Preface to Wordsworth's new edition of his poems, have I been able to comprehend his ideas concerning poetic imagination. I have not been able to raise my mind to the subject, farther than this, that imagination is the faculty by which the poet conceives and produces—that is, images—individual forms, in which are embodied universal ideas or abstractions. This I do comprehend, and I find the most beautiful and striking illustrations of this faculty in the works of Wordsworth himself.

The incomparable twelve lines, "She dwelt among the untrodden ways," ending, "The difference to me!" are finely imagined. They exhibit the powerful effect of the loss of a very obscure object upon one tenderly attached to it. The opposition between the apparent strength of the passion and the insignificance of the object is delightfully conceived, and the object itself well portrayed.

A sonnet by Shelley (published 1816)

To Wordsworth

Poet of Nature, thou hast wept to know
  That things depart which never may return:
Childhood and youth, friendship, and love's first glow,
  Have fled like sweet dreams, leaving them to mourn.
These common woes I feel. One loss is mine,
  Which thou too feel'st, yet I alone deplore.
Thou wert as a lone star whose light did shine
  On some frail bark in winter's midnight roar:
Thou hast like to a rock-built refuge stood
Above the blind and battling multitude:
In honoured poverty thy voice did weave
  Songs consecrate to truth and liberty.
Deserting these, thou leavest me to grieve,
  Thus, having been, that thou shouldst cease to be.

From Coleridge's *Biographia Literaria (1817)*, Chapter XXII

I cannot here enter into a detailed examination of Mr Wordsworth's works; but I will attempt to give the main results of my own judgment after an acquaintance of many years, and repeated perusals. And though to appreciate the defects of a great mind it is necessary to understand previously its characteristic excellences, yet I have already expressed myself with sufficient fulness, to preclude most of the ill effects that might arise from my pursuing a contrary arrangement. I will therefore commence with what I deem the prominent *defects* of his poems hitherto published.

The first *characteristic, though only occasional* defect, which I appear to myself to find in these poems is the INCONSTANCY of the *style*. Under this name I refer to the sudden and unprepared transitions from lines or sentences of peculiar felicity (at all events striking and original) to a style, not only unimpassioned but undistinguished. He sinks too often and too abruptly to that style which I should place in the second division of language, dividing it into the three species; *first*, that which is peculiar to poetry; *second*, that which is only proper in prose; and *third*, the neutral or common to both. . . .

. . . The business of the writer, like that of a painter whose subject requires unusual splendour and prominence, is so to raise the lower and neutral tints, that what in a different style would be the *commanding* colours, are here used as the means of that gentle *degradation* requisite in order to produce the effect of a *whole*. Where this is not achieved in a poem, the metre merely reminds the reader of his claims in order to disappoint them; and where this defect occurs frequently, his feelings are alternately startled by anticlimax and hyper-climax.

[Coleridge gives examples to illustrate this point, ending with *Resolution and Independence*.]

Indeed this fine poem is *especially* characteristic of the author. There is scarce a defect or excellence in his writings of which it would not present a specimen. But it would be unjust not to repeat that this defect is only occasional. From a careful reperusal of the two volumes of poems, I doubt whether the objectionable passages would amount in the whole to one hundred lines; not the eighth part of the number of pages. In *The Excursion* the feeling of incongruity is seldom excited by the diction of any passage considered in itself, but by the sudden superiority of some other passage forming the context.

The second defect I can generalize with tolerable accuracy, if the reader will pardon an uncouth and new-coined word. There is, I should say, not seldom a *matter-of-factness* in certain poems. This may be divided into, *first*, a laborious minuteness and fidelity in the representation of objects, and their positions, as they appeared to the poet himself; *secondly*, the insertion of accidental circumstances, in order to the full explanation of his living characters, their dispositions and actions; which circumstances might be necessary to establish the probability of a statement in real life, where nothing is taken for granted by the hearer, but appear superfluous in poetry, where the reader is willing to believe for his own sake. . . .

The second division respects an apparent minute adherence to *matter-of-fact* in characters and incidents; a *biographical* attention to probability, and an *anxiety* of explanation and retrospect. Under this head I shall deliver, with no feigned diffidence, the results of my best reflection on the great point of controversy between Mr Wordsworth and his objectors; namely, on THE CHOICE OF HIS CHARACTERS. I have already declared and, I trust, justified, my utter dissent from the mode of argument which his critics have hitherto employed. To *their* question, Why did you choose such a character, or a character from such a rank of life? the poet might in my opinion fairly retort: why with the conception of my character did you make wilful choice of mean or ludicrous associations not furnished by me, but supplied from your own sickly and fastidious feelings? How was it, indeed, probable, that such arguments could have any weight with an author, whose plan, whose guiding principle, and main object it was to attack and subdue that state of association, which leads us to place the chief value on those things in which man DIFFERS from man, and to forget or disregard the high dignities which belong to HUMAN NATURE, the sense and the feeling which *may* be, and *ought* to be, found in *all* ranks? The feelings with which, as Christians, we contemplate a mixed congregation rising or kneeling before their common Maker, Mr Wordsworth would have us entertain at *all* times, as men, and as readers; and by the excitement of this lofty yet prideless impartiality in *poetry*, he might hope to have encouraged its continuance in *real life*. The praise of good men be his! In real life, and, I trust, even in my imagination, I honour a virtuous and wise man, without reference to the presence or absence of artificial advantages. Whether in the person of an armed baron, a laurel'd bard, &c., or of an old pedlar, or still older leech-gatherer, the same qualities of head and heart must claim the same reverence. And even in poetry I am not conscious that I have ever suffered my feelings to be disturbed or offended by any thoughts or images, which the poet himself has not presented.

But yet I object nevertheless and for the following reasons. First, because the object in view, as an *immediate* object, belongs to the moral philosopher, and would be pursued, not only more appropriately, but in my opinion with far greater probability of success, in sermons or moral essays, than in an elevated poem. It seems, indeed, to destroy the main fundamental distinction, not only between a poem and prose, but even between philosophy and works of fiction, inasmuch as it proposes *truth* for its immediate object, instead of *pleasure*. Now till the blessed time shall come, when truth itself shall be pleasure, and both shall be so united as to be distinguishable in words only, not in feeling, it will remain the poet's office to proceed upon that state of association, which actually exists as *general*; instead of attempting first to *make* it what it ought to be, and then to let the pleasure follow. But here is unfortunately a small *Hysteron-Proteron*. For the communication of pleasure is the introductory means by which alone the poet must expect to moralize his readers. Secondly: though I were to admit, for a moment, *this* argument to be groundless, yet how is the moral effect to be produced, by merely attaching the name of some low profession to powers which are *least* likely, and to qualities which are assuredly not *more* likely, to be found in it? The poet, speaking in his own person, may at once delight and improve us by sentiments which teach us the independence of goodness, of wisdom, and even of genius, on the favours of fortune. And having made a due reverence before the throne of Antonine, he may bow with equal awe before Epictetus among his fellow-slaves—

—and rejoice
In the plain presence of his dignity.

Who is not at once delighted and improved, when the POET Wordsworth himself exclaims,

O many are the poets that are sown
By Nature; men endowed with highest gifts,

The vision and the faculty divine,
Yet wanting the accomplishment of verse,
Nor having e'er, as life advanced, been led
By circumstance to take unto the height
The measure of themselves, these favour'd beings,
All but a scatter'd few, live out their time
Husbanding that which they possess within,
And go to the grave unthought of. Strongest minds
Are often those of whom the noisy world
Hears least.

Excursion B.I

To use a colloquial phrase, such sentiments, in such language, do one's heart good; though I for my part, have not the fullest faith in the *truth* of the observation. . . .

. . . . . .

Third; an undue predilection for the *dramatic* form in certain poems, from which one or other of two evils result. Either the thoughts and diction are different from that of the poet, and then there arises an incongruity of style; or they are the same and indistinguishable, and then it presents a species of ventriloquism, where two are represented as talking, while in truth one man only speaks.

The fourth class of defects is closely connected with the former; but yet are such as arise likewise from an intensity of feeling disproportionate to *such* knowledge and value of the objects described, as can be fairly anticipated of men in general, even of the most cultivated classes; and with which therefore few only, and those few particularly circumstanced, can be supposed to sympathize. In this class, I comprise occasional prolixity, repetition, and an eddying, instead of progression, of thought. . . .

Fifth and last; thoughts and images too great for the subject. This is an approximation to what might be called *mental* bombast, as distinguished from verbal: for, as in the latter there is a disproportion of the expressions to the thoughts, so in this there is a disproportion of thought to the circumstance and occasion. This, by the bye, is a fault of which none but a man of genius is capable. It is the awkwardness and strength of Hercules with the distaff of Omphale.

It is a well-known fact, that bright colours in motion both make and leave the strongest impressions on the eye. Nothing is more likely too, than that a vivid image or visual spectrum, thus originated, may become the link of association in recalling the feelings and images that had accompanied the original impression. But if we describe this in such lines, as

> They flash upon that inward eye,
> Which is the bliss of solitude!

in what words shall we describe the joy of retrospection, when the images and virtuous actions of a whole well-spent life pass before that conscience which is indeed the *inward* eye: which is indeed "*the bliss of solitude*"? Assuredly we seem to sink most abruptly, not to say burlesquely, and almost as in a *medley*, from this couplet to—

> And then my heart with pleasure fills,
> And dances with the *daffodils.*

[Coleridge gives another example from *Gipsies.*]

The last instance of this defect (for I know no other than these already cited) is from the Ode, where, speaking of a child, "a six years' darling of a pigmy size," he thus addresses him:

> Thou best philosopher, who yet dost keep,
> Thy heritage! Thou eye among the blind,
> That, deaf and silent, read'st the eternal deep,
> Haunted for ever by the Eternal Mind,—

Mighty Prophet! Seer blest!
On whom those truths do rest,
Which we are toiling all our lives to find!
Thou, over whom thy immortality
Broods like the day, a master o'er a slave,
A presence that is not to be put by!

Now here, not to stop at the daring spirit of metaphor which connects the epithets "deaf and silent" with the apostrophized *eye*: or (if we are to refer it to the preceding word, philosopher) the faulty and equivocal syntax of the passage; and without examining the propriety of making a "master *brood* o'er a slave," or the *day* brood *at all*; we will merely ask, what does all this mean? In what sense is a child of that age a *philosopher*? In what sense does he *read* "the eternal deep"? In what sense is he declared to be "*for ever haunted*" by the Supreme Being? or so inspired as to deserve the splendid titles of a *mighty prophet*, a *blessed seer*? By reflection? by knowledge? by conscious intuition? or by *any* form or modification of consciousness? . . .

Though the instances of this defect in Mr Wordsworth's poems are so few, that for themselves it would have been scarce just to attract the reader's attention toward them; yet I have dwelt on it, and perhaps the more for this very reason. For being so very few, they cannot sensibly detract from the reputation of an author who is even characterized by the number of profound truths in his writings, which will stand the severest analysis; and yet few as they are, they are exactly those passages which his *blind* admirers would be most likely, and best able, to imitate. But WORDSWORTH, where he is indeed Wordsworth, may be mimicked by Copyists, he may be plundered by Plagiarists; but he can not be imitated, except by those who are not born to be imitators. For without his depth of feeling and his imaginative power his *sense* would want its vital warmth and peculiarity; and without his strong sense, his *mysticism* would become *sickly*—mere fog, and dimness!

To these defects which, as appears by the extracts, are only occasional, I may oppose, with far less fear of encountering the dissent of any candid and intelligent reader, the following (for the most part correspondent) excellences. First, an austere purity of language both grammatically and logically; in short a perfect appropriateness of the words to the meaning. . . . [Here his argument becomes more general: he does not give examples from Wordsworth.]

The second characteristic excellence of Mr W's work is: a correspondent weight and sanity of the Thoughts and Sentiments, won—not from books, but—from the poet's own meditative observation. They are *fresh* and have the dew upon them. His muse, at least when in her strength of wing, and when she hovers aloft in her proper element,

> Makes audible a linked lay of truth,
> Of truth profound a sweet continuous lay,
> Not learnt, but native, her own natural notes!
>
> S.T.C.

Even throughout his smaller poems there is scarcely one which is not rendered valuable by some just and original reflection.

See . . . the two following passages in one of his humblest compositions:

> O Reader! had you in your mind
> Such stores as silent thought can bring,
> O gentle Reader! you would find
> A tale in every thing;

and

> I've heard of hearts unkind, kind deeds
> With coldness still returning;

Alas! the gratitude of men
Has oftener left me mourning;

or in a still higher strain the six beautiful quatrains,

Thus fares it still in our decay:
And yet the wiser mind
Mourns less for what age takes away
Than what it leaves behind.

The Blackbird in the summer trees,
The Lark upon the hill,
Let loose their carols when they please,
Are quiet when they will.

With nature never do *they* wage
A foolish strife; they see
A happy youth, and their old age
Is beautiful and free!

But we are pressed by heavy laws;
And often, glad no more,
We wear a face of joy, because
We have been glad of yore.

If there is one who need bemoan
His kindred laid in earth,
The household hearts that were his own
It is the man of mirth.

My days, my Friend, are almost gone,
My life has been approved,
And many love me; but by none
Am I enough beloved;

or the sonnet on Buonaparte; or finally (for a volume would scarce suffice to exhaust the instances) the last stanza of the poem on the withered Celandine:

To be a prodigal's favourite—then, worse truth,
A miser's pensioner—behold our lot!
O man! that from thy fair and shining youth
Age might but take the things youth needed not.

Both in respect of this and of the former excellence, Mr Wordsworth strikingly resembles Samuel Daniel, one of the golden writers of our golden Elizabethan age, now most causelessly neglected: Samuel Daniel, whose diction bears no mark of time, no distinction of age, which has been, and as long as our language shall last, will be so far the language of the to-day and for ever, as that it is more intelligible to us, than the transitory fashions of our particular age. A similar praise is due to his sentiments. No frequency of perusal can deprive them of their freshness. For though they are brought into the full day-light of every reader's comprehension, yet are they drawn up from the depths which few in any age are privileged to visit, into which few in any age have courage or inclination to descend. If Mr Wordsworth is not equally with Daniel alike intelligible to all readers of average understanding in all passages of his works, the comparative difficulty does not arise from the greater impurity of the ore, but from the nature and uses of the metal. A poem is not necessarily obscure, because it does not aim to be popular. It is enough, if a work be perspicuous to those for whom it is written, and

Fit audience find, though few.

To the "Ode on the intimations of immortality from recollections of early childhood" the poet might have prefixed the lines which Dante addresses to one of his own Canzoni—

Canzon, io credo, che saranno radi
Che tua ragione intendan bene,
Tanto lor sei faticoso ed alto.

O lyric song, there will be few, think I,
Who may thy import understand aright:
Thou art for *them* so arduous and so high!

But the ode was intended for such readers only as had been accustomed to watch the flux and reflux of their inmost nature, to venture at times into the twilight realms of consciousness, and to feel a deep interest in modes of inmost being, to which they know that the attributes of time and space are inapplicable and alien, but which yet can not be conveyed save in symbols of time and space. For such readers the sense is sufficiently plain, and they will be as little disposed to charge Mr Wordsworth with believing the Platonic pre-existence in the ordinary interpretation of the words, as I am to believe, that Plato himself ever meant or taught it....

Third (and wherein he soars far above Daniel) the sinewy strength and originality of single lines and paragraphs: the frequent *curiosa felicitas* of his diction. . . . This beauty, and as eminently characteristic of Wordsworth's poetry, his rudest assailants have felt themselves compelled to acknowledge and admire.

Fourth: the perfect truth of nature in his images and descriptions, as taken immediately from nature, and proving a long and genial intimacy with the very spirit which gives the physiognomic expression to all the works of nature. Like a green field reflected in a calm and perfectly transparent lake, the image is distinguished from the reality only by its greater softness and lustre. Like the moisture or the polish on a pebble, genius neither distorts nor false-colours its objects; but on the contrary brings out many a vein and many a tint, which escapes the eye of common observation, thus raising to the rank of gems what had been often kicked away by the hurrying foot of the traveller on the dusty high road of custom.

Let me refer to the whole description of skating, especially to the lines

> So through the darkness and the cold we flew,
> And not a voice was idle: with the din
> Meanwhile the precipices rang aloud;
> The leafless trees and every icy crag
> Tinkled like iron; while the distant hills
> Into the tumult sent an alien sound
> Of melancholy, not unnoticed, while the stars
> Eastward were sparkling clear, and in the west
> The orange sky of evening died away.

Or to the poem on the green linnet. What can be more accurate yet more lovely than the two concluding stanzas?

> Upon yon tuft of hazel trees,
> That twinkle to the gusty breeze,
> Behold him perched in ecstasies,
>   Yet seeming still to hover;
> There! where the flutter of his wings
> Upon his back and body flings
> Shadows and sunny glimmerings
>   That cover him all over.
>
> While thus before my eyes he gleams
> A brother of the leaves he seems;
> When in a moment forth he teems
>   His little song in gushes:
> As if it pleased him to disdain
> And mock the form which he did feign
> While he was dancing with the train
>   Of leaves among the bushes.

Or the description of the blue-cap, and of the noon-tide silence; or the poem to the cuckoo; or, lastly, though I might multiply the references to ten times the number, to the poem, so completely Wordsworth's, commencing

> Three years she grew in sun and shower, &c.

Fifth: a meditative pathos, a union of deep and subtle thought with sensibility; a sympathy with man as man; the sympathy indeed of a contemplator, rather than a fellow-sufferer or co-mate (*spectator, haud particeps*) but of a contemplator, from whose view no difference of rank conceals the sameness of the nature; no injuries of wind or weather, or toil, or even of ignorance, wholly disguise the human face divine. The superscription and the image of the Creator still remain legible to *him* under the dark lines, with which guilt or calamity had cancelled or cross-barred it. Here the man and the poet lose and find themselves in each other, the one as glorified, the latter as substantiated. In this mild and philosophic pathos, Wordsworth appears to me without a compeer. Such he *is*: so he *writes*. . . .

[Coleridge gives examples quoting stanzas from *The Mad Mother* to illustrate this "blending, *fusing* power of the Imagination and Passion."]

Last, and pre-eminently, I challenge for this poet the gift of IMAGINATION in the highest and strictest sense of the word. In the play of *Fancy*, Wordsworth, to my feelings, is not always graceful, and sometimes recondite. The *likeness* is occasionally too strange, or demands too peculiar a point of view, or is such as appears the creature of predetermined research, rather than spontaneous presentation. Indeed his fancy seldom displays itself as mere and unmodified fancy. But in imaginative power, he stands nearest of all modern writers to Shakespeare and Milton; and yet in a kind perfectly unborrowed and his own. To employ his own words, which are at once an instance and an illustration, he does indeed to all thoughts and to all objects

add the gleam,
The light that never was, on sea or land,
The consecration, and the poet's dream.

I shall select a few examples as most obviously manifesting this faculty; but if I should ever be fortunate enough to render my analysis of imagination, its origin and characters, thoroughly intelligible to the reader, he will scarcely open on a page of this poet's works without recognizing, more or less, the presence and the influences of this faculty.

[Coleridge gives an example from *Yew Trees*, and then speaks of the "effect of the old man's figure in the poem *Resolution and Independence*," quoting the lines

> While he was talking thus, the lonely place,
> The old man's shape, and speech, all troubled me:
> In my mind's eye I seemed to see him pace
> About the weary moors continually,
> Wandering about alone and silently.

He also refers to some of the sonnets, and quotes from the Immortality Ode and from *The White Doe of Rylstone*, to illustrate the imaginative powers of Wordsworth.]

The following analogy will, I am apprehensive, appear dim and fantastic, but in reading Bartram's Travels, I could not help transcribing the following lines as a sort of allegory or connected simile and metaphor of Wordsworth's intellect and genius.—"The soil is a deep, rich, dark mould, on a deep stratum of tenacious clay; and that on a foundation of rocks, which often break through both strata, lifting their back above the surface. The trees which chiefly grow here are gigantic black oak; *magnolia magni-floria*; *fraxinus excelsior*; *platane*; and a few stately tulip trees." What Mr Wordsworth *will* produce, it is not for me to prophesy: but I could pronounce with the liveliest convictions what he is capable of producing. It is the FIRST GENUINE PHILOSOPHIC POEM.

... I have advanced no opinion either for praise or censure, other than as texts introductory to the reasons which compel me to form it. Above all, I was fully convinced that such a criticism was not only wanted; but that, if executed with adequate ability, it must conduce, in no mean degree, to Mr Wordsworth's *reputation*. His *fame* belongs to another age, and can neither be accelerated nor retarded. How small the proportion of the defects are to the beauties, I have repeatedly declared; and that no one of them originates in deficiency of poetic genius. Had they been more and greater, I should still, as a friend to his literary character in the present age, consider an analytic display of them as *pure gain*; if only it removed, as surely to all reflecting minds even the foregoing analysis must have removed, the strange mistake, so slightly grounded, yet so widely and industriously propagated, of Mr Wordsworth's turn for SIMPLICITY!

From a letter from Keats to John Hamilton Reynolds, dated Sunday, 3 May, 1818

And here I have nothing but surmises, from an uncertainty whether Miltons apparently less anxiety for Humanity proceeds from his seeing further or no than Wordsworth: And whether Wordsworth has in truth epic passion, and martyrs himself to the human heart, the main region of his song—In regard to his genius alone—we find what he says true as far as we have experienced and we can judge no further but by larger experience—for axioms in philosophy are not axioms until they are proved upon our pulses: We read fine things but never feel them to the full until we have gone the same steps as the Author. . . .

. . . with your patience, I will return to Wordsworth—whether or no he has an extended vision or a circumscribed grandeur—whether he is an eagle in his nest, or on the wing

—And to be more explicit and to show you how tall I stand by the giant, I will put down a simile of human life as far as I now perceive it; that is, to the point to which I say we both have arrived at—Well—I compare human life to a large Mansion of Many Apartments, two of which I can only describe, the doors of the rest being as yet shut upon me. The first we step into we call the infant or thoughtless Chamber, in which we remain as long as we do not think—We remain there a long while, and notwithstanding the doors of the second Chamber remain wide open, showing a bright appearance, we care not to hasten to it; but are at length imperceptibly impelled by the awakening of this thinking principle within us—we no sooner get into the second Chamber, which I shall call the Chamber of Maiden-Thought, than we become intoxicated with the light and the atmosphere, we see nothing but pleasant wonders, and think of delaying there for ever in delight: However among the effects this breathing is father of is that tremendous one of sharpening one's vision into the heart and nature of Man—of convincing one's nerves that the world is full of Misery and Heartbreak, Pain, Sickness and oppression—whereby this Chamber of Maiden Thought becomes gradually darken'd and at the same time on all sides of it many doors are set open—but all dark—all leading to dark passages—We see not the ballance of good and evil. We are in a Mist, *We* are now in that state—We feel the "burden of the Mystery," To this Point was Wordsworth come, as far as I can conceive when he wrote "Tintern Abbey" and it seems to me that his Genius is explorative of those dark Passages. Now if we live, and go on thinking, we too shall explore them—he is a Genius and superior [to] us, in so far as he can, more than we, make discoveries, and shed a light in them—Here I must think that Wordsworth is deeper than Milton—though I think it has depended more upon the general and gregarious advance of intellect, than individual greatness of Mind.

From the Rev. Francis Wrangham's review of *Peter Bell* in *The British Critic*, June 1819

The sentiments with which we regard Mr Wordsworth as a poet, have long been before the public, in one of our earliest numbers; and a fuller consideration of his writings leaves us still satisfied with the opinions we there expressed. We think that there is no one of the present day, and none but the few giants of preceding ages, who have excelled him in some of his productions; in these and in parts of others he has displayed a splendour and purity of diction, a force, and skilful harmony of measure, with a depth, a truth, a tenderness, and a solemn sublimity of sentiment, which in their union remind us forcibly of the happiest, and most golden moments of the immortal Petrarch. Competent judges will not complain of this praise as exaggerated; and they only, who are miserably ignorant of the capabilities of a simple style, or (to speak more correctly) of the meaning of the term simplicity of style, will be surprized to hear us make mention of a diction which they have been accustomed to hear characterized as fit only for the mouths of nurses and infants. But without entering into that argument, which is foreign to our present purpose, we will satisfy ourselves with opening a single volume as it lies before us, and recommending those who doubt *the fact* to the perusal of *Ruth*, or an exquisite little poem, beginning "Three years she grew in sun and shower." If they have formed their notions of simplicity in style from the pages of modern criticism, we can promise them at least the pleasure of a surprise from the perusal of these poems.

Still in our consideration of what Mr Wordsworth might have been from what he sometimes is, we confess, regretfully, that he seems to us to have failed; not merely failed in the acquisition of present popularity, which he justly values at a very low rate, (for to the poet, beyond all other writers, the favourable judgment of an artificial and fashion-mongering age, offers but a doubtful assurance of real and abiding fame,) but also in our opinion he has not laid grounds for his permanent and unambiguous rank as an English Classic so high, as his peculiar powers, and the meritorious study which he has bestowed in the cultivation of them would have led us to anticipate for them. In every age, so long as our language be intelligible, whether living or dead, Wordsworth will have enthusiastic admirers, and to go a step farther, there will always be among them such admirers as a poet may with reason be most proud of; but we are much in error if in any age the ablest of those admirers will be able satisfactorily to answer the objections urged against him by candid and feeling readers of a different persuasion. We say this, reasoning partly from our own feelings, but still more from those of the ablest and fairest judges whom we have been able to consult; we scarcely ever met with a single person, whose opinion on the subject we valued, and who was open to express it, that could say he had read any whole poem of Wordsworth's composition, longer than a mere sonnet, without being obliged to get over, and subdue, in some part of it, offensive and disturbing feelings; to forget something that shocked his taste, and checked that full current of admiration, which the remainder excited; the latter feeling perhaps after all predominated, yet the mind was left in a state of incomplete satisfaction.

We are ourselves warm, very warm admirers of Wordsworth; yet if our opinion be worth asking, we must give it nearly in the words which we have written above. This is a fact, of which those who "care for such things," will consider it worthy of inquiry to ascertain the causes; and as we have never, we believe, attempted to develope them, though perhaps they may be deduced from our former reasoning, we will take the opportunity which *Peter Bell* affords us, to say a few words upon it. We see no cause for departing from the account which we have before given of the principles, on which Mr Wordsworth's poetical system is built; they seem to us to be two in number, with an important corollary deducible from them; we perfectly agree in the truth and importance of the two first, and we are precluded from denying the abstract truth, though we doubt of the practical expediency of the last. The principles are, first, that "whatsoever material or temporary exists before our senses, is capable of being associated in our minds with something spiritual and eternal;" and secondly, that it is the business of the poet to see all things with a view to this capability of association, and to familiarize the process to his own, and to his reader's mind; the corollary is, that if all things are equally capable of the process, and in the availing itself of that capability, the true and essential excellence of poetry consists, then the commonest external thing, the most every day occurrence of life, or the meanest appearance of nature is equally capable of being made the ground-work or subject of poetry with the noblest and most uncommon. . . .

These principles then are not only true, but so far as poetry itself may be considered as one among many engines bestowed upon man by God for the improvement of his moral nature, no less than the mere adornment of his earthly existence, they must undoubtedly be ranked among moral, and highly important truths. Nor if we look at poetry merely as a source of intellectual pleasure, can we doubt that these principles are in that point of view equally considerable. We will not affirm that no pleasure is derivable from a merely exact delineation of any scene of nature or art, but we are sure that it is lame and poor to that vivid, and, as it were, electric delight, which the mind receives from a description, acting, not so much by itself, and in finished details, as by rousing the creative power within, and enabling it to see in more perfect beauty that which is only sketched, and faintly traced by the describer. . . .

Simple and self-evident as these propositions now are to ourselves, they were certainly lost sight of by the majority of our intermediate poets from the Restoration down to a late period; laborious and unimpassioned description clothed in a conventional set of terms, and a language artificial, and often grossly misapplied, were substituted for the natural and individual, though highly cultivated, and highly raised poetry, which had gone before. So far then as our author revived, enforced, and exemplified these principles, so far as he manfully protested against, and very ingeniously demonstrated, the abuses of modern poetic diction by the indiscriminate and conventional use of those terms, metaphors, and figures, which had their merit in ancient poetry, from the propriety and dramatic truth of their application, so far as he evinced that it was as absurd to make passion and imagination speak the language of poetical *convention* as it would be to confine them to the terms of the schools or the courts; thus far he is entitled to our highest praises, and our warmest thanks; he by so doing unfettered the tongue of the Muse, and replaced in her hand the sceptre of power.

But when we come to the practical consequences which he has always maintained, and too often exemplified, we must in honesty hold a more measured language, and admit, that we see in them the excesses, from which no manliness or strength of mind seems able to guard the reviver of an old, or the inventor of a new system. We have said that we cannot deny the abstract truth of his corollary: if it be true that all things are capable of the process, and that in pursuing the process lies the true business of the poet, then any thing, that which is low as well as that which is high, is capable of being the subject of poetry. We grant it, and we grant no more; Wordsworth, as it appears to us, has advanced one step farther, and in that step the fallacy lies; he has substituted the words 'more fit for' in the place of 'capable of,' and has therein committed the same error which a statuary would, who, because all stone was capable of the process, in the performance of which his art lay, should therefore choose to execute his groupes in granite, rather than in Parian marble. . . . He has not suffered his poetry to be the expression merely of his natural and unperverted feelings; but *he has devoted it to the developement and maintenance of a system*. Because he has discovered and maintained successfully, that good poetry may be written on a celandine or a daisy, he seems to have acted as if better poetry could be written on them than on subjects of a higher degree; he has neglected to take into the account that poetry is a communicative art, that the state of the recipient is to be considered, as well as that of the communicant; that it is little to have mixed up all the essential ingredients of poetic pleasure if they are to be neutralized or overpowered by certain accompanying feelings of disgust or ridicule.

We are aware that the poet himself will deny the grounds of our conclusion; he will declare, perhaps, that though his writings are in faithful adherence to a certain system, yet he writes with unshackled freedom, that it is an unconscious adherence, and undeviating, only because the system itself is built upon the laws of our nature. Such an answer, it is evident, will apply with equal force to a false and a true system; it is making the inveteracy of the habit its justification; but, indeed, with all our old, our unfeigned, our respectful, and even affectionate deference for Wordsworth, we are bold to say that he is no competent judge in this matter. That he writes under the impulse of a glowing and real enthusiasm we do not intend to deny; on the contrary, we are very sure that he feels whatever he describes himself as feeling in the contemplation of a bird's nest, or the sudden gleaming of a bunch of daffodils, but we cannot therefore conclude either that the thoughts which they excite are so important, as that they should form the principal subject of a wise man's contemplations; or that it is proper for a poet to make such feelings the principal topic of his communications to the world.

. . . . . .

Two remarks remain to be made, one addressed to readers, the other with great respect to the poet himself. To the former we would say, that if they have formed their opinions of Wordsworth from public reputation, from illiberal and unjust criticism, from any thing but an attentive and impartial study of his writings, they impeach their own justice; have done the poet great wrong, and themselves yet greater. We have stated our objections to certain of his opinions, and we repeat that we think he has shewn a perverse preference for the maintenance and exemplification of a system to the yielding to the nobler and more genial current of his natural feelings. Still, if we reject from the list of his poems whatever are most open to these objections, those in which the inventor or reviver of a system predominates over the natural poet, enough and more than enough will yet remain in the volumes of Wordsworth, to reward with the richest fruits that poetry can bestow, a candid and attentive reader. It is pitiable and maudlin folly to consider poetry as the mere recreation of idleness, in which it is a fault if the mind is called upon for a moment's exertion; it is prejudice to take up our opinions for granted, and without examination, upon the word of a single critic; it is injustice for a single fault of taste to reject all the writings of any poet; let our readers only stand clear of this folly, and avoid this prejudice and this injustice, and we promise them that they will find in Wordsworth, poems, which it is a misfortune at least, we will not venture to say a disgrace, to be incapable of feeling and admiring.

We have also to address a few words to the poet himself. His writings are devoted to the cause of religion and morality, and in that holy cause we scarcely know a more zealous, a more fearless, or more eloquent advocate; it is quite refreshing to turn from the tawdry voluptuousness of one contemporary poet, or the gloomy misanthropy of another; the vague aspirations of this man, the cold scepticism of that, or the shocking blasphemy of a third, to the pure, manly, single-minded morality of Wordsworth. We give him credit too for feeling as he writes, and we are sure, that to promote virtue and purity, is, with him, beyond all profit, all praise, all pleasure. Upon this ground we take our stand, and we beseech him to consider, that whatever prevents his general acceptation, diminishes his power of doing good; we think he must be satisfied by a trial of so many years, that while he writes as he writes now, projecting his system at every angle, and presenting so many sides obvious to the perversions of ridicule and malice, he may indeed have a few passionate admirers, whose zeal and weight may suffice to console wounded vanity, but he never can have that general influence, nor produce that powerful effect, which of all living poets he is by nature most capable of producing. We do not prescribe the manner or the measure of alteration to the poet, we appeal to the man and the moralist, whether some alteration, some yielding to prejudices, if they be permanent, some departure from the very *summum jus* of abstract truth, be not both possible and expedient.

From Thomas Love Peacock's *The Four Ages of Poetry* (1820)

[In this essay, he divides poetry into four ages: the ages of iron, gold, silver, and brass, comparing the modern age to that of brass.]

Thomson and Cowper looked at the trees and hills which so many ingenious gentlemen had rhymed about so long without looking at them, and the effect of this operation on poetry was like the discovery of a new world. Painting shared the influence, and the principles of picturesque beauty were explored by adventurous essayists with indefatigable pertinacity. The success which attended these experiments, and the pleasure which resulted from them, had the usual effect of all new enthusiasms, that of turning the heads of a few unfortunate persons, the patriarchs of the age of brass, who, mistaking the prominent novelty for the all-important totality, seem to have ratiocinated much in the following manner: "Poetical genius is the finest of all things, and we feel that we have more of it than any one ever had. The way to bring it to perfection is to cultivate poetical impressions exclusively. Poetical impressions can be received only among natural scenes: for all that is artificial is anti-poetical. Society is artificial, therefore we will live out of society. The mountains are natural, therefore we will live in the mountains. There we shall be shining models of purity and virtue, passing the whole day in the innocent and amiable occupation of going up and down hill, receiving poetical impressions, and communicating them in immortal verse to admiring generations." To some such perversion of intellect we owe that egregious confraternity of rhymesters, known by the name of the Lake Poets; who certainly did receive and communicate to the world some of the most extraordinary poetical impressions that ever were heard of, and ripened into models of public virtue, too splendid to need illustration. They wrote verses on a new principle; saw rocks and rivers in a new light; and remaining studiously ignorant of history, society, and human nature, cultivated the phantasy only at the expense of the memory and the reason; and contrived, though they had retreated from the world for the express purpose of seeing nature as she was, to see her only as she was not, converting the land they lived in into a sort of fairy-land, which they peopled with mysticisms and chimaeras. This gave what is called a new tone to poetry, and conjured up a herd of desperate imitators, who have brought the age of brass prematurely to its dotage.

The descriptive poetry of the present day has been called by its cultivators a return to nature. Nothing is more impertinent than this pretension. Poetry cannot travel out of the regions of its birth, the uncultivated lands of semi-civilized men. Mr Wordsworth, the great leader of the returners to nature, cannot describe a scene under his own eyes without putting into it the shadow of a Danish boy or the living ghost of Lucy Gray, or some similar phantastical parturition of the moods of his own mind.

In the origin and perfection of poetry, all the associations of life were composed of poetical materials. With us it is decidedly the reverse. We know too that there are no Dryads in Hyde-Park nor Naiads in the Regent's-canal. But barbaric manners and supernatural interventions are essential to poetry. Either in the scene, or in the time, or in both, it must be remote from our ordinary perceptions. While the historian and the philosopher are advancing in, and accelerating, the progress of knowledge, the poet is wallowing in the rubbish of departed ignorance, and raking up the ashes of dead savages to find gewgaws and rattles for the grown babies of the age. Mr Scott digs up the poachers and cattle-stealers of the ancient border. Lord Byron cruises for thieves and pirates on the shores of the Morea and among the Greek islands. Mr Southey wades through ponderous volumes of travels and old chronicles, from which he carefully selects all that is false, useless and absurd, as being essentially poetical; and when he has a commonplace book full of monstrosities, strings them into an epic. Mr Wordsworth picks up village legends from old women and sextons; and Mr Coleridge, to the valuable information acquired from similar sources, superadds the dreams of crazy theologians and the mysticisms of German metaphysics, and favours the world with visions in verse, in which the quadruple elements of sexton, old woman, Jeremy Taylor, and Emanuel Kant are harmonized into a delicious poetical compound. Mr Moore presents us with a Persian, and Mr Campbell with a Pennsylvanian tale, both formed on the same principle as Mr Southey's epics, by extracting from a perfunctory and desultory perusal of a collection of voyages and travels, all that useful investigation would not seek for and that common sense would reject.

These disjointed relics of tradition and fragments of second-hand observation, being woven into a tissue of verse, constructed on what Mr Coleridge calls a new principle (that is, no principle at all), compose a modern-antique compound of frippery and barbarism, in which the puling sentimentality of the present time is grafted on the misrepresented ruggedness of the past into a heterogeneous congeries of unamalgamating manners, sufficient to impose on the common readers of poetry, over whose understandings the poet of this class possesses that commanding advantage, which, in all circumstances and conditions of life, a man who knows something, however little, always possesses over one who knows nothing.

A poet in our time is a semi-barbarian in a civilized community. He lives in the days that are past. His ideas, thoughts, feelings, associations, are all with barbarous manners, obsolete customs, and exploded superstitions. The march of his intellect is like that of a crab, backward. The brighter the light diffused around him by the progress of reason, the thicker is the darkness of antiquated barbarism, in which he buries himself like a mole, to throw up the barren hillocks of his Cimmerian labours. The philosophic mental tranquillity which looks round with an equal eye on all external things, collects a store of ideas, discriminates their relative value, assigns to all their proper place, and from the materials of useful knowledge thus collected, appreciated, and arranged, forms new combinations that impress the stamp of their power and utility on the real business of life, is diametrically the reverse of that frame of mind which poetry inspires, or from which poetry can emanate. The highest inspirations of poetry are resolvable into three ingredients: the rant of unregulated passion, the whining of exaggerated feeling, and the cant of factitious sentiment: and can therefore serve only to ripen a splendid lunatic like Alexander, a puling driveller like Werter, or a morbid dreamer like Wordsworth.

A parody written by Hartley Coleridge (S. T. Coleridge's son) of one of the "Lucy" poems

He lived amidst th' untrodden ways
  To Rydal Lake that lead;
A bard whom there were none to praise,
  And very few to read.

Behind a cloud his mystic sense,
Deep hidden, who can spy?
Bright as the night when not a star
Is shining in the sky.

Unread his works—his "Milk White Doe"
With dust is dark and dim;
It's still in Longmans' shop, and oh!
The difference to him.

From the Journal of Sir Walter Scott, an entry for 1827

Jan. 1st. God make this a happy year to the King and country, and to all honest men!

I went with all our family to-day to dine as usual at the kind House of Huntly Burn; but the same cloud which hung over us on Saturday still had its influence. The effect of grief upon [those] who, like myself and Sir A.F.,[1] are highly susceptible of humour, has, I think, been finely touched by Wordsworth in the character of the merry village teacher Matthew—whom Jeffrey profanely calls the hysterical schoolmaster. But, with my friend Jeffrey's pardon, I think he loves to see Imagination best when it is bitted and managed and ridden upon the *grand pas*. He does not make allowance for starts and sallies and bounds when Pegasus is beautiful to behold though sometimes perilous to his rider. Not that I think the amiable Bard of Rydal shows judgment in chusing such subjects as the popular mind cannot sympathise in. It is unwise and unjust to himself. I do not compare myself, in point of imagination, with Wordsworth—

[1] Sir Adam Ferguson (1771–1855), friend of Sir Walter, and with him at Edinburgh University.

far from it; for [his] is naturally exquisite, and highly cultivated by constant exercise. But I can see as many castles in the clouds as any man, as many genii in the curling smoke of a steam engine, as perfect a Persepolis in the embers of a sea-coal fire.

From John Stuart Mill's "Thoughts on Poetry and its Varieties," in *The Monthly Repository*, January and October 1833

[The essay was reprinted in his *Dissertations and Discussions.*]

The difference, then, between the poetry of a poet, and the poetry of a cultivated but not naturally poetic mind, is, that in the latter, with however bright a halo of feeling the thought may be surrounded and glorified, the thought itself is always the conspicuous object; while the poetry of a poet is Feeling itself, employing Thought only as a medium of its expression. In the one, feeling waits upon thought; in the other, thought upon feeling. The one writer has a distinct aim, common to him with any other didactic author; he desires to convey the thought, and he conveys it clothed in the feelings which it excites in himself, or which he deems most appropriate to it. The other merely pours forth the overflowing of his feelings; and all the thoughts which those feelings suggest are floated promiscuously along the stream.

It may assist in rendering our meaning intelligible, if we illustrate it by a parallel between the two English authors of our own day, who have produced the greatest quantity of true and enduring poetry, Wordsworth and Shelley. Apter instances could not be wished for; the one might be cited as the type, the *exemplar*, of what the poetry of culture may accomplish: the other as perhaps the most striking example ever known of the poetic temperament. How different, accordingly, is the poetry of these two great writers! In Wordsworth, the poetry is almost always the mere setting of a thought. The thought may be more valuable than the setting, or it may be less valuable, but there can be no question as to which was first in his mind: what he is impressed with, and what he is anxious to impress, is some proposition, more or less distinctly conceived; some truth, or something which he deems such. He lets the thought dwell in his mind, till it excites, as is the nature of thought, other thoughts, and also such feelings as the measure of his sensibility is adequate to supply. Among these thoughts and feelings, had he chosen a different walk of authorship (and there are many in which he might equally have excelled), he would probably have made a different selection of media for enforcing the parent thought: his habits, however, being those of poetic composition, he selects in preference the strongest feelings, and the thoughts with which most of feeling is naturally or habitually connected. His poetry, therefore, may be defined to be, his thoughts, coloured by, and impressing themselves by means of, emotions. Such poetry, Wordsworth has occupied a long life in producing. And well and wisely has he done so. Criticisms, no doubt, may be made occasionally both upon the thoughts themselves, and upon the skill he has demonstrated in the choice of his media: for, an affair of skill and study, in the most rigorous sense, it evidently was. But he has not laboured in vain: he has exercised, and continues to exercise, a powerful, and mostly a highly beneficial influence over the formation and growth of not a few of the most cultivated and vigorous of the youthful minds of our time, over whose heads poetry of the opposite description would have flown, for want of an original organization, physical or mental, in sympathy with it.

On the other hand, Wordsworth's poetry is never bounding, never ebullient; has little even of the appearance of spontaneousness: the well is never so full that it overflows. There is an air of calm deliberateness about all he writes, which is not characteristic of the poetic temperament: his poetry seems one thing, himself another; he seems to be poetical because he wills to be so, not because he cannot help it: did he will to dismiss poetry, he need never again, it might almost seem, have a poetical thought. He never seems *possessed* by any feeling; no emotion seems ever so strong as to have entire sway, for the time being, over the current of his thoughts. He never, even for the space of a few stanzas, appears entirely given up to exultation, or grief, or pity, or love, or admiration, or devotion, or even animal spirits. He now and then, though seldom, attempts to write as if he were; and never, we think, without leaving an impression of poverty: as the brook which on nearly level ground quite fills its banks, appears but a thread when running rapidly down a precipitous declivity. He has feeling enough to form a decent, graceful, even beautiful decoration to a thought which is in itself interesting and moving; but not so much as suffices to stir up the soul by mere sympathy with itself in its simplest manifestation, nor enough to summon up that array of "thoughts of power" which in a richly stored mind always attends the call of really intense feeling. It is for this reason, doubtless, that the genius of Wordsworth is essentially unlyrical. Lyric poetry, as it was the earliest kind, is also, if the view we are now taking of poetry be correct, more eminently and peculiarly poetry than any other: it is the poetry most natural to a really poetic temperament, and least capable of being successfully imitated by one not so endowed by nature.

From a letter from Robert Browning to Harriet Martineau, dated 16 February, 1846

[Browning's bitterness at Wordsworth's comfortable and prosy old age is also reflected in the famous lyric, *The Lost Leader*, where the great poet is shown betraying his art by becoming a figure of the Establishment—

Just for a handful of silver he left us,
Just for a riband to stick in his coat.]

Was ever such a '*great*' poet before? Put one trait with the other—the theory of rural innocence—alternation of 'vulgar trifles' with dissertating with style of "the utmost grandeur that *even you* can conceive" (speak for yourself, Miss M!)—and that amiable transition from two o'clock's grief at the death of one's brother to three o'clock's happiness in the "extraordinary mesmeric discourse" of one's friend. All this, and the rest of the serene and happy inspired daily life which a piece of "unpunctuality" can ruin, and to which the guardian "angel" brings as crowning qualification the knack of poking the fire adroitly—of this—what can one say but that—no, best hold one's tongue and read the *Lyrical Ballads* with finger in ear. Did not Shelley say long ago "He had no more *imagination* than a pint-pot"—though in those days he used to walk about France and Flanders like a man? *Now*, he is "most comfortable in his worldly affairs" and just this comes of it! He lives the best twenty years of his life after the way of his own heart—and when one presses in to see the result of the rare experiment—what the *one* alchemist whom fortune has allowed to get all his coveted materials and set to work at last in earnest with fire and melting-pot—what *he* produces after all the talk of him and the like of him;

why, you get *pulvis et cinis*—a man at the mercy of tongs and shovel!

From a conversation recorded by Canon H. D. Rawnsley in 1870, and included in a paper to the Wordsworth Society in 1882

"Now tell me," said I, "what was the poet like in face and make?"

". . . He was much to look at like his son William; he was a listy[1] man was his son, mind ye. But for a' he was a sizeable man, was the father, he was plainish featured, and was a man as had no pleasure in his faace. Quite different Wudsworth was from li'le Hartley.[2] Hartley always had a bit of smile or twinkle in his faace, but Wudsworth was not lovable in the faace by noa means, for o' he was a sizeable man, mind ye." . . .

"Was he," I said, "a sociable man, Mr Wordsworth, in the earliest times you can remember?"

"Wudsworth, . . . for a' he had noa pride nor nowt, was a man who was quite one to hissel, ye kna. He was not a man as folks could crack[3] wi', nor not a man as could crack wi' folks. But there was another thing as kep' folks off, he had a ter'ble girt deep voice, and ye might see his faace agaan[4] for long enuff. I've knoan folks, village lads and lasses, coming over by the old road above which runs from Grasmere to Rydal, flayt a'most to death there by Wishing Gaate to hear the girt voice a groanin' and mutterin' and thunderin' of a still evening. And he had a way of standin' quite still by the rock there in t'path under Rydal, and folks could hear sounds

[1] lusty. [2] Hartley Coleridge, the son of S. T. Coleridge.
[3] chat. [4] working.

like a wild beast coming from the rocks, and childer were scared fit to be dead a'most. . . . He was a gay good walker, and for a' he had latterly a pony and phaeton, I never once seed him in a conveyance in whole of my time. But he was never a mountain man. He wud gae a deal by Pelter-bridge and round by Red Bank, but he was most ter'ble fond of under Nab, and by old high road to Swan Inn and back, and very often came as far as Dungeon Ghyll. You've happen heerd tell of Dungeon Ghyll; it was a vara favourite spot o' Wudsworth's, now, was that, and he onst made some potry[1] about a lamb as fell over. And I dar say it was true enuff o' but the rhymes, and ye kna they was put in to help it out. . . ."

"Did you ever see Mr Wordsworth out walking—round Pelter-bridge way?"

"Ay, ay, scores and scores o' times. But he was a lonely man, fond o' goin' out wi' his family, and saying nowt to noan of 'em. When a man goes in a family way he keeps togither wi' 'em, but many's a time I've seed him a takin' his family out in a string, and niver geein' the deariest bit of notice to 'em; standin' by hissel' and stoppin' behind agapin', wi' his jaws workin' the whoal time; but niver no crackin' wi' 'em, nor no pleasure in 'em,—a desolate-minded man, ye kna. Queer thing that, mun, but it was his hobby, ye kna. It was potry as did it. We all have our hobbies—some for huntin', some cardin',[2] some fishin', some wrestlin'. He niver followed nowt nobbut a bit o' skating, happen. Eh, he was fond of going on in danger times;—he was always first on the Rydal, however; but his hobby, ye mun kna, was potry. It was a queer thing, but it would like enough cause him to be desolate; and I'se often thowt that his brain was that fu' of sic stuff, that he was forced to be always at it

[1] "The Idle Shepherd-boys; or Dungeon-Ghyll Force," written in 1800.
[2] card-playing.

whether or no, wet or fair, mumbling to hissel' along the roads."

"Do you think," I asked, "that he had any friends among the shepherds?"

"Naay, naay, he cared nowt about folk, nor sheep, nor dogs (he had a girt fine one, weighed nine stone, to guard the house), not no more than he did about claes he had on—his hobby was potry."

"How did he generally dress?"

"Well, in my time them swaller-lappeted ones were i' vogue, but he kep' to all-round plain stuff, and I remember had a cap wi' a neb[1] to it. He wore that most days."

"Did you ever read his poetry, or see any books about in the farmhouses?" I asked.

"Ay, ay, time or two. But ya're weel aware there's potry and potry. There's potry wi' a li'le bit pleasant in it, and potry sic as a man can laugh at or the childer understand, and some as takes a deal of mastery to make out what's said, and a deal of Wudsworth's was this sort, ye kna. You could tell fra the man's faace his potry would niver have no laugh in it. His potry was quite different work from li'le Hartley. Hartley 'ud goa running along beside o' the brooks and mak his, and goa in the first oppen door and write what he had got upo' paper. But Wudsworth's potry was real hard stuff, and bided a deal of makking, and he'd keep it in his head for long enough. Eh, but it's queer, mon, different ways folks hes of making potry now. Folks goes a deal to see where he's interred; but for my part I'd walk twice distance over Fells to see where Hartley lies. Not but what Mr Wudsworth didn't stand very high, and was a well-spoken man enough, but quite one to himself." . . .

[1] peak.

Samuel Taylor Coleridge

(1772–1834)

The spell which Coleridge cast over many of his contemporaries seems not to have worked so well with his reviewers. As a personality, a talker, a fountain of ideas on every subject from superstition to science, as one of the most remarkably talented figures of the age, he was regarded with veneration by all who knew him (and sometimes with exasperation by those who knew him better). Talfourd's account of his conversation and reading of his poems at one of Lamb's famous supper parties, where he appears like his own visionary bard in *Kubla Khan*, is only one of the many descriptions of his magnetic presence. Hazlitt in *My First Acquaintance with Poets*, an essay too well known to be reprinted here, gives a fuller picture, and the letters and memoirs of the period contain innumerable references to his genius. A collection of such observations, called significantly *Coleridge the Talker*, edited by Armour and Howes (Ithaca, N.Y., 1940), is an excellent guide to his character and discourse, and the impact he made on those who met him.

But as a poet he met a less happy fate at the hands of the reviewers, most of whom were at first baffled and enraged by what Hazlitt, reviewing *Christabel* in *The Edinburgh Review* (September 1816), calls a "mixture of raving and driv'ling." His early poems before the publication of *Lyrical Ballads* received polite notice, as he tells us in the first chapter of *Biographia Literaria*: "They were received with a degree of favour, which, young as I was, I well know was bestowed on them not so much for any positive merit, as because they were considered buds of hope, and promises of better works to come." (The remainder of this passage is given below.)

These early poems were apprentice-work, mainly in the style of late eighteenth-century poetry, and made no demands on the understanding of his critics. Confronted, however, with *Lyrical Ballads*, most of the critics assumed this to be the work of one author, and *The Ancient Mariner* was given fairly rough handling.

> . . . The strangest story of a cock and bull that we ever saw on paper: yet, though it seems a rhapsody of unintelligible wildness and incoherence (of which we do not perceive the drift, unless the joke lies in depriving the wedding guest of his share of the feast), there are in it poetical touches of an exquisite kind.

writes the critic of *The Monthly Review* (May 1799) in a more kindly spirit than most of his colleagues. Wordsworth, in one of his least attractive egotistical moments, in a letter[1] to his publisher, Joseph Cottle, was inclined to put much of the blame for the attacks on *Lyrical Ballads* on the inclusion of *The Ancient Mariner*:

> From what I can gather it seems that *The Ancyent Marinere* has upon the whole been an injury to the volume, I mean that the old words and the strangeness of it have deterred readers from going on. If the volume should come to a second edition I would put in its place some little things which would be more likely to suit the common taste.

Blackwood's, true to form, published a parody of the poem in February 1819, only to describe it, in October of the same year, as "by far the most wonderful . . . and the most touching of all the productions of its author."

[1] Dated 24 June, 1799.

The first reviews of *Christabel*, on its long-delayed appearance in 1816, show even less understanding of Coleridge's gifts. He was accused of plagiarism, he was parodied (again by *Blackwood's* in 1819, who had a taste for this kind of insult), and generally attacked for writing nonsense. It was a singularly ill-fated poem, and cost Coleridge a good deal of torment, both in its composition and in its subsequent treatment at the hands of his critics. In his preface to the poem he defends himself against the charges of plagiarism:

> For there is amongst us a set of critics, who seem to hold, that every possible thought and image is traditional; who have no notion that there are such things as fountains in the world, small as well as great; and who would therefore charitably derive every rill they behold flowing, from a perforation made in some other man's tank.

But this had little effect, except perhaps to turn the attack to the second point made in his preface—the innovation in the poem of a principle of metre by which the accents, and not the syllables, are counted in each line. Far from appreciating its experimental quality and its true originality, such critics as Hazlitt in *The Edinburgh Review* (September 1816) and the reviewer in *The Monthly Review* (January 1817) interpreted it as an insult to all thinking men, and a wretched concoction of "rude unfashioned stuff."

It was not until 1834 that a commentary on his poetry appeared which showed particular distinction, and this was written by his nephew Henry Nelson Coleridge, and published just after the poet's death in August 1834 in *The Quarterly Review*. He does not rhapsodize over the poetry in the fulsome style of *Blackwood's*, but goes straight to the essential greatness of Coleridge:

> No writer has ever expressed the great truth that man makes his world, or that it is the imagination which shapes and colours

all things—more vividly than Coleridge. Indeed, he is the first who, in the age in which we live, brought forward that position into light and action.

P.H.

From Chapter I of *Biographia Literaria* (1817)

In 1794,[1] when I had barely passed the verge of manhood, I published a small volume of juvenile poems. They were received with a degree of favour, which, young as I was, I well know was bestowed on them not so much for any positive merit, as because they were considered buds of hope, and promises of better works to come. The critics of that day, the most flattering equally with the severest, concurred in objecting to them obscurity, a general turgidness of diction, and a profusion of new coined double epithets. The first is the fault which a writer is the least able to detect in his own compositions: and my mind was not then sufficiently disciplined to receive the authority of others, as a substitute for my own conviction. Satisfied that the thoughts, such as they were, could not have been expressed otherwise, or at least more perspicuously, I forgot to enquire, whether the thoughts themselves did not demand a degree of attention unsuitable to the nature and objects of poetry. This remark however applies chiefly, though not exclusively, to the "Religious Musings." The remainder of the charge I admitted to its full extent, and not without sincere acknowledgments both to my private and public censors for their friendly admonitions. In the after editions, I pruned the double epithets with no sparing hand, and used my best efforts to tame the swell and glitter both of thought and diction;

[1] In the editon of 1847 this was altered to 1796 (the correct date).

though in truth, these parasite plants of youthful poetry had insinuated themselves into my longer poems with such intricacy of union, that I was often obliged to omit disentangling the weed, from the fear of snapping the flower. From that period to the date of the present work I have published nothing, with my name, which could by any possibility have come before the board of anonymous criticism. Even the three or four poems, printed with the works of a friend, as far as they were censured at all, were charged with the same or similar defects, though I am persuaded not with equal justice; with an EXCESS OF ORNAMENT, in addition to STRAINED AND ELABORATE DICTION. May I be permitted to add, that, even at the early period of my juvenile poems, I saw and admitted the superiority of an austerer and more natural style, with an insight not less clear, than I at present possess. My judgment was stronger than were my powers of realizing its dictates; and the faults of my language, though indeed partly owing to a wrong choice of subjects, and the desire of giving a poetic colouring to abstract and metaphysical truths, in which a new world then seemed to open upon me, did yet, in part likewise, originate in unfeigned diffidence of my own comparative talent.—During several years of my youth and early manhood, I reverenced those, who had re-introduced the manly simplicity of the Greek, and of our own elder poets, with such enthusiasm as made the hope seem presumptuous of writing successfully in the same style. Perhaps a similar process has happened to others; but my earliest poems were marked by an ease and simplicity, which I have studied, perhaps with inferior success, to impress on my later compositions.

From Chapter XIV of *Biographia Literaria* (1817)

During the first year that Mr Wordsworth and I were neighbours, our conversations turned frequently on the two cardinal points of poetry, the power of exciting the sympathy of the reader by a faithful adherence to the truth of nature, and the power of giving the interest of novelty by the modifying colours of imagination. The sudden charm, which accidents of light and shade, which moon-light or sunset diffused over a known and familiar landscape, appeared to represent the practicability of combining both. These are the poetry of nature. The thought suggested itself—(to which of us I do not recollect)—that a series of poems might be composed of two sorts. In the one, the incidents and agents were to be, in part at least, supernatural; and the excellence aimed at was to consist in the interesting of the affections by the dramatic truth of such emotions, as would naturally accompany such situations, supposing them real. And real in this sense they have been to every human being who, from whatever source of delusion, has at any time believed himself under supernatural agency. For the second class, subjects were to be chosen from ordinary life; the characters and incidents were to be such as will be found in every village and its vicinity, where there is a meditative and feeling mind to seek after them, or to notice them, when they present themselves.

In this idea originated the plan of the *Lyrical Ballads*; in which it was agreed, that my endeavours should be directed to persons and characters supernatural, or at least romantic; yet so as to transfer from our inward nature a human interest and a semblance of truth sufficient to procure for these shadows of imagination that willing suspension of disbelief for the moment, which constitutes poetic faith. Mr Wordsworth, on the other hand, was to propose to himself as his object, to give the charm of novelty to things of every day, and to excite a feeling analogous to the supernatural, by awakening the mind's attention to the lethargy of custom, and directing it to the loveliness and the wonders of the world before us; an inexhaustible treasure, but for which, in consequence of the film of familiarity and selfish solicitude, we have eyes, yet see not, ears that hear not, and hearts that neither feel nor understand.

With this view I wrote *The Ancient Mariner*, and was preparing among other poems, *The Dark Ladie*, and the *Christabel*, in which I should have more nearly realized my ideal, than I had done in my first attempt. But Mr Wordsworth's industry had proved so much more successful, and the number of his poems so much greater, that my compositions, instead of forming a balance, appeared rather an interpolation of heterogeneous matter. Mr Wordsworth added two or three poems written in his own character, in the impassioned, lofty, and sustained diction, which is characteristic of his genius. In this form, the *Lyrical Ballads* were published; and were presented by him as an experiment, whether subjects, which from their nature rejected the usual ornaments and extra-colloquial style of poems in general, might not be so managed in the language of ordinary life as to produce the pleasurable interest, which it is the peculiar business of poetry to impart.

A letter from Charles Lamb to Wordsworth, 30 January, 1801, on the reappearance of *Lyrical Ballads*, in two volumes

. . . I am sorry that Coleridge has christened his Ancient Marinere, 'a poet's Reverie'—it is as bad as Bottom the Weaver's declaration that he is not a lion, but only the scenical representation of a lion. What new idea is gained by this title but one subversive of all credit—which the tale should force upon us—of its truth!

For me, I was never so affected with any human tale. After first reading it, I was totally possessed with it for many days. I dislike all the miraculous part of it; but the feelings of the man under the operation of such scenery, dragged me along like Tom Piper's magic whistle. I totally differ from your idea that the Marinere should have had a character and profession. This is a beauty in Gulliver's Travels, where the mind is kept in a placid state of little wonderments; but the Ancient Marinere undergoes such trials as overwhelm and bury all individuality or memory of what he was—like the state of a man in a bad dream, one terrible peculiarity of which is, that all consciousness of personality is gone. Your other observation is, I think as well, a little unfounded: the Marinere, from being conversant in supernatural events, *has* acquired a supernatural and strange cast of *phrase*, eye, appearance, &c., which frighten the "wedding guest." You will excuse my remarks, because I am hurt and vexed that you should think it necessary, with a prose apology, to open the eyes of dead men that cannot see.

To sum up a general opinion of the second volume, I do not feel any one poem in it so forcibly as the Ancient

Marinere, the Mad Mother, and the Lines at Tintern Abbey in the first.

From a letter from Coleridge to Thomas Wedgwood, 14 January, 1803

In simple earnest, I never find myself alone within the embracement of rocks & hills, a traveller up an alpine road, but my spirit courses, drives, and eddies, like a Leaf in Autumn: a wild activity, of thoughts, imaginations, feelings, and impulses of motion, rises up from within me—a sort of *bottom-wind*, that blows to no point of the compass, & comes from I know not whence, but agitates the whole of me; my whole Being is filled with waves, as it were, that roll & stumble, one this way, & one that way, like things that have no common master. I think, that my soul must have pre-existed in the body of a Chamois-chaser; the simple image of the old object has been obliterated—but the feelings, & impulsive habits, & incipient actions, are in me, & the old scenery awakens them. The farther I ascend from animated Nature, from men, and cattle, & the common birds of the woods, & fields, the greater becomes in me the Intensity of the feeling of Life; Life seems to me then a universal spirit, that neither has, nor can have, an opposite. God is every where, I have exclaimed, & works every where; & where is there *room* for Death? In these moments it has been my creed, that Death exists only because Ideas exist, that Life is limitless Sensation; that Death is a child of the organic senses, chiefly of the Sight; that Feelings die by flowing into the mould of the Intellect, & becoming Ideas; & that Ideas passing forth into action re-instate themselves again in the world of Life. And I do believe, that Truth lies inveloped in these loose generalizations.—I do not think it possible, that any bodily pains could eat out the love & joy, that is so substantially part of me, towards hills, & rocks, & steep waters! And I have had some Trial.

From a letter from Dorothy Wordsworth to Thomas de Quincey, dated Grasmere, Monday, 1 May, 1809

I was called downstairs and found Miss Hutchinson[1] reading Coleridge's *Christabel* to Johnny[2]—She was tired, so I read the greatest part of it: he was excessively interested especially with the first part, but he asked "why she could not say her prayers in her own room," and it was his opinion that she ought to have gone "directly to her Father's room to tell him that she had met with the Lady under the old oak tree and all about it."

From the review of *Christabel; Kubla Khan, a Vision; The Pains of Sleep*, in *The Monthly Review*, January 1817

In a very circumstantial though short preface, Mr Coleridge informs us that *Christabel* was written long ago; that consequently all marks of plagiarism[3] which may be dis-

[1] Sara Hutchinson, Wordsworth's sister-in-law.

[2] Johnny, Wordsworth's son, was not quite seven (*b*. June 1803).

[3] The charges of plagiarism brought by the reviewers against *Christabel* caused great indignation to Coleridge and his friends. Dorothy Wordsworth in a letter to Lady Beaumont (27 October, 1805) refers to the resemblance between Scott's recently published *Lay of the Last Minstrel* and Coleridge's as yet unpublished *Christabel*. "My Brother and Sister think that the Lay being published first, it will tarnish the freshness of *Christabel*, and considerably injure the first effect of it." According to her account, Scott had heard recitations of *Christabel*, had been much impressed, and had unconsciously imitated it.

covered in it are only chance coincidences; and also that the metre of *Christabel*, though irregular, still has a "method in its madness," and "counts the accents, not the syllables, in each line." This variation from every former rule of versification is called "a new principle"; and the reader is to be reasoned into a belief that a line of ten syllables is no longer than one of five, if there be no more *emphatic* syllables (for this is all that the author means by accent) in the one than in the other.

We have long since condemned in Mr Scott and in Miss Holford,[1] and in fifty other males and females, the practice of arbitrary pronunciation, assumed as a principle for regulating the length or rhythm of a verse; and we hereby declare to all whom it may concern, that they are guilty of neither more nor less than bombastic *prose*, and not even conscious of *bombastic* verse, who rest their hopes on the acquiescence of their readers in their own "arbitrary pronunciation." Let those readers only weigh and measure a few of Mr Coleridge's lines in this poem of *Christabel*, which unfortunately was so long delayed in its publication, and which really did *not* pilfer anything from previous poems. Let them form their opinion; and then let them say whether Mr Coleridge originally conceived, or surreptitiously obtained, such superb ideas!

> 'Tis the middle of night by the castle clock!
> And the owls have awaken'd the crowing cock;
> Tu-whit!—Tu-whoo!
> And hark, again! the crowing cock,
> How drowsily it crew.

Are we to be told that this is *nature*? "Avec permission, Monsieur," etc., etc., (as Voltaire said in Dr Moore's *Travels*), we do not allow the plea. When Virgil describes the dead

[1] Miss Holford (1778–1852) a now forgotten authoress, friend and correspondent of Southey.

hour of night, when Homer in a still bolder manner strikes out the scene before us; when Shakespeare, boldest, truest, and yet gentlest of all, presents the same picture to our eyes; they all fill their canvas with living objects, and with actual sounds: but they are all equally above that imitative harmony, that affected adaptation of sound to sense, which nothing but German music and German poetry[1] could ever have attempted. They would have started with horror and astonishment from such an effort, in any language, as that which Mr Coleridge is constantly making; namely, to dignify meanness of conception, to versify the flattest prose, and to teach the human ear a new and discordant system of harmony.

We shall give the public one opportunity of judging of this extravagant but not ingenious production:—

> Yea, she doth smile, and she doth weep,
> Like a youthful hermitess,
> Beauteous in a wilderness,
> Who, praying always, prays in sleep.
> And if she move unquietly,
> Perchance, 'tis but the blood so free,
> Comes back and tingles in her feet.
> No doubt, she hath a vision sweet.
> What if her guardian spirit 'twere?
> What if she knew her mother near?
> But this she knows, in joys and woes,
> That saints will aid if men will call:
> For the blue sky bends over all!

This precious production is not finished, but we are to have more and more of it in future! It would be truly astonishing that such rude unfashioned stuff should be tolerated, and still more that it should be praised by men of genius, (witness

[1] Cf. Southey's description of *The Ancient Mariner*: "a Dutch attempt at German sublimity" (*Critical Review*, October 1798).

Lord Byron[1] and some others), were we not convinced that every principle of correct writing, as far as poetry is concerned, has been long *given up*; and that the observance, rather than the breach, of such rules is considered as an incontrovertible proof of rank stupidity. It is grand, in a word, it is sublime, to be lawless; and whoever writes the wildest nonsense in the quickest and newest manner is the popular poet of the day! Whether this sentence be considered as a positive truth, or as a splenetic effusion, by the different parties who *now* divide the literary world, we think that the time is fast approaching when all minds will be agreed on it; and when any versifier who widely differs from the established standard of our nobler authors will be directly remanded into that Limbo of vanity from which he most certainly emerged.

The fragment of *Kubla Khan* is declared to have been composed in a dream, and is published as the author wrote it. Allowing every possible accuracy to the statement of Mr Coleridge we would yet ask him whether this extraordinary fragment was not rather the effect of rapid and instant composition after he was awake, than of memory immediately recording that which he dreamt when asleep? By what process of consciousness could he distinguish between such composition and such reminiscence? Impressed as his mind was with his interesting dream, and habituated as he is (notwithstanding his accidental cessation from versifying) to the momentary production of verse, will he venture to assert that he did not *compose*, and that he did *remember*, the lines before us? Were they dreamt, or were they spontaneously poured forth instantly after the dream,

> Without stop or stay,
> Down the rocky way
> That leads, etc. etc.,

[1] Byron in a note to *The Siege of Corinth* in 1816 calls *Christabel* "that wild and singularly original and beautiful poem."

His "psychological curiosity," as he terms it, depends in no slight degree on the establishment of the previous fact which we have mentioned: but the poem itself is below criticism. We would dismiss it with some portentous words of Sir Kenelm Digby, in his observations on Browne's *Religio Medici*:—"I would have much ado to believe what he speaketh confidently: that he is more beholding to Morpheus for learned and rational as well as pleasing dreams, than to Mercury for smart and facetious conceptions."

The Pains of Sleep, a little poem at the end of the pamphlet, has some better verses in it than its predecessors. Without in the least approving the spirit, we admire the simplicity of the following lines:

[Here are quoted the first two stanzas of the poem.]

We close the slight publication before us with unmingled regret. The author of *Remorse* may perhaps be able to explain our feeling better than ourselves: but that so much superior genius should be corrupted and debased by so much execrable taste must be a subject of sincere lamentation to every lover of the arts, and to every friend of poetry.

From a letter from S.T.C. to the Rev. F. Wrangham, dated 5 June, 1817, in which he complains of Hazlitt's treachery in reviewing *Christabel*

The praise or dispraise of Reviews or indeed of any one whom I do not personally love, is utterly indifferent to me, and always has been. But I cannot be indifferent to starvation; a very eminent Bookseller was consulted by a brother of the trade concerning me—and his answer was—these words (You may safely conclude that the exaggeration in the first part excited a strange sort of smile and stare on my part) "I have heard from several of our first rate men, Lord Byron was one, and Mr W. Scott another, that taking him all in all, Mr C. is the greatest man we have; but *I* would not have a work of his, if it were given me ready printed etc., for the 'Quarterly Review' takes no notice of his works or but in a half in half way that damns a man worse than anything: and *our* 'Review' [the *Edinburgh*] is decided to write him down"—Before the "Christabel" was published, Jeffrey wrote to Anacreon Moore,[1] begging him, as a favour, to supply a grand quiz of the poem; and tho' purchased by Merry,[2] Gifford would not let it be reviewed in the "Quarterly"!

From Chapter XXIV of *Biographia Literaria* (1817)

Strange as the delusion may appear, yet it is most true, that three years ago I did not know or believe that I had an enemy in the world; and now even my strongest sensations of gratitude are mingled with fear, and I reproach myself for being too often disposed to ask,—Have I one friend?—During the many years which intervened between the composition and the publication of the *Christabel*, it became almost as well known among literary men as if it had been on common sale; the same references were made to it, and the same liberties taken with it, even to the very names of the imaginary persons in the poem. From almost all of our most celebrated poets, and from some with whom I had no personal acquaintance, I either received or heard of expressions of admiration that, (I can truly say,) appeared to myself utterly disproportionate to a work, that pretended to be nothing more than a common Faery Tale. Many, who had allowed no merit to my other poems, whether printed or

[1] Tom Moore, the poet.

[2] *I.e.*, Murray.

manuscript, and who have frankly told me as much, uniformly made an exception in favour of the *Christabel* and the poem entitled *Love*. Year after year, and in societies of the most different kinds, I had been entreated to recite it; and the result was still the same in all, and altogether different in this respect from the effect produced by the occasional recitation of any other poems I had composed.—This before the publication. And since then, with very few exceptions, I have heard nothing but abuse, and this too in a spirit of bitterness at least as disproportionate to the pretensions of the poem, had it been the most pitiably below mediocrity, as the previous eulogies, and far more inexplicable.—This may serve as a warning to authors, that in their calculations on the probable reception of a poem, they must subtract to a large amount from the panegyric, which may have encouraged them to publish it, however unsuspicious and however various the sources of this panegyric may have been. And, first, allowances must be made for private enmity, of the very existence of which they had perhaps entertained no suspicion—for personal enmity behind the mask of anonymous criticism: secondly for the necessity of a certain proportion of abuse and ridicule in a Review, in order to make it saleable, in consequence of which, if they have no friends behind the scenes, the chance must needs be against them; but lastly and chiefly, for the excitement and temporary sympathy of feeling, which the recitation of the poem by an admirer, especially if he be at once a warm admirer and a man of acknowledged celebrity, calls forth in the audience. For this is really a species of animal magnetism, in which the enkindling reciter, by perpetual comment of looks and tones, lends his own will and apprehensive faculty to his auditors. They *live* for the time within the dilated sphere of his intellectual being. It is equally possible, though not equally common, that a reader left to himself should sink below the poem, as that the poem left to itself should flag beneath the feelings of the reader.—But, in my own instance, I had the additional misfortune of having been gossiped about, as devoted to metaphysics, and worse than all, to a system incomparably nearer to the visionary flights of Plato, and even to the jargon of the Mystics, than to the established tenets of Locke. Whatever therefore appeared with my name was condemned beforehand, as predestined metaphysics.

From Sir Thomas Noon Talfourd's *Letters of Charles Lamb, with a Sketch of his Life* (1837)[1]

There Coleridge sometimes, though rarely, took his seat; and then the genial hubbub of voices was still: critics, philosophers, and poets, were contented to listen; and toil-worn lawyers, clerks from the India House, and members of the Stock Exchange, grew romantic while he spoke. Lamb used to say that he was inferior then to what he had been in his youth; but I can scarcely believe it; at least there is nothing in his early writing which gives any idea of the richness of his mind so lavishly poured out at this time in his happiest moods. Although he looked much older than he was, his hair being silvered all over, and his person tending to corpulency, there was about him no trace of bodily sickness or mental decay, but rather an air of voluptuous repose. His benignity of manner placed his auditors entirely at their ease, and inclined them to listen delighted to the sweet, low tone in which he began to discourse on some high theme. Whether he had won for his greedy listener only some raw lad, or

[1] Talfourd is here describing the famous Wednesday night parties given by Charles Lamb in the Temple. See Hazlitt's account in "On the Conversation of Authors" of these evenings, presided over by Lamb, "the most delightful, the most provoking, the most witty and sensible of men".

charmed a circle of beauty, rank, and wit, who hung breathless on his words, he talked with equal eloquence; for his subject, not his audience, inspired him. At first his tones were conversational; he seemed to dally with the shadows of the subject and with fantastic images which bordered it; but gradually the thought grew deeper, and the voice deepened with the thought; the stream gathering strength, seemed to bear along with it all things which opposed its progress, and blended them with its current; and stretching away among regions tinted with ethereal colours, was lost at airy distance in the horizon of the fancy. His hearers were unable to grasp his theories, which were indeed too vast to be exhibited in the longest conversation; but they perceived noble images, generous suggestions, affecting pictures of virtue, which enriched their minds and nurtured their best affections. Coleridge was sometimes induced to recite portions of "Christabel," then enshrined in manuscript from eyes profane, and gave a bewitching effect to its wizard lines. But more peculiar in its beauty than this, was his recitation of Kubla Khan. As he repeated the passage—

> A damsel with a dulcimer
> In a vision once I saw;
> It was an Abyssinian maid,
> And on her dulcimer she played,
> Singing of Mount Abora!

his voice seemed to mount, and melt into air, as the images grew more visionary, and the suggested associations more remote.

From Shelley's *Letter to Maria Gisborne* (1820)

> You will see Coleridge; he who sits obscure
> In the exceeding lustre and the pure

Intense irradiation of a mind,
Which, with its own internal lightning blind,
Flags wearily through darkness and despair—
A cloud-encircled meteor of the air,
A hooded eagle among blinking owls.

From Chapter I of Thomas Love Peacock's *Nightmare Abbey* (1818)

Another occasional visitor, much more to Mr Glowry's[1] taste, was Mr Flosky, a very lachrymose and morbid gentleman, of some note in the literary world, but in his own estimation of much more merit than name. The part of his character which recommended him to Mr Glowry was his very fine sense of the grim and the tearful. No one could relate a dismal story with so many minutiae of supererogatory wretchedness. No one could call up a *raw-head and bloody-bones* with so many adjuncts and circumstances of ghastliness. Mystery was his mental element. He lived in the midst of that visionary world in which nothing is but what is not. He dreamed with his eyes open, and saw ghosts dancing round him at noontide. He had been in his youth

[1] Mr Glowry is the host and owner of Nightmare Abbey. His famous guest, Mr Flosky, is a malicious sketch of Coleridge, who also appears in *Headlong Hall* (the first of Peacock's novels) as Mr Panscope, "the chemical, botanical, geological, astronomical, mathematical, metaphysical, meteorological, anatomical, physiological, galvanistical, musical, pictorial, bibliographical, critical philosopher, who had run through the whole circle of the sciences, and understood them all equally well."

Peacock's disgust at what he felt was the turncoat political attitude of Wordsworth, Coleridge, and Southey (who had all once enthusiastically supported the French Revolution) accounts for the sharpness of his attack in *Nightmare Abbey*, and more especially in *Melincourt*, where Coleridge appears as the ridiculous Mr Mystic, of Cimmerian Lodge, lost in a fog of metaphysics.

an enthusiast for liberty, and had hailed the dawn of the French Revolution as the promise of a day that was to banish war and slavery, and every form of vice and misery, from the face of the earth. Because all this was not done, he deduced that nothing was done; and from this deduction, according to his system of logic, he drew a conclusion that worse than nothing was done; that the overthrow of the feudal fortresses of tyranny and superstition was the greatest calamity that had ever befallen mankind; and that their only hope now was to rake the rubbish together, and rebuild it without any of those loopholes by which the light had originally crept in. To qualify himself for a coadjutor in this laudable task, he plunged into the central opacity of Kantian metaphysics, and lay *perdu* several years in transcendental darkness, till the common daylight of common sense became intolerable to his eyes. He called the sun an *ignis fatuus*; and exhorted all who would listen to his friendly voice, which were about as many as called "God save King Richard,"[1] to shelter themselves from its delusive radiance in the obscure haunt of Old Philosophy. This word Old had great charms for him. The good old times were always on his lips; meaning the days when polemic theology was in its prime, and rival prelates beat the drum ecclesiastic with Herculean vigour, till the one wound up his series of syllogisms with the very orthodox conclusion of roasting the other.

From John Sterling's critique of *Christabel* in *The Athenaeum*, 2 July, 1828, entitled "An Appeal Apologetic from Philip Drunk to Philip Sober"

[Sterling, friend and disciple of Coleridge, shows in this review that he has learnt his critical approach from his

[1] Cf. *Richard II*, Act V, Scene 2.

master. "To Coleridge," he wrote in 1836, "I owe *education*. He taught me to believe that an empirical philosophy is none, that Faith is the highest Reason, that all criticism, whether of literature, laws, or manners, is blind, without the power of discerning the organic unity of the object." This is one of the few reviews before H. N. Coleridge that show any real understanding of Coleridge's method.]

It is common to hear everything which Mr Coleridge has written condemned with bitterness and boldness. His poems are called extravagant; and his prose works, poems too, and of the noblest breed, are pronounced to be mystical, obscure, metaphysical, theoretical, unintelligible, and so forth; just as the same phrases have over and over been applied, with as much sagacity, to Plato, St Paul, Cudworth,[1] and Kant.[2] But *Christabel* is the only one of his writings which is ever treated with unmingled contempt; and I wish to examine with what justice this feeling has been excited. In the first place it should be remembered, that, at the time when it was written, the end of the last century, no attempt had been made in England by a man of genius for a hundred and fifty years to embody in poetry those resources which feudal manners and popular superstitions supply to the imagination. To those who care not for the mythology of demoniac terrors and wizard enchantment, Mr Coleridge did not write. He did not write for Bayles[3] and Holbachs;[4] nor did

[1] Ralph Cudworth (1617–88), Cambridge Platonist, whose doctrine of "plastic nature" had much influence on Coleridge's thought.

[2] Immanuel Kant (1724–1804), the German transcendental philosopher, also a powerful influence on Coleridge.

[3] Pierre Bayle (1647–1706), sceptical philosopher of the Enlightenment.

[4] Baron d'Holbach (1723–89), called by Voltaire "the personal enemy of God." His *Système de la nature* (1770), sceptical and atheistical, was much admired by Shelley.

he write for Glanvils[1] or Jameses:[2] but for those who, not believing the creed of the people, not holding that which was in a great degree the substantial religion of Europe for a thousand years, yet see in these superstitions the forms under which devotion presented itself to the minds of our forefathers, the grotesque mask assumed for a period, like the veil on the face of Moses, as a covering for the glory of God. Persons who think this obsolete faith to be merely ridiculous, will of course think so of *Christabel*. He who perceives in them a beauty of their own, and discovers all the good to which in those ages they were necessary accompaniments, will not object to have them represented, together with all the attributes and associations which rightly belong to them, and in which genius, while it raises them from their dim cemetery, delights again to array them.

That much of the machinery of the poem is, in the eyes of a natural philosopher or a woman of fashion, trivial or laughable, bears not upon the question. The fullest persuasion of the impossibility of every occurrence in the tale is not in the least incompatible with that kind of faith which is amply sufficient for the demands of the poet. It admits of much question, whether the mind be in the more healthy and natural state, when it is disposed to treat with scorn and ridicule whatever lies beyond the limit of its own convictions, or when it studies with affection and interest every shape and mode of human belief, and attempts to trace out and sympathize with that germ of good and truth, which lies somewhere amid the roots of every article of popular credence. But the latter is at all events the only condition of feeling on which poetry pretends to act; and he who brings

[1] Joseph Glanvill (1636–80), a rationalistic divine who was an original F.R.S. in 1664.

[2] This may refer to Thomas James (1573–1629), librarian of Bodley and Fellow of New College, Oxford.

a mind bristling with demonstration or experiment to receive the impact of a creative imagination, acts as iniquitously as Laertes fighting with a sword against the foil of Hamlet.

The very first lines of *Christabel* are frequently selected as objects of ridicule. Be it remembered that they are the opening of a tale of witchery, and that, unless they are read in that good faith and singleness of heart, with which a child would listen to such a story, they are not heard with the predisposition to which alone the author addressed himself.

[Sterling then defends *Christabel* against the charges of absurdity, by quoting at some length to show how the opening lines are "admirably calculated for bringing before the reader the 'witching hour of night,' with all that thrilling and ghost-ridden feeling which is the proper recipient of the mysterious story."]

The next lines to these are beautiful specimens of a kind of excellence which runs through the whole poem, the presentation of the clearest and brightest pictures by the smallest number of words.

> She stole along, she nothing spake;
> The breezes they were still also;
> And nought was green upon the oak,
> But moss and rarest mistletoe.
> She kneels beneath the huge oak tree,
> And in silence prayeth she.

A hundred stanzas of details would not make plainer the terror and devotion of the lovely lady, and the silent dimness of the ancient oak. All that follows for two pages is in a style of the most concise and brilliant perfection; and no poet whatsoever of our day has given us, in four times the space, the same quantity and variety of living imagery as is treasured in these thirty or forty lines. The description of the fiendish damsel, if such she were, is given in three words, with a grace and distinctness which no one but Spenser could have equalled, and which would have cost him many more words to convey. Her narrative is a masterly counterfeiting of the effect which terror produces, in leading the sufferer to dwell on unimportant, as much as on important particulars, and also exhibits the attempt which she makes, after the manner of all skilful liars, to add evidence to her story by minute details, together with the superfluity of epithet and adjuration, and shows her consciousness of falsehood by the over-anxiety to secure credence. I am perfectly convinced that no play of our day by any other writer,—nor is this saying much,—contains a passage so dramatic as the tale told by Geraldine. The circumstances which follow are all of them imagined with the highest beauty and fitness. Christabel had a terrible dream about evils befalling her lover. She went out into the forest to pray beneath an ancient oak, and found there a lady in distress, who told her a story of unprovoked outrage and suffering. Then mark how the narrative, throughout the variety of its pictures, so full of minute and elegant tracery, is filled with indications of something unearthly and dangerous in the character of the stranger. In the first place, by the belief of our ancestors, the evil powers could harm no one who had not consented in some way to their design, and submitted to their influence. Therefore, after the tale of Geraldine, come these lines:—

> Stretch forth thy hand (thus ended she,)
> And help a wretched maid to flee.
> Then Christabel stretched forth her hand,
> And comforted fair Geraldine.

Then again, in entering the castle through the wicket in the gate,

The gate that was ironed within and without,
Where an army in battle array had marched out,
The lady sank, belike through pain;
And Christabel, with might and main,
Lifted her up, a weary weight,
Over the threshold of the gate.
Then the lady rose again,
And moved as she were not in pain.

Then, as they cross the court,

Outside her kennel the mastiff old
Lay fast asleep in moonshine cold.
The mastiff old did not awake,
Yet she an angry moan did make.

Every line in this portion of the poem is filled with some strong under-import; and how completely do we perceive, in the next paragraph, the tokens we should expect of a supernatural and evil presence!

They passed the hall, that echoes still,
Pass as lightly as you will.
The brands were flat, the brands were dying,
Amid their own white ashes lying;
But, when the lady passed, there came
A tongue of light, a fit of flame;
And Christabel saw the lady's eye,
And nothing else saw she thereby,
Save the boss of the shield of Sir Leoline tall,
Which hung in a murky old niche in the wall.

The element of fire seems to recognize the presence of the fiend; and the domestic hearth cries aloud, as it were, to the innocent maiden, and lights up the gleaming eye of her destroyer. The following paragraphs are remarkable for their clearness and brightness of description, without any of that detailed and wordy minuteness which injures the corresponding passages of Scott. . . .

Throughout the poem there runs and lives one special excellence, the beauty of single lines and expressions, perfect flowers in themselves, yet interfering as little with the breadth and unity of the general effect, as the primroses and hawthorns of the valley with its sweeping perspective of light and shadow. No one, I imagine, can fail to recognize in it the original germ of the *Lay of the Last Minstrel*; but how superior is it to that spirited and brilliant tale, in the utter absence both of defect and superfluity in the diction,—in the thrilling interest and beauty of every, the slightest circumstance,—in the relation of each atom to the whole,—and in the deep reflection which is the very atmosphere and vital air of the whole composition!

A passage by Sergeant[1] Talfourd, quoted in Joseph Cottle's *Reminiscences of Samuel Taylor Coleridge and Robert Southey* (1847)

Not less marvellously gifted, though in a far different manner, is Coleridge, who by a strange error has usually been regarded of the same [Lake] school. Instead, like Wordsworth, of seeking the source of sublimity and beauty in the simplest elements of humanity, he ranges through all history and science, investigating all that has really existed, and all that has had foundation only in the wildest, and strangest minds, combining, condensing, developing and multiplying the rich products of his research with marvellous facility and skill; now pondering fondly over some piece of

[1] The legal title which had been held by Sir Thomas Noon Talfourd (see p. 245).

exquisite loveliness, brought from an unknown recess, now tracing out the hidden germ of the eldest, and most barbaric theories, and now calling fantastic spirits from the vasty deep, where they have slept since the dawn of reason. The term "myriad-minded" which he has happily applied to Shakespeare, is truly descriptive of himself. He is not one, but legion, "rich with the spoils of time," richer in his own glorious imagination and sportive fantasy. There is nothing more wonderful than the facile majesty of his images, or rather of his world of imagery, which, whether in his poetry or his prose, start up before us, self-raised, and all perfect, like the palace of Aladdin. He ascends to the sublimest truths by a winding track of sparkling glory, which can only be described in his own language.

> The spirit's ladder
> That from this gross and visible world of dust,
> Even to the starry world, with thousand rounds
> Builds itself up; on which the unseen powers
> Move up and down on heavenly ministries—
> The circles in the circles, that approach
> The central sun from ever narrowing orbit.

In various beauty of versification he has never been exceeded. Shakespeare doubtless in liquid sweetness and exquisite continuity, and Milton in pure majesty and classic grace—but this, in one species of verse only; and taking all his trials of various metres, the swelling harmony of his blank verse, the sweet breathing of his gentle odes, and the sybil-like flutter, with the murmuring of his wizard spells, we doubt if even these great masters have so fully developed the sources of the English tongue. He has yet completed no adequate memorial of his Genius, yet it is most unjust to say he has done little or nothing.

To refute this assertion, there are his *Wallenstein*; his love poems of intensest beauty; his *Ancient Mariner*, with his touches of profoundest tenderness amidst the wildest and most bewildering terrors; his holy and sweet tale of *Christabel*, with its enchantments, and richer humanities; the depths, the sublimities, and the pensive sweetness of his *Tragedy*; the heart-dilating sentiments scattered through his *Friend*; and the stately imagery which breaks upon us at every turn of the golden paths of his metaphysical labyrinth. And if he has a power within him mightier than that which even these glorious creations indicate, shall he be censured because he has deviated from the ordinary course of the age in its development, and instead of committing his imaginative wisdom to the press, has delivered it from his living lips? He has gone about in the true spirit of an old Greek bard, with a noble carelessness of self, giving fit utterance to the divine spirit within him. Who that has ever heard can forget him? His mild benignity, the unbounded variety of his knowledge, the fast succeeding products of his imagination, the child-like simplicity with which he rises from the dryest and commonest theme into the wildest magnificence of thought, pouring on the soul a stream of beauty and wisdom to mellow and enrich it for ever? The seeds of poetry, the materials for thinking, which he has thus scattered will not perish. The records of his fame are not in books only, but on the fleshly tablets of young hearts, who will not suffer it to die even in the general ear, however base and unfeeling criticism may deride their gratitude.

From John Wilson's review of Coleridge's *Poetical Works* (3 vols., 1834), in *Blackwood's Magazine*, October 1834

Reflections on having left a Place of Retirement—the *Lime-tree Bower my Prison*—and the *Nightingale*—are all full of the same delight in nature—a delight which grew more and more creative of beauty—making the food it fed on, and devoutly worshipping the only true—that is, the imaginary world. In these and other compositions of equal and kindred excellence, the poet's heart and imagination minister to each other; emotions and images come upon us with united power; and even when metaphysical, more than seems safe in the poetry of passion, there is such a warmth and glow in the winged words, wheeling in airy circles not inextricably involved, that Mind or Intellect itself moves us in a way we should not have believed possible, till we experience the pleasure of accompanying its flights—or rather of being upborne and wafted on its dove-like but eagle-strong wings. The law of association is illustrated in the *Nightingale* more philosophically than by Hartley[1] or Brown[2]—and how profound to the understanding heart is the truth in that one line —sure as Holy Writ—were man but faithful to his Maker,

In nature there is nothing melancholy.

In not one of the poems we have yet quoted or mentioned,

[1] David Hartley (1705–57), the philosopher whose works on the doctrine of association (*Observations on Man*, 1749) influenced both Wordsworth and Coleridge.

[2] Thomas Brown (1778–1820), Professor of Moral Philosophy at Edinburgh in 1810.

can it be truly said that there is any approach to the sublime. Indeed, only in the *Fears in Solitude* might we be justified in expecting such a strain—and the subjects of some of the other pieces necessarily exclude both sentiment and imagery of that character. In the *Fears in Solitude* there is, as we have seen, much stately and sustained beauty; and we are not only roused, but raised by the pealing music. In the happiest passages, even on reflection, we miss little that might or should have been there—though something; and it would be ungrateful to criticise in our cooler moments what so charmed us in our glow, or to doubt the potency of the spell that had so well done its master's work. In much of what we have not quoted—though the whole is above pitch and reach of common powers—there is a good deal of exaggeration, and we fear some untruth—as if sense were sometimes almost sacrificed to sound—and the poet's eyes blinded with the dust raised by the whirlwind of passion, carrying him along the earth, and not up the ether. But in one poem, Coleridge, in a fit of glorious enthusiasm, has reached the true sublime. Out of the Bible, no diviner inspiration was ever worded than the *Hymn before sunrise in the Vale of Chamouni*. We doubt if there be any single strain equal to it in Milton or Wordsworth. If there be, it is Adam's Hymn in Paradise. The instantaneous Impersonation of Mount Blanc into a visible spirit, brings our whole capacity of adoration into power, and we join mighty Nature in praise and worship of God. As the hymn continues to ascend the sky, we accompany the magnificent music on wings up the holy mountain, till in its own shadow it disappears, and

We worship the invisible alone.

. . . While tens of thousands on tens of thousands of copies of poems—of far inferior excellence—in pamphlet shape and size, were fluttering far and wide over all the fashionable and unfashionable world—and Byron—Byron—Byron was in all literary and illiterary parties, morning, noon, and night, the catchword and reply—when Medora, and the names of other interesting lemans of pirates and robbers, were sighed or whispered from all manner of mouths—how seldom was heard the name of Coleridge—and then as if it belonged to some man "in a far countree" and how rarely—though both sounds are beautiful—Christabel and Geraldine—were they murmured by maid and matron! Yet maids and matrons all were devoted to romance, and so sensitive to the preternatural, that they wept to see the moonlight through the ghostlike hand of a heroine who held it up for no other reason in the world than to show that she had died a natural death of love! Byron himself—the idol of the hour—rejoiced to declare *Christabel* singularly wild and beautiful—Scott that it had inspired the *Lay*—all our true poets delighted in the vision which they loved too well to loudly praise—for admiration is mute, or speaks in its trance, but with uplifted eyes. But the sweet, soft, still breath of praise, like that of purest incense, arose from many a secret place, where genius and sensibility abided, and Coleridge, amidst the simpers of the silly, and the laughter of the light, and the scorn of the callous, and the abuse of the brutal, and the blackguardism of the beggar-poor—received the laurel crown woven by the hands of all the best of his brother bards—and wore it ever after cheerfully but without pride—round his lofty forehead —and it was green as ever the day he died.

Christabel is indeed, what Byron said it was, a singularly wild and original poem. No other words could so well characterise it. It did not appear in a dearth, but at a time when a flush of poetry overspread the land. Genius as high, as various, and as new as had ever adorned any era, was then exultingly running its victorious career—taking its far sweeping aerial flights over its native seas and mountains—or bringing within the dominion of its wings the uttermost ends of the earth. . . .

. . . *Christabel* resembles no other poem, except inasmuch as it is a poem. Here was a new species of poetry, and the specimen was felt to be perfect. It was as if some bright consummate flower had been added to the families of the field —discovered growing by itself—with its own peculiar balm, and its own peculiar bloom—mournful as moonlight—delicate as the dawn—yet strong as the day—and in its silken folds, by its own beauty, preserved unwithered in all weathers. Or may we liken the music of *Christabel* to that of some new instrument, constructed on a dream of the harps, on which in forgotten ages the old harpers played—ere all those castles were in ruins—and when the logs now lying black in the mosses were green trees rejoicing in the sky? True, at least, it is that in all the hanging gardens of poetry—Imagination—the head-gardener—declares there is but one single *Christabel*.

What means the poem? Coleridge himself could not have answered that question—for it is a mystery. What is the meaning of any mood of Superstition? Who shall explain Fear? One flutter shall make you dumb as frost. If ghosts from the grave—or fiends from regions deeper than all graves—or if heaven lets visit earth its saints and angels—and such has ever been the creed of Imagination—you must not hope—nay, you will not desire—that such intercommunion as may then befall shall bear any but a strange, wild, sad resemblance to that of life with life—when both are yet mortal—and the voices of both have as yet sounded but on this side of the boundary between time and eternity.

From H. N. Coleridge's review of *The Poetical Works of S. T. Coleridge* (3 vols., 1834), in *The Quarterly Review*, August 1834

[Coleridge died a few days before it was printed, and the *Quarterly* adds a short obituary note at the end of the issue.]

[Coleridge's best poems] are distinguished in a remarkable degree by the perfection of their rhythm and metrical arrangement. The labour bestowed upon this point must have been very great; the tone and quantity of words seem weighed in scales of gold. It will, no doubt, be considered ridiculous by the Fannii and Fanniae[1] of our day to talk of varying the trochee with the iambus, or of resolving either into the tribrach. Yet it is evident to us that these, and even minuter points of accentual scansion, have been regarded by Mr Coleridge as worthy of study and observation. We do not, of course, mean that rules of this kind were always in his mind while composing, any more than that an expert disputant is always thinking of the distinctions of mood and figure, whilst arguing; but we certainly believe that Mr Coleridge has almost from the commencement of his poetic life looked upon versification as constituting in and by itself a much more important branch of the art poetic than most of his eminent contemporaries appear to have done. And this more careful study shows itself in him in no technical peculiarities or fantastic whims, against which the genius of our language revolts; but in a more exact adaptation of the

[1] By this he means the "younger aspirants—male and female—who for the moment enjoy some popularity," who are referred to later in the review, in a passage not given here.

movement to the feeling, and in a finer selection of particular words with reference to their local fitness for sense and sound. Some of his poems are complete models of versification, exquisitely easy to all appearance, and subservient to the meaning, and yet so subtle in the links and transitions of the parts as to make it impossible to produce the same effect merely by imitating the syllabic metre as it stands on the surface. The secret of the sweetness lies within, and is involved in the feeling. It is this remarkable power of making his verse musical that gives a peculiar character to Mr Coleridge's lyric poems. In some of the smaller pieces, as the conclusion of the *Kubla Khan*, for example, not only the lines by themselves are musical, but the whole passage sounds all at once as an outburst or crash of harps in the still air of autumn. The verses seem as if *played* to the ear upon some unseen instrument. And the poet's manner of reciting verse is similar. It is not rhetorical, but musical: so very near recitative, that for any one else to attempt it would be ridiculous; and yet it is perfectly miraculous with what exquisite searching he elicits and makes sensible every particle of the meaning, not leaving a shadow of a shade of the feeling, the mood, the degree, untouched.

. . . The minute study of the laws and properties of metre is observable in almost every piece in these volumes. Every kind of lyric measure, rhymed and unrhymed, is attempted with success; and we doubt whether, upon the whole, there are many specimens of the heroic couplet or blank verse superior in construction to what Mr Coleridge has given us. We mention this the rather, because it was at one time, although that time is past, the fashion to say that the Lake school—as two or three poets, essentially unlike to each other, were foolishly called—had abandoned the old and established measures of the English poetry for new conceits of their own. There was no truth in that charge. . . .

. . . We should not have dwelt so long upon this point of versification unless we had conceived it to be one distinguishing excellence of Mr Coleridge's poetry, and very closely connected with another, namely, fulness and individuality of thought. It seems to be a fact, although we do not pretend to explain it, that condensation of meaning is generally found in poetry of a high import in proportion to perfection in metrical harmony. Petrarch, Spenser, Shakspeare and Milton are obvious instances. Goethe and Coleridge are almost equally so. Indeed, whether in verse, or prose, or conversation, Mr Coleridge's mind may be fitly characterized as an energetic mind—a mind always at work, always in a course of reasoning. He cares little for anything, merely because it was or is; it must be referred, or be capable of being referred, to some law or principle, in order to attract his attention. This is not from ignorance of the facts of natural history or science. His written and published works alone sufficiently show how constantly and accurately he has been in the habit of noting all the phenomena of the material world around us; and the great philosophical system[1] now at length in preparation for the press demonstrates, we are told, his masterly acquaintance with almost all the sciences, and with not a few of the higher and more genial of the arts. Yet his vast acquirements of this sort are never put forward by or for themselves; it is in his apt and novel illustrations, his indications of analogies, his explanation of anomalies, that he enables the hearer or reader to get a glimpse of the extent of his practical knowledge. He is always reasoning out from an inner point, and it is the inner point, the principle,

[1] The "great philosophical system" was, in fact, never published. It was a *magnum opus* often discussed in Coleridge's letters, and was to be "an Instrument of Practical Reasoning in the Business of Real Life," a treatise which would incorporate much of his later theological and philosophical writings, including *Biographia Literaria*.

the law which he labours to bring forward into light. If he can convince you or himself of the principle *a priori*, he generally leaves the facts to take care of themselves. He leads us into the laboratories of art or nature as a showman guides you through a cavern crusted with spar and stalactites, all cold and dim, and motionless, till he lifts his torch aloft, and on a sudden you gaze in admiration on walls and roof of flaming crystals and stars of eternal diamond. . . .

We have not yet referred to the *Ancient Mariner*, *Christabel*, the Odes on *France*, and the *Departing Year*, or the *Love Poems*. All these are well known by those who know no other parts of Coleridge's poetry, and the length of our preceding remarks compels us to be brief in our notice. Mrs Barbauld, meaning to be complimentary, told our poet, that she thought the *Ancient Mariner* very beautiful, but that it had the fault of containing no moral. "Nay, madam," replied the poet, "if I may be permitted to say so, the only fault in the poem is that there is *too much*! In a work of such pure imagination I ought not to have stopped to give reasons for things, or inculcate humanity to beasts. *The Arabian Nights* might have taught me better." They might—the tale of the merchant's son who puts out the eyes of a genii by flinging his date-shells down a well, and is therefore ordered to prepare for death—might have taught this law of imagination; but the fault is small indeed; and the *Ancient Mariner* is, and will ever be, one of the most perfect pieces of imaginative poetry, not only in our language, but in the literature of all Europe. We have, certainly, sometimes doubted whether the miraculous destruction of the vessel in the presence of the pilot and hermit, was not an error, in respect of its bringing the purely preternatural into too close contact with the actual framework of the poem. The only link between those scenes of out-of-the-world wonders, and the wedding guest, should, we rather suspect, have been the blasted, unknown being himself who described them. There should have been no other witnesses of the truth of any part of the tale, but the Ancient Mariner himself. This by the way: but take the work altogether, there is nothing else like it; it is a poem by itself; between it and other compositions, in *pari materia*, there is a chasm which you cannot overpass; the sensitive reader feels himself insulated, and a sea of wonder and mystery flows round him as round the spell-stricken ship itself. It was a sad mistake in the able artist—Mr Scott, we believe—who in his engravings has made the ancient mariner an old decrepit man. That is not the true image; no! he should have been a growthless, decayless being, impassive to time or season, a silent cloud—the wandering Jew. The curse of the dead men's eyes should not have passed away. But this was, perhaps, too much for any pencil, even if the artist had fully entered into the poet's idea. Indeed, it is no subject for painting. The *Ancient Mariner* displays Mr Coleridge's peculiar mastery over the wild and preternatural in a brilliant manner; but in his next poem, *Christabel*, the exercise of his power in this line is still more skilful and singular. The thing attempted in *Christabel* is the most difficult of execution in the whole field of romance—witchery by daylight; and the success is complete. Geraldine, so far as she goes, is perfect. She is *sui generis*. The reader feels the same terror and perplexity that Christabel in vain struggles to express, and the same spell that fascinates her eyes. Who and what is Geraldine—whence come, whither going, and what designing? What did the poet mean to make of her? What could he have made of her? Could he have gone on much farther without having had recourse to some of the ordinary shifts of witch tales? Was she really the daughter of Roland de Vaux, and would the friends have met again and embraced?

Alas! they had been friends in youth;
But whispering tongues can poison truth;
And constancy lives in realms above;
And life is thorny—and youth is vain—
And to be wroth with one we love
Doth work like madness in the brain.
And thus it chanced, as I divine,
With Roland and Sir Leoline.
Each spake words of high disdain
And insult to his heart's best brother:
They parted—ne'er to meet again!
But never either found another
To free the hollow heart from paining;—
They stood aloof, the scars remaining,
Like cliffs which had been rent asunder:—
A dreary sea now flows between:
But neither heat, nor frost, nor thunder,
Shall wholly do away, I ween,
The marks of that which once has been.

We are not amongst those who wish to have *Christabel* finished. It cannot be finished. The poet has spun all he could without snapping. The theme is too fine and subtle to bear much extension. It is better as it is, imperfect as a story, but complete as an exquisite production of the imagination, differing in form and colour from the *Ancient Mariner*, yet differing in effect from it only so as the same powerful faculty is directed to the feudal or the mundane phases of the preternatural.

From these remarkable works we turn to the love poems scattered through the volumes before us. There is something very peculiar in Mr Coleridge's exhibition of the most lovely of the passions. His love is not gloomy as Byron's, nor gay as Moore's, nor intellectual as Wordsworth's. It is a clear unclouded passion, made up of an exquisite respect and gentleness, a knightly tenderness and courtesy,—pure yet ardent, impatient yet contemplative. It is Petrarch and Shakespeare incorporate—it is the midsummer moonlight of all love poetry.

. . . . . .

. . . We speak of Coleridge, then, as the poet of imagination; and we add, that he is likewise the poet of thought and verbal harmony. That his thoughts are sometimes hard and sometimes even obscure, we think must be admitted; it is an obscurity of which all very subtle thinkers are occasionally guilty, either by attempting to express evanescent feelings for which human language is an inadequate vehicle, or by expressing, however adequately, thoughts and distinctions to which the common reader is unused. As to the first kind of obscurity, the words serving only as hieroglyphics to denote a once existing state of mind in the poet, but not logically inferring what the state was, the reader can only guess for himself by the context, whether he ever has or not experienced in himself a corresponding feeling; and therefore, undoubtedly, this is an obscurity which strict criticism cannot but condemn. But, if an author be obscure, merely because this or that reader is unaccustomed to the mode or direction of thinking in which such author's genius makes him take delight—such a writer must indeed bear the consequence as to immediate popularity; but he cannot help the consequence, and if he be worth anything for posterity, he will disregard it. In this sense almost every great writer, whose natural bent has been to turn the mind upon itself, is —must be—obscure; for no writer, with such a direction of intellect, will be great, unless he is individual and original; and if he is individual and original, then he must, in most cases, himself make the readers who shall be competent to sympathize with him.

Select Bibliography

(in addition to the material from which extracts have been included in the present volume)

LIST OF ABBREVIATIONS

ER: *The Edinburgh Review*
JEGP: *The Journal of English and Germanic Philology*
MLQ: *Modern Language Quarterly*
MLR: *The Modern Language Review*
MP: *Modern Philology*
PMLA: *Publications of the Modern Language Association of America*
PQ: *The Philological Quarterly*
RES: *The Review of English Studies*
SP: *Studies in Philology*.

General Books and Articles

M. H. ABRAMS: *The Mirror and the Lamp: Romantic Theory and the Critical Traditions* (New York, 1953).

U. AMARASINGHE: *Dryden and Pope in the Early Nineteenth Century* (Cambridge, 1962).

A. ANDREWS: *A History of British Journalism* (2 vols., London, 1887).

W. J. BATE: *From Classic to Romantic* (Cambridge, Mass., 1946).

A. S. COLLINS: "The Growth of the Reading Public during the Eighteenth Century," *RES*, II (1926), 284–294; 428–438.

A. S. COLLINS: *The Profession of Letters, 1780–1832* (London, 1928).

R. G. COX: "The Great Reviews," *Scrutiny*, VI (1937), 2–20, 155–175.

R. G. COX: *Nineteenth Century Periodical Criticism* (unpublished Cambridge Ph.D. Dissertation, 1939).

AMY CRUSE: *The Englishman and his Books in the Early Nineteenth Century* (London, 1930).

H. R. FOX BOURNE: *English Newspapers* (2 vols., London, 1887).

L. E. GATES: *Three Studies in Literature* (London, 1899).
W. GRAHAM: *The Beginning of English Literary Periodicals* (New York, 1926).
W. GRAHAM: *English Literary Periodicals* (New York, 1930).
M. JOYCE: *Edinburgh: the Golden Age* (London, 1951).
E. H. LACON WATSON: *Contemporary Comments* (London, 1931).
F. R. LEAVIS: *The Relationship of Journalism to Literature* (unpublished Cambridge Ph.D. Dissertation, 1925).
J. WAIN (editor): *Contemporary Reviews of Romantic Poetry* (London, 1953).
W. S. WARD: "Some Aspects of the Conservative Attitude towards Poetry in English Criticism, 1798–1820," *PMLA*, LX (1945), 386–398.
R. WELLEK: "The Concept of Romanticism in Literary History," *Comparative Literature*, I (1949), 1–23; 147–172.
R. WELLEK: *A History of Modern Criticism, 1750–1950*, Vols. I and II (New Haven, 1955).

On Particular Reviews

Blackwood's Edinburgh Magazine
MARGARET O. W. OLIPHANT: *Annals of a Publishing House* (2 vols., Edinburgh, 1897).

The Eclectic Review
See Conder, below.

The Edinburgh Review
ANON.: "The Edinburgh Review (1802–1902)," *ER*, CXLV (July 1902), 275–318.
W. A. COPINGER: *The Authorship of the First Hundred Numbers of the Edinburgh Review* (Manchester, 1895).
E. SCHNEIDER, I. GRIGGS, and J. D. KERN: "Early Edinburgh Reviewers: A New List," *MP*, XLIII (1946).
L. STEPHEN: "The First Edinburgh Reviewers," in *Hours in a Library*, II (London, 1874).
J. J. WELKER: "The Position of the Quarterlies on Some Classical Dogmas," *SP*, XXXVII (1940), 542–562.
See also Jeffrey, below.

The Examiner

E. Blunden (editor): *Leigh Hunt's Examiner Examined* (London, 1928).

The London Magazine

J. Bauer: *The London Magazine, 1820–29* (Copenhagen, 1953).

S. Butterworth: "The Old London Magazine," *The Bookman*, October 1922, 12–17.

The Monthly Review

B. Nangle: *The Monthly Review: Indexes of Contributors* (London, 1934).

J. W. Robberds: *A Memoir of the Life and Writings of William Taylor* (London, 1843).

The Quarterly Review

W. Graham: *Tory Criticism in the Quarterly Review, 1809–1853* (New York, 1918).

H. Shine and H. C. Shine: *The Quarterly Review under William Gifford* (Chapel Hill, 1949).

S. Smiles: *Memoir and Correspondence of John Murray* (2 vols., London, 1891).

See also Welker's article listed at p. 269 and Gifford, below.

Particular Critics

H. N. Coleridge

W. Graham: "Henry Nelson Coleridge, Expositor of Romantic Criticism," *PQ*, IV (1925), 231–238.

S. T. Coleridge

T. W. Raysor: "Coleridge's Criticism of Wordsworth," *PMLA*, LIV (1939), 496–510.

B. Willey: "Coleridge on Imagination and Fancy," *Proceedings of the British Academy*, XXXII (1946), 174–187.

Conder

E. R. Conder: *Josiah Conder (1789–1855), A Memoir* (London, 1857).

Gifford

R. B. Clark: *William Gifford, Tory Satirist, Critic and Editor* (New York, 1930).

Hazlitt

P. L. CARVER: "Hazlitt's Contributions to *The Edinburgh Review*," *RES*, IV (October 1928), 375–393.

P. P. HOWE: *William Hazlitt* (London, 1922, 1928, 1947 (new edition with introduction by F. Swinnerton)).

J. M. BULLITT: "Hazlitt and the Romantic Conception of the Imagination," *PQ*, XXIV (1945), 343–361.

Jeffrey

R. DANIEL: "Jeffrey and Wordsworth," *Sewanee Review*, 51 (1942), 195–213.

L. E. GATES (editor): *Selections from the Essays of Francis Jeffrey* (Boston, 1894).

J. A. GREIG: *Francis Jeffrey of the Edinburgh Review* (Edinburgh, 1948).

B. GUYER: "The Philosophy of Jeffrey," *MLQ*, XI (1950).

M. Y. HUGHES: "The Humanism of Francis Jeffrey," *MLR*, XI (1921), 243–251.

F. JEFFREY: *Contributions to the Edinburgh Review* (4 vols., London, 1844, 1853).

D. NICHOL SMITH (editor): *Francis Jeffrey's Literary Criticism* (Oxford, 1910).

R. NOYES: *Wordsworth and Jeffrey in Controversy* (Bloomington, Indiana, 1941).

Lockhart

M. C. HILDYARD (editor): *Lockhart's Literary Criticism* (Oxford, 1931).

A. LANG: *The Life and Letters of J. G. Lockhart* (2 vols., London, 1897).

J. G. LOCKHART: *Peter's Letters to his Kinsfolk* (2 vols., London, 1819).

M. LOCKHEAD: *J. G. Lockhart* (London, 1954).

V. WOOLF: "Lockhart's Criticism," in *The Moment, and other Essays* (London, 1947).

John Scott

T. R. HUGHES: "John Scott: Editor, Author and Critic," *London Mercury*, XXI (April 1930), 518–528.

J. ZEITLIN: "The Editor of the *London Magazine*," *JEGP*, XX, 328–354.

John Sterling

A. K. TUELL: *Sterling: a Representative Victorian* (New York, 1941).

Southey

W. GRAHAM: "Robert Southey as Tory Reviewer," *PQ*, II (1923), 97–111.

Wilson

MARY M. GORDON: *Christopher Wilson* (Edinburgh, 1862).

A. L. STROUT: "J. Wilson, Champion of Wordsworth!", *MP*, XXXI (1934), 383–394.

A. L. STROUT: "William Wordsworth and J. Wilson: A Review of their Relations between 1802 and 1817," *PMLA*, XLIX (1934), 143–183.

E. SWANN: *Christopher North* (Edinburgh, 1934).

R. A. WARDLE: "The Authorship of the *Noctes Ambrosianae*," *MP*, XLII (1944), 9–17.

J. WILSON: *Noctes Ambrosianae*, ed. R. S. Mackenzie (5 vols., Edinburgh, 1854–55). (This edition excludes all contributions identified as not Wilson's.)

Wrangham

G. M. HARPER: *William Wordsworth, his Life, Works and Influence* (2 vols., Princeton and London, 1916, 1929 (revised edition)), *passim*.

Wordsworth

M. L. PEACOCK (editor): *The Critical Opinions of William Wordsworth* (Baltimore, 1950).

Criticism of Particular Poets by their Contemporaries

Coleridge

W. GRAHAM: "Contemporary Criticism of Coleridge the Poet," *PMLA*, XXXVIII (1923), 278–289.

Wordsworth

ELSIE SMITH: *An Estimate of William Wordsworth by his Contemporaries* (Oxford, 1932).

DATE DU